TV China

TV CHINA

Edited by Ying Zhu & Chris Berry

Indiana University Press

Bloomington & Indianapolis

This book is a publication of

Indiana University Press
601 North Morton Street
Bloomington, IN 47404-3797 USA

http://iupress.indiana.edu

Telephone orders   800-842-6796
Fax orders   812-855-7931
Orders by e-mail   iuporder@indiana.edu

Library of Congress Cataloging-in-
Publication Data

TV China / edited by Ying Zhu and Chris
Berry.
    p. cm.
    Includes index.
    ISBN 978-0-253-35257-6 (cloth : alk. paper)
— ISBN 978-0-253-22026-4 (pbk. : alk.
paper) 1. Television broadcasting—China.
I. Zhu, Ying, date II. Berry, Chris, date
    PN1992.3.C6Z49 2008
    384.550951—dc22

2008028560

1 2 3 4 5 14 13 12 11 10 09

Contents

TV China

Introduction

YING ZHU & CHRIS BERRY

If radio and film were the emblematic media of the Maoist era, television has rapidly established itself as the medium of "marketized" China. Just twenty years ago, television sets were few and far between, and mostly installed in public places. Now almost every mainland Chinese household has a television set, and television is the main source of news and entertainment for most Chinese. Furthermore, television has pioneered the marketization of the media that has occurred over the last decade. Although television stations are still government-owned, they generate more revenue in taxes for central government than they receive from it, and they also dominate national spending on advertising.

Television has also become the dominant medium in every Chinese-speaking territory outside the mainland: in Hong Kong, Taiwan, Malaysia, and Singapore, and in Chinese communities around the world. The advent of satellite broadcasting, falling trade barriers, and other features of globalization have led to vastly increased circulation of materials among Chinese-speaking territories. The days when diasporic Chinese had never seen a China Central Television news item from Beijing, or mainland audiences had never seen a TVB drama from Hong Kong, are long gone.

While academic research and writing about Chinese television has increased in recent years, there is still significantly less material available in English on Chinese television than there is on Chinese literature or film, for example, and coverage remains sporadic and patchy. This anthology responds to this lack, and to the changes in the nature of Chinese-language broadcasting itself.

The increasing flows of programming, talent, and funding across borders, along with the establishment of transnational satellite-based stations and channels, mean that "Chinese television" today is a global phenomenon. But what does this mean? Satellite and cable packages aimed primarily at migrant communities make selected Chinese-language programming available to viewers with the funds to subscribe in most countries and territories on the planet. A number of Chinese-language stations operate in the United States, and Singapore, Malaysia, Indonesia, and Canada all have Chinese-language stations. Furthermore, Chinese-language programs are not produced only in the core Greater China territories of Hong Kong, Taiwan, and the People's Republic of China. They are also produced in Australia and many other countries, and Chinese cultural programming in other languages is produced in still more.

Global circulation and widespread production of Chinese-language television represents a considerable change. Until quite recently, production was largely confined to Greater China, Singapore, and Malaysia, and circulation was limited by both pre-satellite technological conditions and political barriers. Even within the Greater China zone, the origin, development, and characteristics of television in each territory are made distinct by different political histories, economic structures, and regulatory traditions. For instance, Joseph Chan points out in his essay that whereas Hong Kong's television was dominated by commercial interests from the beginning, in Taiwan the ruling Kuomintang Nationalist Party had a significant influence.

Despite these differences, the timeline of television's ascension to media dominance is similar in Taiwan and Hong Kong. The first Chinese-language television station was a cable channel established in Hong Kong. Rediffusion (Lide, renamed Asia Television—Yazhou Dianshi—in 1982) began operation in 1957 (Kitley 2003: 188). However, television did not really take off in the colony until 1967, when Television Broadcasts Limited (TVB, Dianshi Guangbo) launched its free-to-air service. Rediffusion became free-to-air in 1973. By 1975, 88 percent of Hong Kong households had television sets, and watching television had already overtaken film-going as the most popular leisure activity (Lee 2000: 369), destroying the Cantonese-language film industry for a decade. In Taiwan, television was free-to-air from its beginnings in 1962, when Taiwan Television (Taiwan Dianshi) began broadcasting. Its impact was also limited initially. But when it began to show the local *gezaixi* opera forms that were so popular with the local population and established island-wide coverage in 1965, this changed. Film audiences dropped 30 percent within a year. By 1975, 73 percent of the island's population had television sets and television was the most important medium by almost any measure (Lu 1994).

In contrast, in the People's Republic, although the first television station was set up in Beijing in 1958, broadcasts were interrupted by the ups and downs of political campaigns and development was very slow (Huang and Yu 1997). During mainland China's isolation, Taiwan and more especially Hong Kong established themselves as the centers for production and distribution of television for the Chinese world outside the People's Republic. There, only 925,000 television sets were manufactured between 1958 and Mao's death in 1976, and these were often placed in public halls rather than sold for private home use. The 1980s were the period in which television boomed in the People's Republic. The annual output of television sets had reached 27.67 million by 1989 (Huang 1994: 217). In 1978 there was less than one television receiver per hundred people, and only 10 million had access to television, but by 1996 there was a television receiver for every four people, and 1 billion had access (Hazelbarth 1997: 1). By 2000, this figure had risen to 1.19 billion, representing 92 percent of the population (Li 2001).

In the new century, television is fully established as the dominant medium among all Chinese populations, and the flow of programming to Chinese-speaking populations around the world has increased. If there is a pan-Chinese culture in formation, the global circulation of Chinese television must be one of the factors driving its development. Satellite broadcasts cover much larger geographical areas than standard broadcast signals, often larger than whole nation-states. The People's Republic has embraced the market economy and joined the global market-based economic system, and the World Trade Organization (WTO) and other alliances and treaties have reduced protectionism within that system. As a result, both ideological and protectionist obstacles to the flow of television have decreased. Just a few years ago, most viewers in mainland China had access only to the national Chinese Central Television (CCTV) channels and a local provincial or municipal channel, depending on where they lived. Now the major local channels are made available all over the country by satellite, and each station has a number of channels. Certain Hong Kong–based channels are also permitted, such as Phoenix and Rupert Murdoch's STAR TV.

It would be a mistake, however, to think that the emergent global Chinese television system is a single, unified, homogenous space. The fact that the pan-Asian satellite television station STAR TV had to drop the BBC's World Service Television from its package in 1994 in order to secure access to the mainland makes clear the continued political and ideological divide within the region (Curtin 2007). The poor relations between Taiwan and the mainland also prevent programming from flowing openly between those two territories. However, at least as important as ideological factors are commercial ones. Very few programs from the hundreds of channels operating in the People's Republic can be viewed, say, in the United States. And even fewer can be viewed in Europe, where Chinese populations are even smaller. In other words, as a global phenomenon, Chinese television is more connected than ever before, but locally

specific circumstances still prevail and national television regulatory environments and market territories still need to be taken into account.

In English-language academia, film and literature are almost certainly the
most widely researched aspects of Chinese media and arts. Some literature is
translated, and films are available on DVD with subtitles and in some cases released in cinemas outside China. As a result, they are more accessible to non-
Chinese in general and non-speakers of Chinese in particular. Yet far more Chinese people are watching Chinese-language television every day than are reading
novels or going to movie theaters. Indeed, if they are consuming literature and
film, they are likely to be doing so via television, watching film channels and
dramatic series adapted from literature (Zhu, Keane, and Bai, forthcoming). In
these circumstances, it is clear that much more attention needs to be paid to Chinese television if we are to understand ideology, popular culture, consumerism,
and everyday life in this emerging superpower.

Scholarly interest in Chinese television studies has increased since the late
1990s. The basic facts of a boom driven by the development of the market economy in China and the accompanying advertising industry have been well reported. New scholars are working on a wide variety of topics, from institutional
aspects to programming and reception. Individual essays on particular aspects of
Chinese-language television have been published in a wide variety of journals,
edited anthologies, and volumes on broader topics (for example Curtin 2007;
Donald, Keane, and Hong 2002; Keane, Fung, and Moran 2007; Zhu, Keane, and
Bai, forthcoming; Kitley 2003; Lee 2000; Moran and Keane 2003).

The opening up of space in English-language academia for monographs on
particular aspects of Chinese television is an even more significant indicator of
the maturation of the field. James Lull's pioneering 1991 monograph *China Turned
On* used ethnographic data collected in the 1980s to examine how Chinese families responded to television. Using approaches grounded in contemporary cultural
studies understandings of the audience as active and engaged, Lull discovered
that they were far from passive consumers of the government line, and that in
many cases their readings were actively critical. The first English-language monograph on Hong Kong television, Eric Ma's *Culture, Politics, and Television in Hong
Kong* (1999), was also a study of reception. Ma wanted to investigate how anticipation of the handover to mainland rule in 1997 was affecting Hong Kongers' identities, and he examined this through their response to prime-time television drama.
Other monographs have been more concerned with the political economy of
Chinese television. Junhao Hong's *The Internationalization of Television in China*
(1998) focuses on how both exposure to foreign television programs and practices
and the adoption of the market economy within China have transformed Chinese
television, from the types of programs imported to institutional restructuring and
export efforts. Michael Keane's *Created in China: The Great New Leap Forward*

(2007) puts Chinese television in the larger context of the creative industries and the policies designed to encourage their growth and development as earners of profit and foreign exchange in global competition. Combining the approaches of both political economy and critical and cultural studies, Ying Zhu's *Television in Post-Reform China: Serial Dramas, Confucian Leadership, and the Global Television Market* (2008) explores the dynamic interplay between the fashions and fads of Chinese prime-time dramatic programs and an evolving Chinese cultural milieu and media infrastructure that responds to the imperatives of both the Chinese state's modernization agenda and the expansion of transnational capital and markets.

What has yet to emerge in the field of Chinese television studies is a comprehensive text that addresses the practice, circulation, and consumption of Chinese-language television not only within the cultural-linguistic confines of Greater China but also around the world. *TV China* addresses this urgent need. Our discussion encompasses important geographic centers of Chinese television production and consumption, from the mainland to Hong Kong, Taiwan, and the diaspora, as well as all the major aspects of Chinese television, from institutional factors to programming and reception at both local and transnational levels. The essays gathered here aim to provide basic texts for the teaching of undergraduate and graduate seminars devoted to Chinese television, and they suggest directions for future research and scholarship in this rapidly growing field.

The book is divided into four sections: institution, programming, reception, and "going global." Institutional work on television examines issues such as the political economics of television; government policy from censorship to trade protection; and corporate policy and decision making. The ideological differences and rapid change in different Chinese territories have been highlighted in Chinese television research in this sub-field. In this first section, Joseph Chan's seminal essay provides a much-needed overview of how the Greater China television market is being formed. He focuses on how television from different places is interacting in shaping television in this region and examines the strategies and processes that the major players are adopting to exploit this regional market. Chan also goes beyond Greater China to examine how television programs from its important neighbors Japan and South Korea are affecting regional dynamics. He further discusses the implications of the resulting patterns for our understanding of television regionalization and globalization.

While Chan thinks institutionally across the region, Junhao Hong, Yanmei Lü, and William Zou concentrate on a particular institution. They trace the evolution of China Central Television (CCTV), which to this day remains the only national television network in the People's Republic, as a microcosm of the momentous changes that have overtaken Chinese television during the transition from narrowcasting and propaganda to satellite and commercials. In this way, Hong, Lü, and Zou situate the changes in CCTV within China's overall political, economic, and societal transformations. Given CCTV's leading position, there can be no doubt that its transformation reflects changes in China's overall television industry.

Finally, Karen Wilkins's essay investigates the institutional and programming aspects of the Hong Kong television industry, considering continuities and changes across the political transition in 1997. Many commentators assume that changes in television practices and policies must be due to the transfer of sovereignty, but others also highlight the impact of the Asian economic crisis in the same year. Informed by a number of broad theoretical approaches, including sociological and political-economic conceptualizations of the television industry, Wilkins's study weighs these different accounts in the balance. A political-economic history of Hong Kong, as well as of its television industry, is situated within broader parameters of globalization processes.

The second section focuses on programming. Because Chinese television transforms so rapidly, much of the work in this area investigates new genres and their socio-political impact. Chris Berry's essay asks what sort of space Shanghai Television's Documentary Channel (Jishi Pindao) opens up in the culture of China. Rather than deploy an idealized and overly ideological concept like the "public sphere," he utilizes Foucault's ideas on how power is productive. On this basis, he argues that the public space provided by the Documentary Channel is the product of "marketized" (shichanghua) socialist China—in which the state and the market complement each other—as surely as the old model of television as the "mouthpiece of the party" was a response to the needs of centralized socialist society.

Hsiu-Chuang Deppman's essay discusses the transnational cultural and social significance of the popular Taiwanese drama serial Meteor Garden. She argues that the generic combination of the comic book, fairytale, and TV drama and the seductive appearance of the stars in the serial make Meteor Garden an interesting case study of new narrative strategies in popular culture. Based on a Japanese manga (comic), Meteor Garden was a hit not only among global Chinese television audiences but also among other Asian audiences. Analyzing programs like this allows us to highlight the driving forces as well as the characteristics of both transnational Chinese and Asian identity and youth culture.

Finally, Xinyu Lu's essay examines the enormously popular Chinese New Year's Eve variety show as a unique genre in Chinese television. She discusses both the program itself and the popular and critical discourses surrounding it. She argues that the contemporary Chinese New Year's Eve variety show manufactures an ideology of "Chineseness" that is designed to bind together Chinese populations around the world. The program is well established, but, as she demonstrates, it has changed with the drive toward "marketization" and global audiences. A new rhetoric marginalizes the old socialist classes of peasants and workers in favor of new entrepreneurs, and pan-Chinese cultural heritage is invoked in the name of patriotism, at least as much as the specific revolutionary history of the People's Republic was emphasized in the past.

The third section focuses on the reception of Chinese television. As our previous discussion has already indicated, scholars in Chinese television studies initiated the field with work driven by interest in television's cultural impact and its viewership patterns. Haiqing Yu's essay is a reexamination of the micro-politics of Chinese journalism in the television industry as a practice linking audiences to television within the context of media reforms. She argues that post-1989 journalists in China are media intellectuals who engage in a mediation journalism characterized by a double-time narration that decodes and recodes messages that they transmit between the state and the society, between the representatives and the under-represented of the nation. She further argues that mediation journalism in Chinese television is rooted in the way that Chinese modernity has been written in Chinese intellectual history. Yu examines mediation journalism through case studies of Chinese journalists' strategies in framing the news stories of AIDS and SARS.

Janice Xu's essay examines the role of television in the construction of new class identities in contemporary China. Xu discusses the growth of program genres like infomercials, "consumer education" programs, and lifestyle programs that cater to the needs of "the new elite" and the aspirations of the emerging urban middle class. She argues that these programs embrace icons of global consumer culture and enable viewers to imagine and construct new individual identities, and at the same time define their endeavors for empowerment and self-expression in the sphere of consumption. She argues further that Chinese television reinforces the increasingly visible class divisions in society by segmenting audiences into different socio-economic groups.

Tongdao Zhang's essay provides a historical overview of audience research in China as part of his own determination to develop research that serves social as well as economic interests. As he recounts, television reception study originated in China in 1982 as a yet-to-be-defined academic discipline. In that year, a group of communication scholars were commissioned by media organizations in Beijing to conduct research on television viewing patterns in the Beijing area. Audience research grew in the 1980s and 1990s mostly in the service of television stations' commercial interests. The late 1990s witnessed the cultivation of reception study as an academic discipline, with university-based scholars applying Western sociological methods to the field of Chinese audience research. Zhang argues that reception study since 2000 has begun to integrate both quantitative and qualitative methodologies to examine the Chinese audience's viewing patterns, social structure, cultural values, and so forth.

As befits our emphasis on Chinese television as a global phenomenon, *TV China*'s final section spotlights the transnational practice and circulation of Chinese-language television. Here, a major question is what effect the new availability of programming from the "home" culture (if not always home nation-state) has had on Chinese migrant communities. Amy Lee's essay explores the ways in which production contexts intersect with reception contexts to discursively construct a transnational diasporic imaginary. In particular, Lee is interested in the ways in which the circulation of Hong Kong television dramas to overseas Chinatowns has mediated inter-Asian and cross-racial relations in a transpacific and diasporic framework. Her essay follows a cultural studies approach that takes into account the discursive work of television as well as the ways in which the cultural contexts of production and consumption are themselves discursively constructed and understood. In particular, her essay provides textual analysis of what she terms the "travel narrative" constructed by a cluster of television dramas produced by Hong Kong's Television Broadcasts Limited. She argues that, in the American context, the circulation of such travel narratives from Hong Kong television in Chinatowns has produced a cross-border geography of shared cultural imaginaries and disjunctive modernities, which in turn have mediated formations of Chinese immigrant identities.

Cindy Wong's essay asks how media and movement are related through an investigation of the ever more widespread phenomenon of Chinese ethnic diasporic television stations, such as Jade, Phoenix, and CCTV, which supply satellite programs to Chinese households across the U.S. and around the world. In particular, Wong examines the Chinese satellite television community in the northeast U.S., especially the Philadelphia metropolitan area. By comparing the history of Chinese journalism in the U.S. with that of other ethnic media as well as analyzing how television participates in a multi-media environment, she shows how hybrid ethnic identities are promoted, formed, and challenged amongst diasporic Chinese populations. Her essay also underscores complexities in the construction of a dynamic global Chinese identity that must grapple with differences of nation and language as well as global movement.

Finally, Ying Zhu's essay reminds us that Chinese-language television dramas are both agents and beneficiaries of a transnational market commonly understood as the sum of two parts. The major production territories of Hong Kong, Taiwan, and China make up the first part, sometimes referred to as "Greater China" or the "pan-Chinese" region. The overseas communities of the global Chinese diaspora make up the second part. Some Chinese-language television production now occurs in the diaspora, but the distinct domestic media industries that grew up in Hong Kong, Taiwan, and China while they were divided along political and economic lines for most of the past century remain the centers of Chinese media production. Looking at television dramas from each of the three, her essay utilizes a "cultural-linguistic markets" framework to explore forces conducive to the global circulation of Chinese television drama, and the cultural and economic ramifications of this circulation. She discusses how the emergence of a Chinese cultural-linguistic market, together with other cultural-linguistic markets, complicates global cultural flows and power dynamics. Do emerging cultural-linguistic markets challenge the global dominance of mainly American-made cultural products in English? Are we witnessing the dawn of global cultural diversity, or is this just cultural imperialism refashioned in a new pact that carves the world into a few cultural-linguistic spheres of influence, and marginalizes other cultures? Her essay ultimately asks what all this means for the future of transnational Chinese-language media practices.

The boundaries between the sections are far from absolute. Programs have impacts on audiences, and institutional analysis can be transnational. Furthermore, we have aimed to provide balanced coverage in terms of cultural geography, research area, and methodology (ranging from political economy to ethnography and textual analysis). However, our book does not claim to be comprehensive. In particular, Hong Kong and Taiwanese television remain under-explored, compared with our extensive coverage of television in China. This limitation is reflected in the broader field of Chinese-language television studies, and is perhaps a byproduct of what is conventionally understood as the mainland's "cultural hegemony" in the twenty-first century.

However, we hope that each of the essays here opens up more questions across the field of global Chinese television studies. If Xinyu Lu's work shows us how the Spring Festival gala for Chinese New Year has changed as a program, do the Hong Kong audiences Karin Wilkins is interested in and the diasporic audiences that Cindy Wong looks at in Philadelphia watch it? And if so, do they make it part of their New Year's ritual, or are they critical of it? If Chris Berry can depict Shanghai Television's Documentary Channel as opening a public space conditioned by the interests of the party-state apparatus and the market, what are the different ideas of the public circulating in Chinese television cultures? How does the public space of the Documentary Channel compare, for example, with that established by Taiwan's Public Television? If a program like *Meteor Garden*, analyzed here by Hsiu-Chuang Deppman, is pioneering new transnational youth identities across Asia, what is the impact of non-Chinese programming on cultural change and generational difference? Haiqing Yu's focus on journalistic practices in Chinese television news opens up a wide area of research on labor practices and subjectivities in television. Work like Joseph Chan's demonstrates the deeper economic interests driving transnational television in Greater China, but what is the experience of employees of satellite channels, and how do television producers see their role in inter-Chinese relations? What would it reveal to examine these questions in individual institutions like CCTV, examined by Junhao

Hong and his colleagues here, or other genres apart from news, like the historical drama serials Ying Zhu investigates? These are just some of the many ways in which we hope *TV China* stirs up more curiosity about the most important Chinese cultural medium today—Chinese television.

References

Curtin, Michael. 2007. "Reterritorializing Star TV in the PRC." In *Playing to the World's Biggest Audience: The Globalization of Chinese Film and TV*. Berkeley: University of California Press, 192–210.

Donald, Stephanie Hemelryk, Michael Keane, and Yin Hong, eds. 2002. *Media in China: Consumption, Content and Crisis*. London: Routledge Curzon.

Hazelbarth, Todd. 1997. *The Chinese Media: More Autonomous and Diverse—Within Limits; An Intelligence Monograph*. Washington, D.C.: Central Intelligence Agency, Center for the Study of Intelligence.

Hong, Junhao. 1998. *The Internationalization of Television in China: The Evolution of Ideology, Society, and Media since the Reform*. New York: Praeger.

Huang, Yu. 1994. "Peaceful Evolution: The Case of Television Reform in Post-Mao China." *Media, Culture and Society* 16, no. 2: 217–241.

Huang, Yu, and Xu Yu. 1997. "Broadcasting and Politics: Chinese Television in the Mao Era, 1958–1978." *Historical Journal of Film, Radio and Television* 17, no. 4: 563–574.

Keane, Michael. 2007. *Created in China: The Great New Leap Forward*. London: Routledge.

Keane, Michael, Anthony Fung, and Albert Moran. 2007. *New Television, Globalization and the East Asian Imagination*. Hong Kong: Hong Kong University Press.

Kitley, Philip, ed. 2003. *Television, Regulation and Civil Society in Asia*. London: Routledge.

Lee, S. N. Paul. 2000. "Hong Kong Television: An Anchor for Local Identity." In *Television in Contemporary Asia*, ed. David French and Michael Richard, 363–383. Thousand Oaks, Calif.: Sage.

Li, Xiaoping. 2001. "Significant Changes in the Chinese Television Industry and Their Impact in the PRC: An Insider's Perspective." Washington, D.C.: Working Paper of the Center for Northeast Asian Policy Studies, the Brookings Institution. Available at Columbia International Affairs Online, http://www.ciaonet.org/wps/lix01 (accessed 10 September 2002).

"List of Chinese Language Television Channels." n.d. http://en.wikipedia.org/wiki/List_of_Chinese_language_television_channels (accessed 14 September 2007).

Lu, Fei-yi. 1994. "Dianshi: Meijia jingzheng de shenglizhe" [Television: Victor in the Media Competition]. In *Taiwan dianying: Zhengzhi, jingji, meixue* [Taiwan Cinema: Politics, Economics, Aesthetics], 148–153. Taipei: Yunliu.

Lull, James. 1991. *China Turned On: Television, Reform and Resistance*. New York: Routledge.

Ma, Eric Kit-wai. 1999. *Culture, Politics, and Television in Hong Kong*. London: Routledge.

Moran, Albert, and Michael Keane, eds. 2003. *Television across Asia: TV Industries, Program Formats, and Globalisation*. London: Routledge Curzon.

Zhu, Ying. 2008. *Television in Post-Reform China: Serial Dramas, Confucian Leadership, and the Global Television Market.* London: Routledge.

Zhu, Ying, Michael Keane, and Ruoyun Bai, eds. Forthcoming. *TV Drama in China: Unfolding Narratives of Tradition, Political Transformation and Cosmopolitan Identity.* Hong Kong: Hong Kong University Press.

Institution

Toward Television Regionalization in Greater China and Beyond

JOSEPH M. CHAN

The patterns in which television products are internationalized have drawn unfailing interest from scholars, researchers, and policymakers over the last few decades. This interest is due to the important ideological influence that television is assumed to have in identity politics. One major approach to transborder television is derived from the theory of media imperialism, which stresses the asymmetrical relationship between the Western centers and the peripheries of the East and the homogenization of culture (Schiller 1969; Boyd-Barrett 1977, 1998). Underlying this critical stance is the perception that cultural sovereignty and cultural diversity are at risk. Since the 1980s, studies have called for reconsideration of media imperialism because of the rediscovery of the nation-state, the audience's active reception of televisual texts, and the elaboration of more sophisticated patterns of television interactions across borders (e.g., C.-C. Lee 1980; Straubhaar 1991; Sinclair, Jacka, and Cunningham 1996; Barker 1997).

Although globalization is an elusive concept (Hamelink 1999; Held and McGrew 2002), it is central to contemporary discourse on world media and culture (Richards and French 2000; Barker 1997; Tomlinson 1999). The surge in such discourse has renewed interest in the role of the nation-state and the issue of cultural homogenization in this age of globalized communication. To both critical theorists and theorists of globalization, the nation-state is susceptible to the influence of transnational agencies and is rapidly losing its relevancy as communication technologies transcend national boundaries and overcome distance (Golding 1994; Waters 1995; Wriston 1992; Held and McGrew 2002). At the same time, the proliferation of Hollywood products in the cultural market has led some researchers to lament the standardization of culture, resulting in what one characterizes as "the unification of the world under the signs of Mickey Mouse and Bruce Willis" (Gitlin 2002: 21).

Is there a role for the nation-state as television becomes more globalized? Will this globalization result in the homogenization of television culture? Informed by these two general questions, this study attempts to illustrate, through the formation of the Greater China television market, how the nation-state is all but dead and how regionalization should be brought in to make up for the deficiencies of the globalization perspective in accounting for the patterns of transborder television. It also aims to provide an account of how the Greater China television market is being formed. I will examine the strategies and processes that the major players adopt in exploiting this regional market. I will also go beyond Greater China to examine how television programs from its important neighbors Japan and South Korea are affecting regional dynamics. And I will discuss the implications of the resulting patterns for our understanding of television regionalization and globalization.

The Centrality of the China Market

The term "Greater China" may be interpreted in several ways, ranging from the political or economic integration of Taiwan, Hong Kong, and mainland China to cultural exchanges among people of Chinese descent around the world (Harding 1993). This essay regards Greater China as "the economic, political and cultural space defined by the interactions among its three primary constituent parts—Hong Kong, Taiwan and mainland China" (J. Chan 1996: 126). Although Hong Kong was reunified in 1997 with China, which also claims Taiwan as an integral part, the three regions represent different political, economic, and cultural systems. I will therefore treat their television configurations separately. Television that spans the regional boundaries can be considered as transborder or transnational, depending on the ownership of a television player.

Among the three constituents of Greater China, Hong Kong and Taiwan are by themselves marginal markets to transnational television corporations because of their small sizes. Hong Kong is a city with 7 million people, and Taiwan is a region populated by about 24 million, about 75 percent of whom live in urban areas. However, because of their general affluence, these two places do not completely escape the eyes of transnational players. To the transnational players, any extended market can only add to their revenue by allowing them to recycle what they have already produced. But mainland China is the market they covet. Indeed, the China market is also what the broadcasters of Hong Kong and Taiwan crave.

The China market owes its appeal to its large size; China's population is four times that of the United States and one-fifth of the whole of humanity. The populations of many of its provinces match, and sometimes surpass, those of large countries in Western Europe. Given that China is still a developing country with the majority of the population living in rural areas, the economic value of the China television market should not be equated with the population size. What is of value to the transnational and cross-border advertisers is primarily the urban population. The television market potential of China is uneven, with the greatest potential located in the big cities in the coastal region.

The value of the China television market is supported by the high rate at which China's economy has been growing since the early 1990s. At the initial stage of Chinese development, transnational advertising was effective only in making brand names known to the public, who, however, had no real purchasing power. Mass consumption became a major urban lifestyle in the metropolitan areas in China in the early 2000s. While the per capita incomes in these areas are meager by Western standards, they allow some Chinese to acquire not just television sets and washing machines but cellular phones, automobiles, and even private apartments. The urban affluent choose their clothing not just to keep warm but also to show their status and identity. Traveling in and outside the country has become a favorite pastime for many people during weekends and vacations. All these consumption trends have rendered television advertising a formidable business that has been growing at a double-digit rate in the last decade (Huang and Green 2000). What attracts the transnational television players is not necessarily the current value of the China market but its potential. It is therefore strategic for transnational players to secure their position in China, even before it fully opens up. An analysis of Greater China television must grant mainland China a central place.

Television Systems in Greater China

The television systems of the three constituent parts of Greater China are as different as their political configurations. Hong Kong was a British colony that was transformed into a Special Administrative Region of China, and it retains autonomy under the scheme of "one country, two systems." Taiwan, a political rival of the Chinese Communist Party for more than half a century, is a new democracy ruled by the Democratic Progressive Party at the time of writing, which ousted the Kuomintang Party in 2000. Mainland China is a socialist nation that is trying to modernize itself through economic reforms and an open-door policy.

Table 1.1 highlights the differences among the television systems in their ownership, policy toward transborder television, audience characteristics, and exports. Television in Hong Kong operates primarily within a market structure whose parameters are set by government regulators (Chan, Ma, and So 1997; So, Chan, and Lee 2000). Unlike regulatory regimes in many other parts of the world, the licensing conditions under which broadcast television was introduced to Hong Kong did not require a certain amount of local content. While the government has set some limits on the publication of pornographic and politically sensitive materials, government interference in mediated content is minimal in practice. Without an explicit and elaborate cultural policy, Hong Kong is virtually a free port in information; the flow of media in and out is scarcely controlled. Consequently, Hong Kong television has to face competition from the world.

Hong Kong has one of the world's largest libraries of Chinese television programs and is an important regional exporter of audiovisual products (To and Lau 1995). Hong Kong television productions have proved to be very popular in overseas Chinese markets, being distributed through videos, cable and satellite television, piracy, and spillover (in the Guangdong area). The major markets include Taiwan, China, Southeast Asian countries, and Chinese overseas communities in North America and Europe. Hong Kong television first made its name in Taiwan, and later, in the 1980s, became popular in China. Hong Kong television programs owe their competitive edge in China and Taiwan to their higher production quality and quick tempo, their inclusion of well-known stars, and their depiction of modern living. However, with the novelty of Hong Kong television waning and domestic products offering increasing competition, only a few television programs from Hong Kong can draw the crowds in China and Taiwan that they once did.

Taiwan has a long history of authoritarian rule that ended as the Kuomintang (KMT), the ruling party, embarked on a liberalization and democratization program in 1987 (Chen 2002). However, television in Taiwan is very susceptible to the influence of the KMT, the military, the government, and the currently ruling Democratic Progressive Party. Control goes with ownership: the board directors and managers of each station have been appointed by people who are closely affiliated with the interested parties. Although these free-to-air broadcasters are controlled one way or the other by political interests, they are run as

Table 1.1. Television Systems in Greater China

	Mainland China	Taiwan	Hong Kong
Television Ownership and Control	State monopoly, all party-controlled; being commercialized	A developing duopoly marked by the co-existence of commercial terrestrial broadcasters and cable operators, as well as a public broadcasting service (TBS). The terrestrial broadcasters, once subject to the heavy influence of the KMT, the government, and the military, became more controlled by some media entrepreneurs in 2006.	All are privately owned with the exception of one quasi-public broadcaster; minimal regulation
Policy toward Transborder Television	Moving from cultural anti-foreignism to a less severe form of cultural protectionism; censorship and quotas; limited landing rights granted to selected transborder television broadcasters	Restricting imports to different fixed ratios in terrestrial television and cable networks; open to HK-run and foreign television channels in cable television, but requiring at least 20% local programs	Foreign ownership of terrestrial television allowed up to a total of no more than 49%; free flow of programs; foreign channels carried on cable networks
Audience Characteristics	Population about 1.3 billion, about 40% urban, very diverse	Population about 24 million, about 75% urban, relatively homogeneous	Population about 7 million, about 95% urban, homogeneous
Program Exports in Greater China	Limited; some programs are popular in Hong Kong and Taiwan; exports via satellite television, videos, and program sales	Some programs are popular in China and Hong Kong; exports via satellite television, videos, program sales, barter, and piracy	The better programs are popular in China and Taiwan; exports via satellite television, videos, program sales, piracy, and spillover

Note: Adapted from Joseph Chan, "Television in Greater China: Structure, Exports, and Market Formation," in *New Patterns in Global Television: Peripheral Vision*, ed. John Sinclair, Elizabeth Jacka, and Stuart Cunningham (Oxford: Oxford University Press, 1996), 126.

profitable enterprises, resulting in a commercial model that has grown out of oligopolistic competition and a government-business alliance (C.-C. Lee 1980). To weaken the media base of the KMT, Taiwanese president Chen Shui-bian in 2004 launched a policy to depoliticize the media sector by requiring political parties or organizations to stop managing television stations. This policy was successfully implemented in 2006, and it is expected to make the market the most important factor in shaping the development of Taiwanese television. As important as the terrestrial broadcasters in Taiwan are the country's cable networks, which enjoy a penetration rate of more than 76 percent and offer more than 90 channels (Chen 2002).

With the gradual opening of the China market and the penetration of satellite television from Hong Kong, Taiwanese broadcasters are developing a more acute sense of international marketing (J. Chan 1996). Taiwanese television dramas, including martial arts stories, period dramas, romances, and contemporary serials, are very popular in China. Taiwanese dramas are characterized by their emphasis on traditional values and virtues such as fidelity, loyalty, thrift, and the like, and this emphasis seems to resonate strongly with the audience in China. Taiwan began exporting television to Hong Kong in 1971. In more recent years, mainland China has become a more important market for Taiwan, and after the early 1990s, Taiwanese programs began to enjoy some revived interest in Hong Kong.

State-owned and party-controlled, television in China has nonetheless seen important changes in the last two decades, such as the relaxation of ideological control and regulation (Pan and Chan 2000; Huang and Green 2000; Wei 2000; Chang 2002). The cultural anti-foreignism that prevailed during the radical years has subsided, making way for the inflow of Western or capitalist ways of life. Before the reforms, the only foreign programs that were shown were imported from other socialist nations (Hong 1998). Today, both broadcast and cable stations are allowed to show programs originating from Hong Kong, Taiwan, the United States, and other parts of the world, provided that they get political clearance from the government and do not exceed prescribed quotas (Liu 1993; J. Chan 1994a), especially during prime time.

In general, only certain television programs from China are popular in Hong Kong and Taiwan. Hong Kong audiences find the Chinese programs dull and their ideological tone overbearing. Not until the late 1990s did Taiwan allow its television stations to broadcast programs from mainland China. Some of the period dramas proved to be rather popular with the Taiwanese audience. China became more aware of the importance of exporting its programs in the 1990s. CCTV, China's state broadcaster, established Channel 4 to broadcast programs over satellite for audiences in Taiwan and Hong Kong. However, the audience for these programs is insignificant.

Major Players

There are three types of television players in Greater China: (1) global players such as News Corporation and AOL Time Warner, which have significant television operations in many parts of the world; (2) regional players such as Phoenix TV, which focus primarily on regional broadcasting; and (3) national players such as China's CCTV and Hong Kong's Television Broadcasts, or TVB (HK-TVB), which treat regional broadcasting as an extension of their domestic operation. The global players may simply make their home programs available in Asia in general and Greater China in particular. CNN, the BBC, HBO, ESPN, MTV, and the Discovery Channel are the notable examples. The global players may also set up specific channels to target the whole of Greater China or its constituent parts. The Chinese Channel of News Corporation's STAR TV and AOL Time Warner's Chinese Entertainment TV are good examples of such channels. The national players form the basic fabric of regional broadcasting as they take part in program trades, joint productions, and local distribution. The more powerful of the national players, such as CCTV and HK-TVB, can set up custom-built channels for regional broadcasting, such as the former's Channel 4 and the latter's TVB8.

Table 1.2 describes some of the more important television players in Greater China. Although Hong Kong pales in market size, it stands out as the center of broadcasting in the region because of its geopolitical position, advanced communication infrastructure, and rule of law. Consequently, it has become the headquarters for quite a few transborder television operations.

Before I proceed to generalize the strategies and processes of transborder television in Greater China, I deem it necessary to give an example of each type of broadcaster (global, regional, and national).

News Corporation's STAR TV: A Global Player

STAR TV, a subsidiary of News Corporation, is the largest satellite broadcaster in Asia, and has been broadcasting forty services in eight languages to more than 300 million viewers in fifty-three countries from its Hong Kong base since 1991. Besides India, China is STAR TV's major target market. Rupert Murdoch's News Corporation made an entry into China in 1996 by forming a transnational alliance, investing in Phoenix TV, STAR TV's joint venture with Liu Changle, a mainland Chinese with a military background (Otmazgin 2005: 499).

It did not take long for STAR TV to realize that its original idea of pan-Asian broadcasting was not feasible. It divided its services into northern and southern arenas in 1994, with China as the main target in the former and India as the main target in the latter. The immediate success of Zee TV, STAR TV's joint venture in India (broadcast in Hindi), further confirmed STAR TV's need

Table 1.2. Transborder Television Players in
Greater China (in alphabetical order)

Television Players and Content	Headquarters	Primary Target Audience
AOL Time Warner		
· CETV*# (entertainment)	Hong Kong	China
· CNN* (news)	U.S.	Greater China
· HBO* (movies)	U.S.	Greater China
· Cinemax Asia* (movies)	U.S.	Greater China
· Cartoon Network (cartoons)	U.S.	Greater China
Asia Plus (entertainment)	Taiwan	Greater China
BBC World* (news)	UK	Greater China
Bloomberg TV Asian Channel* (financial news)	U.S.	China
CCTV	China	
· Channel 4 (general, in Mandarin)		Greater China
· Channel 9 (general, in English)		Greater China, the world
CNBC Asia Pacific* (financial news)	Singapore	Asian region
Discovery	U.S.	
· Discovery Channel* (information)		Greater China
· Animal Planet* (information)		Greater China
Hallmark	U.S.	
· Asia Channel* (movies)		China
· Taiwan Channel (movies)		Taiwan
· Kermit Channel (education)		China, Taiwan
Japan Entertainment TV* (JETV) (entertainment)	Japan	China, Taiwan
Macau Five Star TV* (youth programs, news, entertainment)	Macau	China
MTV Mandarin*# (music)	U.S.	China, Hong Kong, Taiwan
NHK World Premium* (general)	Japan	China
Phoenix TV	Hong Kong	
· Phoenix Chinese*# (general, entertainment)		China, Hong Kong
· Phoenix Movie*# (movies)		China, Hong Kong
· Phoenix InfoNews* (news)		Greater China

Television Players and Content	Headquarters	Primary Target Audience
STAR TV	Hong Kong	
· STAR Movie* (movies)		Greater China
· STAR World (entertainment)		Hong Kong, Taiwan
· STAR Sports* (sports)		Greater China
· Channel V* (music)		Greater China
· ESPN* (sports)		Greater China
· National Geographic* (science, geography)		Greater China
· Adventure One (adventuring)		Hong Kong
· Fox News* (news)		China, Hong Kong
· Xing Kong Wei Shi*# (entertainment, in Mandarin)		China
· STAR Mandarin Movies (movies, in Mandarin)		Taiwan
· STAR Chinese Channel (general, in Mandarin)		Taiwan
Taipei International Satellite TV	Taiwan	Eastern parts of China and North America
· CTV, TTV, CTS (general)		
· News & Info Channel (news)		
· Movies Channel (movies)		
· Family Channel (education)		
· CSTV (general)		
· MSTV (propaganda)		
TVB	Hong Kong	
· TVB8* (entertainment)		China
· Xing He Channel* (drama)		China
· TVBS (general)		Taiwan
· TVBS Newsnet (news)		Taiwan
· TVBS Golden (entertainment, music)		Taiwan

* with landing rights in three-star or better hotels and selected entities in China
# with landing rights in Guangdong Province

to go local. As a result, STAR TV continually sought joint venture opportunities in the region. Reinforcing this effort is the success of Phoenix TV in China. After struggling for more than a decade, STAR TV is less a regional broadcaster and more a conglomeration of half a dozen local broadcasters slugging it out market by market (Hughes 1998: 6).

In late 2001, STAR TV's venture into China made another breakthrough when its new entertainment channel Xing Kong Wei Shi, a 24-hour Mandarin channel, was granted landing rights in Guangdong Province. The channel was launched in early 2002, via cable television operators, to a million Guangdong households. In return, News Corporation's Fox Cable Networks carry China Central Television's (CCTV) English-language channel CCTV 9 in the U.S.

Phoenix TV: A Regional Player

Phoenix TV was a joint venture between News Corporation's STAR TV and two other corporations with strong China backgrounds. It was listed on Hong Kong's second board, the Growth Enterprise Market (GEM), in October 2000, with Liu Changle as its founder and CEO. The Phoenix channels are targeted to Chinese viewers around the world, although mainland China is the company's primary market. It took Phoenix TV four years to become receivable, through either cable TV or direct satellite, in about 42 million mainland households, or 13 percent of households with television sets in China (Dwyer 2000: 49).

One important reason for Phoenix's popularity is that it provides a programming mix that the state broadcaster, CCTV, fails to provide. Its competitive edge is due largely to its lively variety shows and the relatively liberal way Phoenix treats news and talk shows, which appeal to more educated viewers. Legally, Phoenix TV is only allowed to broadcast to certain restricted areas, but in reality many cable operators carry its channels illegally. Phoenix allows them to download its programs free of charge. The turning point for Phoenix's venture into the China market came in early September 2001, when two Phoenix channels were given approval to broadcast in Guangdong through its cable television network (*South China Morning Post* 2001b). In the few years since its inception, Phoenix has grown into a five-channel station, offering general programs, movies and other entertainment, and news. While it has yet to secure landing rights in Taiwan, it received limited landing rights for the whole of China at the end of 2002 (K. S. Chan 2003).

HK-TVB: A "National"-Turned-Regional Player

The Hong Kong–based TVB plays a significant role in the development of transborder television in Greater China. It owes its influence to its active international marketing efforts and the popularity of its programs. Like those of its local competitor, Asia TV (ATV), TVB's broadcast signals have spilled over into Guangdong since the mid-1980s, outcompeting the domestic broadcasters (J. Chan 2000b). Such penetration was achieved without open permission from the central authorities, but the Chinese government formally gave TVB and ATV landing rights in Guangdong in 2003. However, it remains to be seen whether arrangements will be made for Hong Kong channels to translate their popularity in Guangdong into advertising dollars. Meanwhile, the Chinese channels, as a whole, have risen to the challenge posed by their Hong Kong counterparts, recovering a significant audience share. TVB indicated its ambition in regional broadcasting by launching Galaxy in 1998, which included two 24-hour Mandarin-language satellite channels, TVB8 and TVB Xing He Channel. The footprint of these satellite channels covers China, Southeast Asia, Australia, Europe, and North America (Tang 1998: 3).

TVB8 features a combination of entertainment, infotainment, and musical programs that are popular in most Chinese communities. Both TVB8 and the Xing He Channel were first encrypted, severely restricting their audience on the mainland, but in 2001 TVB revamped TVB8 and made it a free-to-air channel (*South China Morning Post* 2001a). TVB's launching of a channel called TVB Super (TVBS) for the extensive cable networks in Taiwan in 1993 was more profitable (Frank-Keyes 1993). By tailor-making its programs for the Taiwan market, TVBS quickly emerged as a formidable television player in Taiwan, and its performance is known to have an important impact on the partisan terrestrial broadcasters.

Formation of Regional Television

In Western Europe, transborder television is generally received through cable networks or direct-to-home satellite broadcasting. These forms of transmission prevail because European regulators do not forbid consumers to receive signals broadcast from foreign countries. As mainland China restricts foreign media, only individuals or other entities willing to defy the rules can receive DBS (direct broadcast satellite) signals. In the 1990s, foreign broadcasters were formally allowed, at best, to have their programs carried on cable networks at three-star hotels or better and in work units engaged in foreign exchange. STAR TV and Phoenix TV had such permission. But few people can watch such programs. They achieve greater penetration when community and city cable networks take the risk of carrying the satellite signals on their own. Some do this because they are badly in need of programs, both to fill airtime and to attract subscribers with more appealing programming. Such penetration fluctuates with the varying enforcement of the regulations.

It is wrong to assume that China is totally successful in fending off transborder television. Instead, what results is a form of "suppressive openness," meaning that some audiences were made accessible to foreign broadcasters despite restrictive regulation (J. Chan 1996). Regulations were not enforced because the nation-state had lost its political will to do so and the network operators might have chosen to ignore the regulations. When legal defiance is common enough, "suppressive openness" may be legalized and changed into "regulated openness." This began to happen when China formally allowed some foreign broadcasters, including Phoenix TV, AOL Time Warner's Entertainment Television (CETV), the Hong Kong–based Asia TV (ATV), and Television Broadcasts (TVB), to have their signals downlinked to Guangdong cable networks.

This permission marks an important change in China's policy toward foreign broadcasting. Penetration is allowed on a massive scale as long as reception is confined to a predefined area, in this case Guangdong. It can be argued that this is merely a formalization of Hong Kong television's spillover: many people in the Pearl River Delta were already tacitly allowed to receive Hong Kong television signals (J. Chan 2000b). Indeed, the signals were carried by the cable networks in Guangzhou and elsewhere, only with the Hong Kong advertising replaced by local ads.

Trade in television programming has long been recognized and regulated in Greater China. Hong Kong was the first to export its programs, sending them to both mainland China and Taiwan. Although they were highly popular there, cultural protectionism on both sides of the Taiwan Strait has led to restrictions on the proportion of imported programs, especially during prime time. Program trade is therefore only partially subject to the dictates of the market and never became a significant source of revenue for television stations in any of the three regions. However, trade remains a formal channel through which the three regions share programming. The strong transborder appeal of some programs, such as martial arts shows from Hong Kong and costume dramas from mainland China and Taiwan, demonstrates that Greater China has the potential to be a unified television market.

The quota on imported programs in China has led television players in Hong Kong, Taiwan, and elsewhere to form joint production units with Chinese television stations or production houses to produce programs for consumption in all three regions. Forming joint ventures helps them not only evade the quotas but also make the most of the advantages of each place. For instance, the costume drama *Princess Huanzhugege* is a joint production made with Taiwanese capital, shot in China, with actors and production personnel from all three places. It proved to be a great success and has inspired many others to follow suit. Because China wants to separate television transmission from production, it has encouraged the growth of private or semi-private production houses. Ownership of production houses is not as tightly controlled as ownership of television stations, which makes it possible for international corporate players to become involved in television production and financing in China. But the right to broadcast programs remains in the hands of the television station and the party.

The penetration of television in Greater China can take other, more subtle forms, such as piracy and format imitation. In their attempt to attract subscribers, the cable networks in some of the more remote towns in mainland China go so far as to broadcast pirated Hong Kong and Taiwanese television programs, which they obtain by recording them off the air in the Pearl River Delta and Fujian Province. These programs are duplicated as videos and broadcast without official permission. Some of the more popular television series are pirated and sold as videos. People maintain libraries of these videos and circulate them among friends. With the introduction of broadband, some television programs are put on the Internet for people to download. This is most common among university students who have ready access to the Internet.

In Hong Kong and Taiwan, television format, such as that of the British program *Who Wants to Be a Millionaire?*, is sometimes officially imported and paid for. But most of the time, television programs from the West and Japan are important sources of inspiration for television in Greater China. The transfer of television format and even content can thus take place via diffusion, resulting in the convergence of television forms. Programs from around the world are readily available to television producers and managers, who use them as models. Some Chinese are surprised to find, when they travel overseas, that the "innovative formats" they see at home are regular features on Western television.

Transborder Television Strategies

As mentioned earlier, cracking the China market is the most important goal for transborder television players from outside China. Several strategies are emerging. Self-censorship, like that of STAR TV, is essential in order to avoid antagonizing the Chinese government. Rupert Murdoch's decision to take the BBC off of STAR's China programming package has widely been interpreted as an attempt to appease the Chinese government in order to get permission to get into the mainland. His persistent efforts finally paid off when China gave STAR TV limited landing rights and did not object its forming a joint venture, Phoenix TV, with two China-linked corporations. Television players' desire to avoid ideology results in the depoliticization of their programming. Similarly, CETV boasts that it offers entertainment only, staying away from sex and news, while Phoenix TV carries news but it also takes care not to step too far beyond the Chinese Communist Party's ideological boundaries. It openly admits that it has a team in Shenzhen, the city neighboring Hong Kong, to review its programs to ensure that they abide by China's general censorship standards.

Another common strategy of transborder television is to headquarter in Hong Kong. Hong Kong became the broadcasting hub of the region for several reasons. It is where regional satellite television pioneer STAR TV started, and it has always been open to foreign ownership and imported programs. Centrally located in Asia, it has a state-of-the-art communication infrastructure. In addition, it has a vibrant domestic television industry teeming with personnel who are knowledgeable about television in both Greater China and the West. The rule of law also guarantees that transborder television is largely a level playing field. Although Taiwan aspires to be the broadcasting hub of the Asia-Pacific region, its project is endangered by the island's relatively weak legal tradition and shaky political environment. Headquartering in Hong Kong also offers political advantages, because it is a Special Administrative Region of China with autonomy in its internal affairs. This enables Phoenix TV, among others, to broadcast news and information that would have been forbidden were it located in China, giving it a competitive edge over CCTV. Localization is an important lesson to be learned in satellite broadcasting. STAR TV initially dreamed of becoming a pan-Asian broadcaster, with one set of programs for the whole Asia-Pacific region. It learned very soon that this strategy would not work, as Asian culture and regulatory standards are so diversified that country-specific programming is warranted (J. Chan 1994b).

The success of Zee TV, a subsidiary of STAR TV, in India and the later success of Phoenix TV in mainland China offer more evidence of the need for localization. Programming can be localized at various levels, including language, packaging, program mix, marketing strategies, and the like. CETV intends to employ production houses in mainland China to provide programs. TVB of Hong Kong repackages and dubs some of its Cantonese programs for Galaxy. Without some form of localization, it is virtually impossible for a transborder television broadcaster to appeal to a significant proportion of the audience in a given market.

Transborder broadcasters cannot just wait for formal approval to enter China's television market. The lure of profit has motivated all parties to search for new ways of exploiting the leeway that is allowed within the Chinese system. While they may keep on prodding the Beijing authorities for permission, they often resort to the strategy of networking (*guanxi*) to surmount the difficulty. Networking is mobilized as a way to evade formal restrictions, allowing players to downlink foreign satellite television signals, exchange programs for advertising time, and form joint ventures in production or other aspects of the television business. All these arrangements would not be possible without understanding on both sides and the intricate connections that the Chinese partner has with the television regulators and personnel in China. By the creative use of such intricate webs of social connections, China is opening itself up to Hong Kong and Taiwanese television in an evolutionary manner, attesting to the subversive forces of networking and profiteering.

The Impact of Japanese and Korean Television

The Greater China transborder television market does not stop at geographical boundaries. There are growing signs that it extends to include productions from its neighbors Korea and Japan, many of whose programs, through videos and television, have gained large followings, first in Taiwan, then in Hong Kong, and finally in China, among the middle classes and the younger generation. Inspired by these productions, producers in Greater China imitate their formats. The pressing need for programs to fill up the rapidly expanding airtime in mainland China has spurred the importation of programs from Japan and Korea. The development of regional cable and satellite networks such as News Corporation's STAR TV (Warner 1997: 5) and Japan Entertainment Television, Inc. (JET TV) has provided the necessary infrastructure for the pan-Asian distribution of drama programs. The popularization of Japanese and Korean television is a result of what Otmazgin calls "regional dynamism," or economic activities without formal agreement between the governments (Otmazgin 2005: 499).

Japan has for decades been the largest television exporter in the region (Eunmi 1999). Japanese cartoons, game shows, "reality" shows, dramas, and so on have been well received in different parts of the region since the 1970s. Studies show that Japanese television programs, particularly animated ones, are more appealing in Asia than their American counterparts (*Asiaweek* 1996). As well as a regional economic and financial center, Japan is also the leader of popular culture in the region. The influence of Japanese television programming in Greater China increased after the phenomenal success of a new breed of "trendy," or idol, dramas that emerged in the mid-1990s. Qualitatively different from the traditional costume drama, which emphasized artistic creation, this genre is treated by its producers as a cultural commodity designed to score high ratings, promote brand products, and appease program sponsors. Popular comics such as *Tokyo Love Story* and *GTO* (*Great Teacher Onizuka*) that have already captured a large group of young readers are adapted for television. Producers also deliberately cast young idols and feature attractive lifestyles in order to appeal to youngsters. As well as providing the young audience with a storyline, popular Japanese idol dramas are complemented by a chain of derivative cultural commodities, including videos and theme music, as well as artifacts featured in the drama (Tong 2000). The marketing of these spin-off products adds impetus to the formation of the "Haryu Tribe," or fans of Japanese popular culture, and paves the way for the popularization of the Japanese lifestyle in general.

While Japanese idol dramas have a strong influence in the Greater China region, Taiwan has been the keenest consumer of Japanese cultural products because of its status as a former Japanese colony and its traditional ties with Japan's cultural legacy. However, Japanese culture's entry into Taiwan is not straightforward. The KMT government banned Japanese-language television programming after Japan severed its diplomatic relations in favor of mainland China in 1972. For the next two decades, the Taiwanese audience could view Japanese TV programs only when they were illegally transmitted by the cable networks. This ban was lifted in 1993 when Taiwan's cable television industry was put under formal and open regulation, thereby making way for the influx of Japanese television programs and a variety of cultural products (Iwabuchi 2002: 122).

News Corporation's STAR TV was the first international broadcaster to introduce Japanese drama programs to Taiwan. In 1997, five cable channels offered specialized Japanese programming around the clock. Without the rapid development of cable and satellite television networks in Taiwan, it is likely that the penetration of Japanese television programming would have been hindered.

Hong Kong, noted for its strong indigenous television culture, is also susceptible to the influence of Japanese television drama. The annual reports of the Hong Kong Broadcasting Authority indicate that programming imported from Japan was a staple for both terrestrial and pay TV channels around the turn of the millennium. Although only a few selected Japanese idol dramas could be aired on terrestrial television, the impact of Japanese idol dramas on the development of Hong Kong popular culture is noticeable (Ha 2000). Pirated Japanese television dramas circulated widely on video and VCD through an "open" black market. It was estimated at one time that there were more than two hundred video shops in Hong Kong selling pirated Japanese television dramas. A million copies were confiscated by the Customs and Excise Department of Hong Kong in 1998–1999. Major Japanese television stations, such as Fuji TV and TBS, even sent delegates to Hong Kong to exert pressure on the government to tackle the problem of video piracy.

The influence of Japanese television drama is also revealed through a tide of "cultural confluence" (Otmazgin 2005: 499), the mixing of regional and local cultures. In Hong Kong, storylines from popular Japanese television dramas are adapted or modified (*Tai Kung Pao* 1998). News about Japanese television idols is prominently displayed in Hong Kong's daily newspapers and entertainment weeklies. Japanese idols are offered roles in Hong Kong movies. In exchange, Hong Kong talents are invited to appear in Japanese dramas, as singer Faye Wong was by Fuji Television (*Southern Metro Daily* 2001). This strategic move revealed how this Japanese television station treasured its regional market in Greater China.

It took only a few years for pirated Japanese television dramas to spread from Hong Kong to mainland China. While the historical hostility between China and Japan served to reinforce Beijing's restrictions on imported programs, some popular Japanese television dramas scored high ratings when they were shown on provincial television channels during fringe time. For example, *Tokyo Love Story*, *101-kai me no puropozu*, and others were well received in Shanghai during 1998. Related media products such as popular magazines, theme music, and VCDs also had wide appeal (Yao 2000). Japanese television dramas further penetrated mainland China by taking advantage of China's policy of separating production from transmission. Fuji TV, for instance, agreed to co-produce with some Chinese provincial television stations Chinese versions of some popular Japanese dramas. Cultural hybridization also resulted when the storylines of Japanese dramas were appropriated for local productions.

The prevalence of Japanese television drama in Greater China is understandable in view of Japan's long-standing role as a regional economic and cultural center. South Korea's emergence as an audio-visual center is more surprising, because it occurred in spite of competition from the country's giant neighbors China and Japan. It is even more ironic that Japan and China have turned out to be the largest buyers of Korean soap opera (Shin 2005). Japan only lifted restrictions on importing Korean television programs in 1998. A Korean soap opera tragedy titled *Winter Sonata* gained huge popularity in Japan in 2003 and created what was called the "Winter Sonata Syndrome" among local audiences. Japan's public broadcaster, NHK, aired it twice on its satellite channel in that year alone. The show generated around US$200 million in Japan in 2004, not counting sales of DVDs, books, travel guides, and broadcasting rights. *Winter Sonata*'s leading man, Bae Yong-joon, was identified by Dentsu, Japan's largest advertising agency, as "the country's fourth biggest hit product" in the first half of 2004 (B.-M. Lee 2004). These cultural products even melted down the traditional political hostility between the two countries (Endo and Matsumoto 2004: 1). The triumph of *Winter Sonata* in Japan was only part of what the Chinese press in the late 1990s called the "Korean Wave": the growing impact of Korean popular culture in East Asia in general and China in particular. Korean popular culture takes the form of television dramas, movies, pop music, online games, food, fashion, and pop idols.

The emergence of the Korean Wave in Asia can be viewed as the result of a revitalized interest in Asian cultural products among Asian people who share a similar process of modernization (Russell 2003: 8). But this explanation is at best partial. As a matter of fact, the government of South Korea played a vital role in promoting the Korean Wave. After the Asian economic crisis, it realized that the culture industry was key to fueling the country's economic growth, and that it could be used to promote the country's image as well as attract foreign investment. The government consequently stepped up its investment in the entertainment industry from US$8.5 billion in 1999 to US$43.5 billion in 2003 (Onishi 2005: 3). The Ministry of Culture and Tourism provides various supports to private companies to help them create new, innovative cultural content and enter overseas markets (Yang 2006). In addition to investing directly, the Korean government also actively promotes Korean cultural products and exports them to other Asian countries. It is no coincidence that *Jewel in the Palace*, also known as *Daejanggeum*, became the most-watched Korean television drama in Asia (KOIS 2006). When it aired in Hong Kong in 2005, the show was watched by nearly half of Hong Kong's 6.9 million people (Frater 2005). Its success testifies that the combination of American production techniques and Confucian values can indeed catapult Korean television drama into countries with similar cultural backgrounds.

Eclipsing the United States and Japan, the Korean Wave spread across various countries in the region and even reached out across the globe. Countries as diverse as the United States, the Philippines, Mexico, Egypt, and Iraq broadcast Korean dramas, subtitled in local languages, through their cable networks and terrestrial television stations (Bruno 2005). According to South Korea's Ministry of Culture and Tourism, drama accounted for 91.8 percent of all broadcasting exported in 2004. This is a steep increase from 76.8 percent in 2002 and 85.7 percent in 2003. The widening appeal of Korean television drama has led the television industry to invest even more in production in an effort to enhance its competitiveness in the regional and world market (B.-M. Lee 2004).

However, signs of backlash against the Korean Wave began to appear in Greater China in 2006. The asymmetrical flow of Korean pop culture to the entire region has redefined Korea's cultural relationship with her neighboring countries, whose TV industries feel great pressure when competing with the American-styled Korean television dramas. Chinese government officials raised concerns over the excessive inflow of Korean culture. Some even hinted that China might stop importing Korean television drama and might cut imports by 50 percent in the future (*Business Korea* 2006). An immediate result was that China's contracts to import Korean soap operas dropped by nearly 30 percent at the 2006 Shanghai TV Festival. Anti-Korea sentiment has also appeared in Taiwan. The Taiwanese regulatory agency, the Government Information Office, is reported to be considering banning soap operas produced by Japan, Korea, China, and Hong Kong during prime time in order to protect local production. They are also considering imposing a 20 percent tariff on Korean programs (Ko 2006).

In order to sustain the Korean Wave, a call was made for Korean stars and producers to change their attitude and seek bilateral relationships and cultural exchange with other Asian countries (*Korea Times* 2005). All these developments show that while it is difficult to imagine how any television system in East Asia can isolate itself from its neighbors, it is premature to view the East Asian television market as one unified whole.

Theoretical Implications and Concluding Remarks

In a nutshell, the patterns of transborder broadcasting in Greater China are very much a reflection of the evolution of changes in the regulatory regimes in its constituent parts. Program trade is the oldest form of television exchange, having begun in the 1980s. When foreign television was banned in China, spillover was an important mode of diffusion, especially in the Pearl River Delta. It was the contest of will between audience and censors that determined the rates of penetration. Piracy also plays an important role in bringing in transborder television. This is true especially for restricted but popular programs like Japanese soap operas. China's granting of landing rights in Guangdong and limited landing rights elsewhere to foreign channels marks the country's willingness to formally allow the entry of transborder television on a relatively large scale.

The occasional success of a few television programs in the whole of Greater China demonstrates that transborder television has strong potential. Television players from the constituent parts are increasingly interacting, resulting in program trades, joint ventures, and other kinds of exchange. It is premature to expect Chinese television to open to the world completely. However, the success of some transborder programs in the region testifies to the existence of common cultural tastes in Greater China. The popular cultures of Taiwan and Hong Kong, including television programs, pop songs, and movies, are very influential in China. The sharing of a common popular culture constitutes and is constituted by regional television. The interactions of television cultures represent what Jonathan Friedman refers to as the consumption of palatable cultural difference (Friedman 2002). Viewers are socialized to the familiar and yet different imported programs, and at the same time they are entertained by products that try to integrate elements from all three places, including artists, producers, formats, and stories.

At this juncture, I would like to return to the questions I raised at the beginning of the chapter in regard to the role of the nation-state and the prospect of cultural homogenization. First of all, the state is facing challenging conditions, such as the expansion of transnational media corporations, the increasing liberalization and privatization of media systems worldwide, and the development of cable and satellite technologies (Waisbord and Morris 2001). These challenges have indeed weakened the capability of nation-states to exercise power and maintain information sovereignty. However, as the case of Greater China attests, it is really too early to declare the state irrelevant. In spite of the advent of communication technologies such as satellite and cable, ideological and regulatory differences still constitute the limiting factor in the formation of the Greater China television market. Political and ideological boundaries continue to prevent the free flow of capital, personnel, and programs between China and the other two Chinese societies. Like other countries that practice media protectionism, China is afraid of external ideological influence that may threaten the status quo, corrupt the public mind, and cause social instability (J. Chan 2000a). China is still wary of alien forces coming from Hong Kong, Taiwan, and the West that may undermine the socialist system. Such ideological concerns result in the prohibition of foreign satellite television reception, censorship, and quota controls. All these restrictions have prevented transborder broadcasters in Hong Kong and Taiwan from taking full advantage of the China market. As in other countries, formal regulation still rests in the hands of the national political and commercial elite (Sreberny-Mo-hammadi et al. 1997). The nation-state continues to play a critical role in regulating communication across national boundaries and the development of a national cultural industry. Indeed, in China and elsewhere the nation-state even plays a key role in managing the globalization process itself (Yan 2002).

Political considerations in Taiwan also hinder the formation of regional television in Greater China. Inherited from an authoritarian rule that guaranteed oligopoly and profit, Taiwan's television system remains extremely susceptible to influence from the major political parties and the government. Taiwan's and China's mutual political suspicions have led to restrictions on program imports from the mainland. Taiwan and China are at a stalemate, trying to outsmart one another in negotiations. The principle of reciprocity has become a tool by which Taiwan tries to prevent Chinese television from penetrating its home market. To this day, Taiwan bans CCTV Channel 4 from its territory, stating that landing rights will be given only under the condition of reciprocity. All these political and ideological barriers across the Taiwan Strait demonstrate the key roles that nation-states may play in the future development of the Greater China television market. As well as passively resisting the domination of transborder television, nation-states can also take a proactive role to establish their own regional television. Though the formation of regional television is mainly driven by the market, the example of South Korea shows that a government can play an important role in guiding and facilitating the culture industry's development. The success of the South Korean government in invigorating its cultural industry is expected to have a demonstration effect on its Asian neighbors.

The second theoretical concern is whether globalization will result in cultural homogenization. My account of the formation of transborder television in Greater China can only provide a partial response to this question, since it is confined to analysis of the industrial and institutional levels. It shows that the globalization of television is an extraordinarily complex phenomenon that must be examined at the local, regional, national, and global levels. Of particular importance in the case of Greater China are the national and regional levels, and in saying this I echo other scholars who have called for attention to regional television (Sinclair, Jacka, and Cunningham 1996; Straubhaar 2002). The multi-level perspective is different from the unidirectional flow conceived by the earlier theory of media imperialism, which saw the U.S. as a dominating center (Schiller 1969; Boyd-Barrett 1998). It represents increasing flows of capital, programs, and cultures in regions defined by geographical location and cultural proximity (Sinclair, Jacka, and Cunningham 1996). The case of Greater China shows that the influence of regional broadcasters is more prominent than that of global players, particularly when the latter make no attempt to offer tailor-made programs. Programs co-produced by regional players are in general more popular than their Western counterparts. The dissemination of television around the world is an uneven process, with America more dominant in certain places. In Greater China, American television does not occupy the largest proportion of screen time, nor does it produce the most-watched programs. Instead, the intensive confluence of both local and regional cultures and the collaborative efforts of different markets have created several "most-watched" regional television programs.

However, television culture is not spreading by simple imitation. The television industries in Greater China are developing differently. In China, television is an integral part of the propaganda machine; in Hong Kong, it is a cultural industry; and in Taiwan, it is transforming itself from a cultural arm of the ruling political party into a more autonomous cultural industry. As television is reconfigured in China, it is beyond doubt that models from the West and Hong Kong are often a source of inspiration. When China borrows from outside, it tends to appropriate what is best suited to its interests, creating a hybrid culture in the process. Pure imitation is rare, and television culture is being Westernized, regionalized, and reinvented at the same time. Parallel to this is transborder broadcasters' need to localize their programs. STAR TV, for instance, has to offer tailor-made content and repackage its programs for specific markets in China and elsewhere. As long as hybridization and localization are a part of transborder broadcasting, there is no reason to expect the homogenization of television culture.

This being said, we should not neglect one thing toward which television cultures are converging. The penetration of transborder television puts pressure on terrestrial and domestic broadcasters by offering alternative programming and more-balanced news reporting. For instance, the popularity of TVBS, a satellite television service initiated by HK-TVB, in Taiwan exerts strong pressure on the Taiwanese terrestrial broadcasters to expand their ideological boundaries by allowing news and commentaries that are more critical of the ruling party and to increase the quotas on Chinese and Hong Kong programming. Similar pressure exists in China. As transborder television gains a foothold in China, terrestrial television has to come up with competitive strategies. Chinese authorities' most logical policy is to give the domestic television operations the same degree of autonomy that their foreign competitors have. That partly explains why CCTV was allowed to broadcast the Second Gulf War live and to give it 24-hour attention. Without a freer hand, CCTV is going to lose more and more viewers to Phoenix TV, which took the war as another opportunity for rapid growth. The market success of CCTV will in turn spark imitations by other Chinese broadcasters. Television innovations from within and without are diffused through China in this way, and this chain reaction inevitably leads to some degree of cultural convergence.

Notes

This is an updated and revised version of Joseph Chan, "Trans-border Broadcasters and TV Regionalization in Greater China: Processes and Strategies," in Transnational Television Worldwide: Towards a New Media Order, *ed. Jean Chalaby (London: I. B. Tauris, 2005), pp. 173–195. This essay devotes more attention to the rise of Japanese and Korean television in Greater China.*

References

Asiaweek. 1996. "Asia Says Japan Is Top of the Pops." 5 January, pp. 35–39.

Barker, Chris. 1997. *Global Television: An Introduction.* Oxford: Blackwell.

Boyd-Barrett, Oliver. 1977. "Media Imperialism: Towards an International Framework for the Analysis of Media Systems." In *Mass Communication and Society,* ed. James Curran, Michael Gurevitch, and Janet Woolacott, 116–135. London: Edward Arnold.

———. 1998. "Media Imperialism Reformulated." In *Electronic Empires: Global Media and Local Resistance,* ed. Daya Kishan Thussu, 157–176. London: Arnold.

Bruno, San. 2005. "Korean TV Dramas Rise in Popularity in North America: YA Entertainment Brings English-Subtitled Dramas to Eager Viewers." PR Newswire (U.S.), 6 July.

Business Korea. 2006. "Hallyu Hits the World!" 1 July.

Chan, Joseph. 1994a. "Media Internationalization in China: Processes and Tensions." *Journal of Communication* 44, no. 3:70–88.

———. 1994b. "National Responses and Accessibility to STAR TV in Asia." *Journal of Communication* 44, no. 3:112–131.

———. 1996. "Television in Greater China: Structure, Exports, and Market Formation." In *New Patterns in Global Television: Peripheral Vision,* ed. John Sinclair, Elizabeth Jacka, and Stuart Cunningham, 126–160. Oxford: Oxford University Press.

———. 2000a. "No Culture Is an Island: An Analysis of Media Protectionism and Media Openness." In *The New Communications Landscape: Demystifying Media Globalization,* ed. Georgette Wang, Jan Servaes, and Anura Goonasekera, 251–264. London: Routledge.

———. 2000b. "When Socialist and Capitalist Television Clash: The Impact of Hong Kong Television on Guangzhou Residents." In *Money, Power, and Media: Communication Patterns and Bureaucratic Control in Cultural China,* ed. Chin-Chuan Lee, 245–270. Chicago: Northwestern University Press.

———. 2005. "Trans-border Broadcasters and TV Regionalization in Greater China: Processes and Strategies." In *Transnational Television Worldwide: Towards a New Media Order,* ed. Jean Chalaby, 173–195. London: I. B. Tauris.

Chan, Joseph, Eric Ma, and Clement So. 1997. "Back to the Future: A Retrospect and Prospects for the Hong Kong Mass Media." In *The Other Hong Kong Report 1997,* ed. Joseph Cheng, 455–482. Hong Kong: Chinese University Press.

Chan, K. S. 2003. "HK Phoenix Satellite Gets China Landing Rights." *Dow Jones International News,* 6 January.

Chang, Tsan-Kuo. 2002. *China's Window on the World: TV News, Social Knowledge, and International Spectacles.* Cresskill, N.J.: Hampton.

Chen, Binghong. 2002. "Changes in the Configuration and Operation of the Television Industry in Taiwan." [In Chinese.] Paper presented to the Conference on the Prospect and Retrospect of Taiwanese Television, National Chengchi University, Taiwan, 31 October–1 November.

Dow Jones International News. 2001. "News Corp's Star TV Gains Landing Rights in South China." 19 December.

Dwyer, Michael. 2000. "TV: The Key to Chinese Puzzle." Australian Financial Review, 24 October, p. 49.

Endo, Fumiko, and Atsuko Matsumoto. 2004. "Currents: TV Dramas Melt Hearts, Thaw Japan-ROK Relations." Daily Yomiuri, 5 December, p. 1.

Eun-mi, Byun. 1999. "Korean Soap Operas Gaining Popularity in Asia." Korea Herald, 21 July.

Frank-Keyes, John. 1993. "TVB 'Super Channel' Hits Taiwan." South China Morning Post, 27 October.

Frater, Patrick. 2005. "Asian Market Finds Its Seoul: Entertainment Sector Reportedly Up 11% Year-on-Year." Daily Variety, 9 October.

Friedman, Jonathan. 2002. "Globalization and the Making of a Global Imaginary." In Global Encounters: Media and Cultural Transformation, ed. Gitte Stald and Thomas Tufte, 13–32. Luton, UK: University of Luton Press.

Gitlin, Todd. 2002. "The Unification of the World under the Signs of Mickey Mouse and Bruce Willis: The Supply and Demand Sides of American Popular Culture." In In Search of Boundaries: Communication, Nation-States, and Cultural Identities, ed. Joseph Chan and Bryce McIntyre, 21–34. Westport, Conn.: Ablex.

Golding, Peter. 1994. "The Communication Paradox: Inequality at the National and International Levels." Media Development 3:7–9.

Ha, Ying Fang. 2000. "The Resurgent Tide of Japanese Drama." [In Chinese.] Wen Wei Po (Hong Kong), 6 September.

Hamelink, Cees. 1999. "The Elusive Concept of Globalization." Global Dialogue 1, no. 1:1–9.

Harding, Harry. 1993. "The Concept of Greater China: Themes, Variations and Reservations." China Quarterly, no. 136:660–686.

Held, Havid, and Anthony McGrew. 2002. Globalization/Anti-globalization. Oxford: Polity.

Hong, Junhao. 1998. The Internationalization of Television in China: The Evolution of Ideology, Society, and Media since the Reform. Westport, Conn.: Praeger.

Huang, Yu, and Andrew Green. 2000. "From Mao to the Millennium: 40 Years of Television in China." In Television in Contemporary Asia, ed. David French and Michael Richards, 267–292. New Delhi: Sage.

Hughes, Owen. 1998. "Davey Says Plan for Development of Pan-Asian TV Network Unchanged—Star Affirms Localization Strategy." South China Morning Post, 8 April.

Iwabuchi, Koichi. 2002. Recentering Globalization: Popular Culture and Japanese Transnationalism. Durham, N.C.: Duke University Press.

Ko, Shu-ling. 2006. "GIO Looking to Take Foreign Soap Operas off Prime Time TV." [In Chinese.] Taipei Times, 11 January.

KOIS (Korean Overseas Information Service), Government Information Agency. 2006. "Korea Beating Japan in IT, Innovation, and Pop Culture: Le Monde." 12 June. http://www.korea.net.

Korea Times. 2005. "The Power of Korean Dramas." 28 October.

Lee, Byung-Min. 2004. "The Investment Opportunity of Korea's Cultural & Content Industry." *Korea Trade & Investment*, 25 November.

Lee, Chin-Chuan. 1980. *Media Imperialism Reconsidered: The Homogenizing of Television Culture*. Beverly Hills, Calif.: Sage.

Lee, Ji-young. 2004. "TV Producers Step Up Investments in Their Shows." 21 August. http://joins.com.

Liu, Yu-li. 1993. "Comparing Cable Television Laws and Regulations in China and Taiwan." [In Chinese.] *Mass Communication Research*, no. 53:209–230.

Onishi, Norimitsu. 2005. "South Korea Adds Culture to Its Export Power." *New York Times*, 29 June, p. 3.

Otmazgin, N. Kadosh. 2005. "Cultural Commodities and Regionalization in East Asia." *Contemporary Southeast Asia* 27, no. 3:499.

Pan, Zhongdang, and Joseph Chan. 2000. "Building a Market-Based Party Organ: Television and National Integration in China." In *Television in Contemporary Asia*, ed. David French and Michael Richards, 232–263. New Delhi: Sage.

Richards, Michael, and David French. 2000. "Globalization, Television and Asia." In *Television in Contemporary Asia*, ed. David French and Michael Richards, 13–28. New Delhi: Sage.

Russell, Mark. 2003. "Korean TV Sector Enters New Era." *Hollywood Reporter*, 18–24 March.

Schiller, Herbert. 1969. *Mass Communication and the American Empire*. Boston: Beacon.

Shin, Hae-in. 2005. "Keeping Up 'Addiction to Korean TV Dramas'; Drama-Makers Should Concentrate on Presenting Dramas Conveying Korean Perspective, Culture." *Korea Herald*, 16 November.

Sinclair, John, Elizabeth Jacka, and Stuart Cunningham. 1996. "Peripheral Vision." In *New Patterns in Global Television: Peripheral Vision*, ed. John Sinclair, Elizabeth Jacka, and Stuart Cunningham, 1–32. Oxford: Oxford University Press.

So, Clement, Joseph Chan, and Chin-Chuan Lee. 2000. "[Mass Media of] Hong Kong SAR (China)." In *Handbook of the Media in Asia*, ed. Shelton Gunaratne, 527–551. New Delhi: Sage.

South China Morning Post. 2001a. "Foreign TV Not So Remote—Guangdong in Line for Foreign TV Broadcasting Breakthrough." 6 September, p. 1.

———. 2001b. "Phoenix One Wing Short." 31 October, p. 1.

Southern Metro Daily (Guangzhou). 2001. "Faye Wong to Be the Actress for Japanese Drama." [In Chinese.] 21 February.

Sreberny-Mohammadi, Annabelle, Dwayne Winseck, Jim McKenna, and Oliver Boyd-Barrett. 1997. "Editor's Introduction: Media in Global Context." In *Media in Global Context: A Reader*, ed. Annabelle Sreberny-Mohammadi, Dwayne Winseck, Jim McKenna, and Oliver Boyd-Barrett, iv–xxviii. London: Arnold.

Straubhaar, Joseph. 1991. "Beyond Media Imperialism: Asymmetrical Interdependence and Cultural Proximity." *Critical Studies in Mass Communication* 8, no. 1:39–59.

———. 2002. "(Re)asserting National Television and National Identity against the Global, Regional, and Local Levels of World Television." In *In Search of Boundaries: Communication, Nation-States, and Cultural Identities*, ed. Joseph M. Chan and Bryce T. McIntyre, 181–206. Westport, Conn.: Ablex.

Tai Kung Pao. 1998. "The Influence of Japanese Drama on Audio-Visual Production." [In Chinese.] 29 December.

Tang, Rose. 1998. "TVB Eyes Fresh Revenue Sources as Adverts Fall." *South China Morning Post*, 28 May, p. 3.

To, Yiu-ming, and Tuen-yu Lau. 1995. "Global Export of Hong Kong Television: Television Broadcasts Limited." *Asian Journal of Communication* 5, no. 2:108–121.

Tomlinson, John. 1999. *Globalization and Culture*. Chicago: University of Chicago Press.

Tong, Ching Siu. 2000. *Japanese Drama at the Frontline*. Taipei: Business Weekly Press.

Waisbord, Silvio, and Nancy Morris. 2001. "Introduction: Rethinking Media Globalization and State Power." In *Media and Globalization: Why the State Matters*, ed. Silvio Waisbord and Nancy Morris, vii–xvi. Lanham, Md.: Rowman and Littlefield.

Warner, Fara. 1997. "Japanese TV Programs Set Pop Culture Trends for the Region's Youth." *Asian Wall Street Journal*, 14 August, p. 5.

Waters, Malcolm. 1995. *Globalization*. London: Routledge.

Wei, Ran. 2000. "China's Television in the Era of Marketization." In *Television in Contemporary Asia*, ed. David French and Michael Richards, 325–346. New Delhi: Sage.

Wriston, Walter. 1992. *The Twilight of Sovereignty*. New York: Macmillan.

Yan, Yunxiang. 2002. "Managed Globalization." In *Many Globalizations: Culture Diversity in the Contemporary World*, ed. Peter Berger and Samuel Huntington, 19–47. Oxford: Oxford University Press.

Yang, Sung-jin. 2006. "Korean Wave in Harmony with Asian Nations: New Plans Envision Increase in Cultural Exchanges with BRICs—Brazil, Russia, India, China." *Korea Herald*, 25 February.

Yao, A'lian. 2000. "The Battle of Local Productions." *Shanghai Youth Daily*, 29 August.

CCTV in the Reform Years: A New Model for China's Television?

JUNHAO HONG, YANMEI LÜ, & WILLIAM ZOU

Founded in 1958 and originally known as Beijing Television, China Central Television (CCTV) is the only national television network in China. Beijing Television was renamed CCTV in 1978, the year when China entered the reform era. Reform has entailed both the introduction of a market sector into China's economy and the adoption of a responsibility system in the state-owned sector, in which each economic unit is expected to be responsible for its own financial viability rather than rely on state support. From 1958 to the late 1970s, CCTV mainly functioned as a mouthpiece for the Chinese Communist Party (CCP), an ideological vehicle through which were advocated continuous political movements such as class struggle, the Anti-Rightist Campaign of 1958, the Great Leap Forward of 1959, and the 1966–1976 Cultural Revolution. Since 1978, like other economic, political, and cultural institutions in China, CCTV has experienced numerous changes: it has undergone organizational restructuring, its financial resources have been redefined, its roles and functions have been adjusted, and its programming content and development strategies have been redesigned in an effort to make it a world-class television network. The significance of the changes that have occurred within CCTV goes far beyond CCTV itself. CCTV is often viewed as a window on China's politics, economy, and society, and changes in CCTV demonstrate that the country has been moving toward a society of mass consumption with a public-oriented civic culture, even while it is sternly maintaining communist ideology. This article examines, accounts for, and considers the implications of what has changed and what has not changed at CCTV since reform began in the late 1970s, with an emphasis on the last fifteen years.

Relaxation of Political Control and Breakthroughs in Program Content

The reform of CCTV has had two phases. The first phase lasted for about fifteen years, from 1978 to 1993. During this time changes were gradual and mostly involved professional, administrative, and technical areas. Nevertheless, these changes paved the way for more substantial and comprehensive changes in the second phase, the ten years since the mid-1990s.

The initial changes were focused on CCTV's *Evening News* (*Xinwen lianbo*). Constant innovation since 1978 has gradually established the authority of CCTV's news broadcasts, which now reach 400 million viewers every day, topping the national news-program ratings. New news magazine programs such as *Observe and Think* (*Guancha yu sikao*) were considered reflections of the national transformation that triggered a wave of investigative reporting in China.

In the early 1980s, special television news reports and documentaries produced by CCTV spurred introspection about China's history, society, and culture. These shows included *The Odyssey of the Great Wall, The Yangtze River, The Grand Canal,* and *He Shang—A River That Dies Young.* They not only raised CCTV's cultural status, but also considerably enhanced its popularity and social influence.

Changes in the news program sector were complemented by new initiatives in entertainment and sports. The Spring Festival Gala, produced by CCTV and broadcast on the eve of the lunar New Year, debuted in 1983 and soon became an indispensable annual cultural ritual for the people. The Spring Festival Gala has remained the most popular television entertainment program in China to date, and is one of the most talked-about events among the public every year.

The new initiatives also included bold moves toward showing imports from Western countries, some of which were still regarded as China's political or ideological enemies. For instance, in the early 1980s CCTV began to broadcast a number of programs imported from the U.S., the former West Germany, and

Japan, such as *The Man from Atlantis*, *Animal World*, *Garrison's Gorillas*, and *Sanshiro Sugata*. This bold move considerably stimulated domestic television production, especially of audience-oriented entertainment programs and television plays and series, laying the foundation for the more recent boom in Chinese television.

Since 1993, the reform of CCTV has become more thorough, as symbolized by the debut of *Oriental Horizon* (*Dongfang shikong*) on 1 May 1993. *Oriental Horizon* was China's first large-scale news magazine program. It comprised four sub-programs: *Son of the Orient*, *Golden Songs of Oriental Horizon* (which was later renamed *Musical TV*, and which was eliminated in 1996 after CCTV restructured its overall programming), *Living Space*, and *Focus*. "Facing the audience sincerely" was the slogan of these programs (Y. Sun 2003). For decades, China's media had been seen as using big but empty words, exaggeration, and repetition. In general, television broadcasting resembled the serious and revolutionary style of the Xinhua News Agency, the official news agency of the CCP and the central government. However, with the advent of CCTV's new programs, the logjam began to shift and the media became more audience-oriented. The systematic redesign of program content followed. For example, *Oriental Horizon* took the risk of hiring several well-known, politically "brave" newspaper and magazine journalists as hosts, including Bai Yansong, Shui Junyi, Fang Hongjin, and Cui Yongyuan, despite the fact that none of them had previous television experience. However, their critical insights on pressing social issues had already put them at the top of many "favorite journalist" polls. They were soon nationally famous television hosts. In particular, *Tell It Like It Is*, China's first talk show, filled a void in the country's television programming and produced a dialogue between the media and the public. It was first hosted by Bai Yansong, Shui Junyi, and Cui Yongyuan, who were later joined by Jing Yidan, Fang Hongjin, and Wang Zhi, a group of new hosts popular with the audience. The live exchanges between these influential hosts and ordinary members of the public on various social issues appeal to the audience. The remarkable success of *Oriental Horizon* resulted in the improvement of many other programs, both inside and outside CCTV. Television as a whole, including news and information programs, entertainment programs, and service programs, began to pay more attention to the public's concerns and treat them with respect.

Since the mid-1990s, CCTV has set out to make more program adjustments. The new reform has three goals. First, it aims to provide more new programs that serve the public's needs and to create new program formats that appeal to the public. Second, it intends to further improve program quality by addressing difficult and timely issues of public concern, and to facilitate more democratic exchange between the government and the public. And, third, it plans to push for more lively, trustworthy, and accessible program formats (Ding 1993: 1).

Focus was launched to meet these goals. It immediately became one of the most eye-catching programs on CCTV because it broadcast many timely, sharp, and in-depth news reports. It aimed to address hot-button issues that concerned the public and to serve as a public watchdog by directly criticizing the bureaucracy and the wrongdoings of party and government officials. Topics as thorny as civilians suing authorities have been covered on the program. These programs provided a platform for the public to vent their anger against the authorities (Zhen zhen you ci 2003). For a long time, *Focus* ranked second only to *Evening News*, attracting about 300 million viewers. It has received hundreds of thousands of telephone calls, letters, faxes, and e-mails voicing the public's opinions and suggesting stories. *Focus* also drew considerable attention from top party and government officials. Former party secretary-general Jiang Zemin, former premiers Li Peng and Zhu Rongji, and the current party secretary-general Hu Jintao have all made phone calls to relevant state agencies to solve problems they saw exposed on the program. Zhu Rongji claimed that he never missed *Focus* and praised it for doing "part of the central government's work," while Hu Jintao described himself as "a faithful viewer" (Yuan and Wang 2004: 4).

In a never-before-seen demonstration of interest, hundreds of viewers gathered at the CCTV gate every day to suggest stories for investigation. By and large, *Focus* enabled public opinion to supervise the nation. It not only received one of the highest ratings in the history of Chinese television but also inspired many similar programs (Yang and Lü 2004: 17). *Focus* was one of the few programs that managed to retain the trust of both the grassroots and the party and government.

Economic Reform and New Management

Since the second phase of CCTV's reform began in the mid-1990s, the "producer system" has been used for most programs. This is a common system of management in advanced countries, but it was a breakthrough in Chinese television. For decades, television production was managed by the party. Almost all the officials at all levels in television stations were appointed by the relevant party organizations. Media professionals were treated as mere operatives. They were not given authority to decide what to produce and how to produce it, but were just told by their party-appointed supervisors to produce what the party needed, in the way the party wanted. Before the adoption of the producer system, television professionals were powerless. The producer system broke with traditional practice by giving them the power to design programs, make decisions concerning program content, control the raising and spending of money, and oversee production and program management (Y. Sun 2003). The new system also gives producers power over staff hiring and firing, financing, and

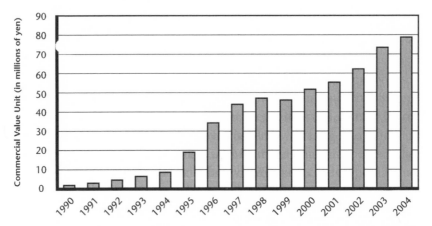

Chart 2.1. CCTV advertising revenue, 1990–2004. *Data obtained from the Television Committee of the China Broadcasting Association, 2005. Commercial value unit: RMB 100 million.*

administration, making them the real core of program management. Since the late 1990s, the producer system has been widely used in all Chinese television organizations. Although this newly introduced system was just one of the fruits of CCTV's reform, it has been a touchstone for measuring how far CCTV has been modernized and internationalized in its concepts, structures, and management (H. Zhang 1997: 2).

Closely related to the adoption of the producer system was the adoption of advertising revenue as television's chief financial resource. This was a big step toward commercialization, which in theory could be viewed as a deviation from Marxist media doctrine. The implementation of the producer system could not have been successful if advertising revenue had not been the chief financial resource. During the reform years, the government began to reduce and then terminate its subsidies to television stations, which had been their sole source of funding. Therefore, television stations had to look elsewhere for financial resources (J. Sun 2002). *Focus* was the first Chinese television program to rely on advertising revenue, but this soon became standard practice.

Now, advertising is CCTV's bread and butter, and commercials on television have become routine. This has made CCTV rich. Not only does it no longer need to ask for funds from the government, but it has even returned surplus revenue to the government. Since the late 1990s, CCTV has contributed RMB 1.2 billion (about US$150 million) to the government in the form of taxes (Y. Lü 2004: 53).

On 11 April 1994, CCTV held the first auction for commercial time, offering fifteen slots in prime-time programs. One was a one-minute slot between

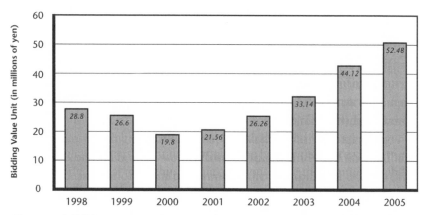

Chart 2.2. CCTV's prime-time commercial spots, 1998–2005. *Data obtained from the Television Committee of the China Broadcasting Association, 2006. Bidding value unit: RMB 100 million.*

Evening News and the popular *Weather Forecast,* and others followed *Weather Forecast.* The minimum bid for each slot was RMB 12 million (about US$1.5 million) per year. More than 190 business entities competed for the fifteen commercial slots. The Kongfuyan Brewery won the most contested auction and paid RMB 30.8 million (about US$3.8 million) per year for a five-second prime-time slot. The auction raised a total of RMB 360 million (about US$45 million) (Yi 1999: 7). In that year, CCTV's total advertising revenue reached RMB 1 billion (about US$125 million). This figure was much greater than the subsidies CCTV would have been allocated by the government for 1994. In 1995, CCTV's total commercial revenue doubled, reaching RMB 2 billion (about US$250 million), showing a healthy development of these newly adopted systems (Y. Lü 2004: 53).

CCTV's eleventh annual auction of prime-time commercial slots, on 18 November 2004, saw the participation of many domestic and foreign companies. Ten times as many international business entities participated in 2004 than in the previous year. The final revenue was RMB 5.3 billion (about US$656 million), an increase of 27.5 percent over the previous year. Advertising revenue alone accounted for more than 50 percent of CCTV's total revenue in 2004.

Pioneered by CCTV, advertising revenue has become the chief financial resource of most television stations in China, a milestone in the history of Chinese television. The beginning of the twenty-first century has witnessed a dramatic surge in CCTV's advertising revenue. It reached RMB 8 billion (about US$1 billion) in 2003 and 2004, taking up almost a third of all the money spent on television advertising in China.

Swift and Broad Expansion

The relaxation of political and economic controls has allowed CCTV to expand swiftly and in many directions in the reform period, particularly over the last two decades, and to become an undisputable world-class television giant.

The breakthroughs in program content and production systems have resulted in many new programs. Advertising revenue has made it possible for new program initiatives to be realized. More programs with good ratings mean more advertising revenue. And more advertising revenue means more programs. Since the reform, CCTV has experienced speedy and healthy development of its programs, infrastructure, finances, and influence.

It took CCTV nearly thirty years to increase its operation from one channel in 1958 to two in 1986. But from 1986 to 2004, less than twenty years, the number of CCTV's channels increased from two to sixteen, an eight-fold expansion. Table 2.1 displays the multiplication of CCTV channels during the reform years.

In addition to the increase in channels, there has also been a significant increase in broadcasting hours during the reform years. For example, according to the *China Radio and Television Yearbook*, there were just 11,310 broadcasting hours in 1990, but there were 163,303 broadcasting hours in 2005, a 14.4-fold increase over fifteen years. On average, CCTV broadcast thirty hours per day in 1990, but about 440 hours per day in 2004. There were only twenty-five programs in 1990, but nearly 400 in 2005, almost a sixteen-fold increase.

Table 2.1. The Increase in CCTV Channels (1958–2004)

Year	Number of Channels
1958	1
1986	2
1989	3
1992	4
1995	6
1996	7
1999	8
2000	9
2001	11
2002	12
2003	14
2004	16

Source: Compiled from *China Radio and TV Yearbook*, 1990–2005.

Now, with a television network of sixteen channels, two of which broadcast twenty-four hours a day, CCTV has become one of the largest, most advanced, most powerful, and most influential television systems in the world. The sixteen broadcasting channels are the News Channel, the Comprehensive Channel, the Economy Channel, the Art and Entertainment Channel, the Sports Channel, the Movie Channel, the Military and Agriculture Channel, the TV Drama Channel, the Science and Education Channel, the Opera Channel, the Society and Law Channel, the Children's Channel, the Music Channel, the International Channel in Chinese, the International Channel in English, and the Spanish and French Channel. Together they offer a variety of information, entertainment, and service programs. In addition, by the end of 2005, CCTV also had eleven subscription channels and twenty-eight online channels. Altogether, the network covered 94.4 percent of China's population and had more than 1.2 billion potential viewers. Each day, 650 million viewers in China watch CCTV. The average Chinese viewer spends 152 minutes per day watching television, and 45 of those minutes are spent watching CCTV programs. Amongst hundreds of other domestic and international TV channels from provincial, local, cable, and satellite broadcasters, CCTV alone accounts for nearly 30 percent of total television-watching time. Besides domestic viewers, programs on two CCTV channels are now accessible in more than 120 countries via satellite and cable transmissions. Worldwide, CCTV Channel 4—the International Channel in Chinese—is received in 10 million households, and CCTV Channel 9—the International Channel in English—in 40 million. With all this expansion, CCTV has indisputably become a potentially powerful player in the global television arena.

The Unchanged Aspects of CCTV

Unfortunately, because of restrictions ranging from the political and ideological to the financial and administrative, the transformation of CCTV has been incomplete (Lu and Pan 2002: 6). There has been little change in its function of serving the party and the priority it gives to putting forth the party's political guidelines.

Remaining a Mouthpiece of the Party

Despite the many significant changes, CCTV is still a party propaganda apparatus (Shi 2004: 59). According to the party, media reform does not mean that the media's role as a mouthpiece is outdated. Rather, the media should perform this role in a new and more effective way, one that suits this era of opening up and reform, with the accompanying globalization, relaxation of political control, and transition from a state economy to a market economy (Hu 2004). It is clear that since the transition from a socialist state economy to a market economy, and especially since China's accession to the World Trade Organization (WTO) in 2001, the functions of the media have gradually become much more diversified; media institutions are no longer simply party propaganda vehicles. However, the reform has not relieved CCTV and other media institutions of their role as a mouthpiece of the CCP.

In 1994, at a national conference on propaganda and ideology, the former party secretary-general Jiang Zemin called on the media to be a tool to "guide" public opinion, and he pointed out that "speaking for the party" should always be the utmost priority of all media institutions (Cheng 2001: 28). Consequently, this task was included in the resolutions of the Sixth Plenary Session of the CCP's Sixteenth Central Committee in 1996 (Ai 2002). CCTV has made it clear to both the party leadership and the public that it will firmly adhere to that principle. In a public announcement, CCTV claimed that its top priority is to follow the guidance of the CCP in order to provide "correct" guidelines to public opinion (Meng 2003). Of course, CCTV was not the only media institution to make such claims. All media institutions in China are owned by the party and government, so they have to act in the same way. Generally speaking, providing "correct" guidelines to public opinion means strengthening party and government monitoring of public opinion through the media (Ling 2003: 28).

During the Cultural Revolution, from 1966 to 1976, the party had total control over the media. However, in theory, there are no essential differences between the regulations used to control CCTV during the Cultural Revolution and those being used during the reform years. For example, the Cultural Revolution regulations required program directors and supervisors to enhance the people's sense of political responsibility and understanding of the class struggle, establish and perfect relevant censorship procedures, and prudently take charge at all levels where pre-examination and final approval of program content were required to ensure that only positive images of the Communist Party, Mao Zedong Thought, socialism, and heroic figures such as revolutionary workers, farmers, and soldiers appeared on screen (Beijing Broadcasting Institute Press 1987: 17). Thirty years later, during the reform years of the mid-1990s, the regulations were similar. For example, they required all program producers to adhere to the socialist direction and the Communist Party's principle that television should be a mouthpiece for the party and government; they held that Marxism-Leninism, Mao Zedong Thought, and Deng Xiaoping Theory are the fundamental guidelines by which policies should be developed to correctly guide public opinion; and they insisted that any adjustments of reporting guidelines and any restructuring of programs be approved by the party's Central Committee. More specifically, they also emphasize that all programs and reports should contribute to the political stability of the nation and the enhancement of communist ideology; that no programs should report the opinions of opposition parties or counter-revolutionaries; and that personal political opinions may not appear in any program (Sun 2005).

As a result of these strict regulations, the proportion of programs with a critical edge, such as *Focus*, declined drastically, from 47 percent of CCTV's programs in 1998 to only 17.5 percent in 2002. One reason for the sharp drop was increasing interference from the authorities, in spite of the party's emphasis on strengthening the media's role as a scrutinizer of society (Jing 2004). Consequently, *Focus* began turning away from social problems and the wrongdoings of party and government officials, attending instead to trivia (Zeng 2004: 14). Most of the programs that used to have a critical edge now focus on providing positive reports highlighting achievements of the party and government and praising the progress of socialist society, much as programs did during the Cultural Revolution forty years ago (Zhu and Xie 2005: 9).

As Yu (2004: 1) observes, the media in China are very bad at providing the public with information. One of the biggest problems is that "pleasant" or "good" things can be covered by the media but "unpleasant" or "bad" things cannot—they are covered up by the party and government and hidden from the public. Despite some improvement, the problem remains, because doing this is a party principle. As a result, politically selective, unrealistic, and untimely reports are still common, and so-called "negative reports" are still under very strict control, depriving the public of their right to information (Fang 2005). When a "negative" thing happens, the authorities decide the time, tone, scale, and even the terms of its reporting, so that all the media can seem the same. Although this kind of control seriously violates the media's freedom and the public's right to know, Chinese media professionals have to put up with it, and they call it "dancing while wearing fetters" (Chi 2005).

Leader-Oriented vs. People-Oriented

Despite numerous changes in CCTV's news programs, most news coverage is still "leader-oriented" rather than "people-oriented." With CCTV's priority still being to serve the political and ideological needs of the party and government, most of its news coverage remains devoted to party and government meetings and the activities of party and government leaders.

A study of CCTV's news programs during one week in November 1999 and one in November 2000 provides some compelling findings. Altogether, there were 129 news stories concerning political affairs, which accounted for 41.6 percent of all news stories. The total time of these stories was 210 minutes, or 52.3 percent of the total news program time (excluding commercials). Thus, on average fifteen minutes of each day was used for reporting political affairs, or more than half of the total news program time. But 35.3 percent of the political news stories were coverage of political leaders' activities. Such coverage accounted for more than one-third of CCTV's most-watched prime-time program, *Evening News*, both in number of stories and in total time. Another 15.6 percent of news stories covered party or government meetings. The rest were other kinds of news stories, such as coverage of domestic political events and international events (Zhou and Xu 2002: 24).

This concentration on party and government leaders and meetings has been heavily criticized by both communications critics and the public. In the view of some critics, CCTV's *Evening News*, which once had the most viewers, has become less appealing in recent years because it has a "machine-made" image. Now, the *Evening News* amounts to coverage of official visits, public appearances, and other routine activities by officials, plus conferences, achievements, and denunciation of Falun Gong. Critical perspectives and timeliness are largely lacking. The surfeit of coverage of party and government meetings is boring audiences, who perceive that news value is being measured by the political level of the meeting and the rank of the officials involved (Guo 2003: 26). This unchanged orientation toward leaders indicates that media reform is only skin-deep. Fortunately, this much disliked concentration on party and government officials rather than the public finally drew the attention of the Central Committee of the Party in 2003, which called a meeting to solve the problem. By and large, the situation has improved since then, though no one expected a total change, given continuing ideological control (Zeng 2004: 14).

Implications

Of the various factors driving the transformation of CCTV, the most important were political. The party's tolerance of the media has increased with the trend toward political democratization.

Deng Xiaoping's call for a further, quicker, and deeper reform in 1992 opened up an opportunity for further relaxation of control over the media, which was viewed as an unprecedented chance for the development of CCTV (Yang 1998: 1). Reacting to Deng's call, a campaign to smash the fetters of outdated concepts was launched across the nation, with news media at the forefront. CCTV's epoch-making news program *Oriental Horizon* appeared in the late spring of 1993 (Yang 2004). The new political and ideological atmosphere prompted the party to tolerate many new initiatives by CCTV and other media institutions during the reform.

CCTV was also forced to change by the pressure of market competition from both domestic and international counterparts. CCTV began to face an adverse environment in the mid-1990s, when a number of television stations and broadcasting companies both at home and abroad began to covet the potentially huge Chinese television market. By 2003, more than thirty overseas media companies had been allowed to operate in China under certain conditions. Head-on rival Hong Kong–based Phoenix Satellite Television spurred CCTV's restructuring and many of its new program initiatives and business approaches from 1996 on. As a privately owned station, Phoenix could not match CCTV's manpower, financial resources, or infrastructure (Y. Chen 2004: 48). However, it was not burdened with the many restrictions imposed on CCTV. Phoenix's nimble and fast development placed tremendous and mounting pressure on CCTV. Intentionally or not, Phoenix made itself so compelling that the media in mainland China could not afford to ignore it and had to transform themselves to compete with it (Z. Chen 2005: 48).

In the meantime, domestic television stations, especially satellite stations operated by various provinces which also have national coverage, also posed serious challenges to CCTV. For example, in 2004 and 2005 Hunan Satellite Television's *Super Girl* became "the hottest TV program" (Chen and Qi 2005) in China. *Super Girl* borrowed the concept and format of a very popular U.S. TV program, *American Idol*, and claimed to be a singing competition for the common people, free of restrictions on height, looks, and age. Millions of young people from primary schools, middle schools, and universities played truant to try out for the program, and it was well received by hundreds of millions of viewers, male and female, young and old. The program has generated an incredible amount of revenue from both commercials and text messages. As much as RMB 112,500 (about US$1,400) was charged for a fifteen-second commercial slot during the show, which was RMB 2,500 (about US$310) more than the highest price for an equivalent slot on CCTV during prime time (Chen and Qi 2005). Competition from other domestic television stations has ended CCTV's long-standing monopoly in the domestic market and forced it to adapt to the new media environment.

The enormous breakthroughs made by provincial satellite television stations by spotting CCTV's blind spots and the market it had ignored have gradually broken down CCTV's loyal audience and eroded its market share. The statistics released by China Media Research (CMR) indicate that, by the end of 2004, more people had access to the satellite television stations of the provinces of Zhejiang, Shandong, Guangdong, Anhui, Sichuan, Fujian, Guizhou and Yunnan than lived in each of those provinces. That means many of them have become some sort of national network. This new situation has had a huge impact on CCTV, forcing it to develop new strategies to maintain its status as the only official national network.

Moreover, in addition to the thirty-one provincial satellite TV stations—or thirty-one unofficial national television networks—there are also a few other types of nationally accessible specialized satellite stations. By the end of 2005, the num-

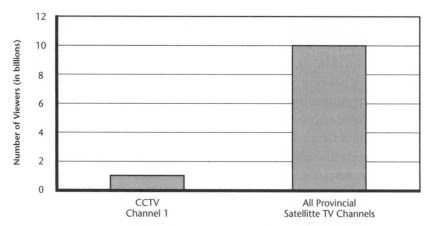

Chart 2.3. CCTV-1's coverage vs. provincial satellite TV stations' coverage. *Data obtained from the China Mainland Information Group, 2006. Unit of coverage: billion people.*

ber of satellite stations accessible nationwide had reached more than fifty. These non-official national networks are competing for shares of the national television audience. More recently, a new round of even fiercer competition started after the State Administration Bureau of Radio, Film, and Television licensed a few more TV stations for nationwide satellite broadcasting, including the News Channel of Shenzhen Television, Southern Television's Cantonese Channel, Hunan Television's Golden Eagle Cartoon Channel, Beijing Television's Cartoon Channel, and Shanghai Television's Cartoon Channel (Lu 2005; X. Zhang 2004). CCTV's only option is to make a comprehensive transformation. Unless it adjusts and strengthens itself to win the competition with both its international and domestic counterparts, CCTV will end up losing its dominant status and the lion's share of the Chinese TV market (Yang 1998: 1).

Conclusion

The transformation of CCTV is painful, but strengthens it and brings benefits (Y. Lü 2004: 52). After years of change beginning in the late 1970s, CCTV has become not only much more developed and market-oriented, but also internationalized and competition-based (Zhu and Xie 2005: 9). Its political role, however, has remained the same, as the Communist Party has maintained its ideological grip. Therefore, neither in theory nor in practice has it been possible for the Chinese media to become a "fourth estate."

In fact, China's media is more like a mirror of politics than a mirror of society. Despite many changes, its fundamental role is still to reflect the political needs of the leaders rather than the needs of the people. This role justified its control by the party and government even during the reform years of the past three decades (Wei 2005). The media sector is still highly centralized, and the news media in particular have little independence (Zhong 2004). It is true that many changes have taken place, such as the transformation of programs, financial structures, and business approaches. However, the essential purpose of all those changes is to enable television to continue as a mouthpiece for the party, albeit more effectively in a new global and domestic environment (Zhong 2004). For instance, to protect the political and ideological role and power of CCTV's *Evening News*, all television stations in China, regardless of whether they are provincial, municipal, local, cable, or satellite, are required to transmit the program (Liu 2002: 19).

When carefully scrutinized, most of the changes can be seen to reflect a top-down model, which means that without permission from the party and government most of them, either in CCTV or in other media institutions, would not have been possible, and it is unrealistic to anticipate a change in this regard in the foreseeable future. Therefore, while the changes in CCTV achieved in the past three decades can be attributed to the favorable environment both at home and abroad in the late twentieth century, and particularly to the relaxation of political control, unfortunately, the media's reliance on the political atmosphere is likely to create difficulties if the political atmosphere becomes less favorable.

References

All references were published in Chinese.

Ai, Honghong. 2002. *On the History of Chinese Radio and Television.* Jinan, China: Shandong University Press.

Beijing Broadcasting Institute Press. 1987. *Selections of Historical Documents on Radio and Television V.* Beijing: Beijing Broadcasting Institute Press.

Chen, Jibao, and Weiwei Qi. 2005. "CCTV Founds Channel Brands by Powerful Means." 7 September. *21st Century Report.* http://www.nanfangdaily.com.cn/jj/20050912/zlygl/200509070100.asp (accessed 2 December 2005).

Chen, Yi. 2004. "'Zero Gap with Nanjing': Basic Reason and Developing Direction." *China Television* 6:48–55.

Chen, Zibai. 2005. "The Phoenix Effect in Chinese Media." http://chinese.mediachina.net/index_news_view.jsp?id=60125 (accessed 2 August 2005).

Cheng, Manli. 2001. "Analysis of the Chinese Communist Party's Thought of News." *Journalism and Communication Studies* 3:24–30.

Chi, Fulin. 2005. "Media Reform Is Accelerated by SARS Crisis." http://www.china-review.com/article-preview.asp?id=1410 (accessed 8 July 2005).

China Radio and TV Yearbook Press. 1990–2005. *China Radio and TV Yearbook.* Beijing: China Radio and TV Yearbook Press.

Ding, Guangen. 1993. "Report at the National Conference of Propaganda Ministers." *Guangming Daily*, 18 January.

Fang, Yanming. 2005. "Political Civilization Construction and Supervision of Public Opinion." http://www.zijin.net/blog/more.asp?name=fym&id=455 (accessed 18 August 2005).

Guo, Yan. 2003. "Breach in the News Reform." *Wuhan Radio and Television Society* 2:26–30.

Hu, Xingrong. 2004. *News Philosophy*. Beijing: Xinhua.

Hu, Zhifeng, and Chun Liu. 2004. "Consultation on Chinese Television—Dialogues of Current Situation and Problems of Chinese Television." *Modern Communication* 1:1–9.

Ji, Bingxuan. 2004. "News Reporting Should Stick to Criterion." *News Battlefront* 3:4–7.

Jing, Yidan. 2004. "One Program and Three Prime Ministers." 6 July. http://www.cctv.com/news/special/C12572/20040706/100420.shtml (accessed 10 August 2005).

Ling, Yan. 2003. "Contradictions and Dialogue Conflicts over Chinese TV System in a Changing Society." *Nanfang Television Study* 1:28–35.

Liu, Chun. 2002. "CCTV, the Aircraft Carrier of Chinese Television: Where Do You Go Ahead?" *Modern Communication* 3:19–20.

Lu, Bin. 2005. "2004 China Media Memo." *Modern Advertisement* 2. http://news.xinhuanet.com/newmedia/2005-02/18/content_2591044.htm (accessed 18 February 2005).

Lü, Peng. 2004. "On the Internationalization of Chinese Television." *Shandong Audiovisual Magazine* 5:4–5.

Lü, Yanmei. 2004. "Yang Weiguang: Television Life (Part Two)." *Modern Communication* 5:52–53.

Lu, Ye, and Zhongdang Pan. 2002. "Imagining the Professional Fame: Constructing Journalistic Professionalism in Social Transformation." *Journalism Study* 4:6–16.

Meng, Jian. 2003. "On the Transformation of Publicity Value of CCTV." *China Journalism Review*. http://www.cjr.com.cn/gb/node2/node26108/index.html (accessed 20 October 2003).

Shi, Tongyu. 2004. "On the Nature of Radio and Television." In *New Explorations of Chinese Radio and Television*, ed. Zhenhua Zhang, 58–93. Beijing: China Radio and Television Press.

Sun, Jinling. 2002. *Questions to Chinese TV Journalists*. Beijing: China Customs Press.

Sun, Yüsheng. 2005. "Something Thinkable and Something Doable: Reflections on *Oriental Horizon* and *Focus*." 13 August. http://www.media-china.com/cmzy/xwpj/taofengxinwenjiang/tf07.htm (accessed 13 August 2005).

———. 2003. *Ten Years*. Beijing: Life, Reading and New Knowledge Sanlian Books.

Wei, Yongzheng. 2005. "Bottom Line of the Current News Reform—A Qualitative Study of the News Media Industry." http://academic.mediachina.net/lw_view.jsp?id=785 (accessed 10 August 2005).

Yang, Weiguang. 1998. "Prelude." In *Outline of China's Television Commentaries*, 1–19. Beijing: China Radio and Television Press.

———. 2004. "Stories behind *Oriental Horizon*." http://www.cctv.com/tvguide/tvcomment/special/C11876/20040316/101734.shtml (accessed 16 March 2004).

Yang, Weiguang, and Yanmei Lü. 2004. "Yang Weiguang: Television Life (Part One)." *Modern Communication* 4:15–18.

Yi, Ling. 1999. "Ten Key People in the Advertising Industry." *New Weekly* 6:7–8.

Yu, Guoming. 2004. "Insight into the Development Trend of China's Media Industry." *Modern Communication* 2:1–5.

Yuan, Zhengming, and Xudong Wang. 2004. "The Development of *Focus*." In *Focus on the Focus*, ed. Zhenzhi Guo and Lifang Zhao, 4–8. Beijing: Qinghua University Press.

Zeng, Zhi. 2004. "The Living Environment and Cultural Puzzlement of TV Media." *Yue Hai Feng Network* 3:14–17.

Zhang, Haichao. 1997. "Some Theoretical Thoughts on the Operation of TV News Programs." *Television Study* 10:2–4.

Zhang, Xiao Zheng. 2004. "Patterns of the Chinese TV Market in the Future." http://www.woxie.com/article/list.asp?id=16743 (accessed 21 June 2004).

Zhen zhen you ci [pseud.]. 2003. "Speaking Glibly." *Development of TV News Programs in China*. 12 November. http://bjlzb.blogdriver.com/bjlzb/9654.html (accessed 5 August 2005).

Zhong, Dajun. 2004. "Press Freedom and the Independence of Judicial Administration and Academy: The Goal of China's Reform Is to Separate the Interest Groups of Government, Industry and Academia." Paper presented at the Seminar of Judicial Progress and Public Opinion Supervision, Beijing, China, 31 October.

Zhou, Xiaopu, and Fujian Xu. 2002. "Analysis and Study of CCTV News Samples." *Modern Communication* 3:23–27.

Zhu, Yujun, and Qinliang Xie. 2005. "Transformation and Elevation: Reinvestigating the TV News Phenomenon in Nanjing." *Modern Communication* 4:9–11.

Hong Kong Television:
Same as It Ever Was?

KARIN GWINN WILKINS

This chapter investigates the institutional and programming aspects of the Hong Kong television industry, questioning the degree to which substantive change might have occurred following the political transition in 1997. At issue here is the complex interplay of political with economic factors, such that despite shedding one governance style for another, the quest for economic profit within the region appears to trump other potential differences.

In recent work Curran (2002) questions the position that the expansion of television services may be fragmenting audiences and disintegrating potentially more cohesive national identities, and that the focus on entertainment, particularly that broadcast through privately operated channels, may create much less informed communities of citizens. Through exemplifying the British experience, his critique compels us to think through the assumptions we make in media studies, based on limited cultural historical cases. Chronicling how media operate across cultures helps us to understand the degree to which certain patterns are historically and socially bound. For example, the assumption that public broadcasting necessarily engages more informative and educational genres than private systems does not hold across media structures in the Middle Eastern region (Wilkins 2004).

The central issue that can be explored across cultural contexts concerns who has the power to define cultural production. The dance between political authorities and economic agents may serve both causes, as each partner bows temporarily to the other's tempo yet never leaves the floor. The television industry in Hong Kong may be so entrenched in a global capitalist system that changes in communication technologies and audience experiences matter less than economic and political concerns.

So what continuities and changes can we identify within the industry? And what do these patterns reveal about power dynamics? In this chapter, I relate programming, consistently lacking in strong political critique, to the economic conditions of the industry as well as to the regulatory environment and to technological changes allowing audiences greater access to television services and channels.

Contrasting conditions across periods of governance allows us to consider the potential influence of political transition. Downing (1996) argues that while most media theories assume stability, transitional moments are paramount in understanding how media work within social systems. Taking a critical approach, the power dynamics manifest in the cultural production of television may be understood as part of a hegemonic process, in which a "dominant" ideology is transmitted. Good's articulation of a critical approach to power in communication theory posits hegemony both as "a theory of consent, which exposes the process," and "as a political strategy, a way of searching for access points to struggle" (1989: 61). This approach to the study of hegemony relies on the basic tenets articulated by Gramsci (1971): that the domination of one group over others within a social system depends upon consent as well as coercion, and that the process of domination is open to disruption, and therefore resistance. Gramsci's attention to ideology might be extended to a view of media "as a terrain of struggle" among powerful forces attempting to control "the direction of society's development" (Downing 1996: 200). Media industries serve as "key actors in the production of consent" (Good 1989: 61), as well as a site for this struggle among competing groups.

Considering the issue of power directs us toward macro-level research, which takes into account the structural relationships across television industries among agents of government, funding, and perhaps communities of viewers. More than a "state or relation to be taken for granted or merely described," power "becomes the central problem for analysis" (Good 1989: 64). Cultural production involves the manufacture and selection of cultural products, which need to be related to "economic and institutional processes" (McAnany and Wilkinson 1992: 742).

The increasing globalization and regionalization of television industries has prompted scholars to concentrate less on the U.S. as a centralized, dominant center of television production (Tunstall 1977; Varis 1984) and more on the emergence of multiple centers of production within and across regions. Although the network of television production and distribution appears to have many more players than the configurations critiqued by earlier dependency critics (such as Schiller 1971, 1993), it continues to be shaped by the economic structure of capitalism. Thus, established with the blessing of colonial or local political elites, cultural imperialism may be seen as "a set of practices enabling the spread of capitalism as an economic system" (Tomlinson 1991: 102).

Hong Kong in Political-Economic Context

Bordering the People's Republic of China (PRC), Hong Kong was a British colony for more than 150 years. As a result of the Opium Wars of the mid-nineteenth century, Hong Kong Island and the southern tip of the Kowloon peninsula were ceded by China to Britain through the Treaty of Nanking in 1842 and the Convention of Peking in 1860; northern Kowloon was then leased to the British government for ninety-nine years in 1898. The British and Chinese governments agreed to transfer jurisdiction of all Hong Kong territories to the PRC on 1 July 1997. According to the Basic Law resolved on in 1990 by British and Chinese leaders, Hong Kong should maintain its existing social and economic systems for fifty years subsequent to this transition.

Eric Ma (2000) describes Hong Kong prior to the transition as dominated by laissez-faire capitalism and guided by minimal government intervention. Culturally, Hong Kong residents were discouraged from identifying too closely with the nations of Britain or China during colonial rule; instead an indigenous culture, marked by achievements within global capitalist systems, was highlighted.

Following the transition, Ma proposes that a "re-sinicization" of Hong Kong occurred, through which Chinese national and cultural identities have been asserted. Televised rituals, such as singing national anthems and national-day celebrations, contributed to this shift in articulation of identity. Curtin (1998) argues that Hong Kong residents had had little chance to participate directly in their own governance, so using television as a central space for participating in the very ritual of the transition, even though indirectly, fit their historical experience.

Among the many structural changes that occurred over the transition, the symbolic presence of the military, particularly as perpetuated through mediated images, illustrates one significant change. Ma explains that during British colonial rule the territory operated as a militarized zone; subsequently the People's Liberation Army (PLA) transitioned from symbolizing repression, given the events of 4 June 1989, toward symbolizing national strength and pride, through the clear presence of troops and public military parades.

Some observers have remarked that the political transition did not bring as many disasters as had been feared (Lee et al. 2002). Instead, the regional economic crisis in Asia dealt a much more devastating blow. Hong Kong in particular was expected to recover quickly, but did not.

The Television Landscape during Colonial Rule

Before 1997, the television industry resonated with the colonial political and capitalist economic structure of the territory. It aimed at economic profit and operated under tight political control. Television during this period promoted an allegedly apolitical cultural identity for Hong Kong, distinguishing residents from British as well as mainland Chinese communities, by providing programming that was largely entertainment.

The television services available to Hong Kong residents during this time were constrained by both the regulatory and the economic conditions of the industry. Just as the broader context of the territory favored private enterprise and free trade, the television stations were commercial, with the government receiving a proportion of advertising or subscription revenues from each broadcasting system. Wealthy owners dominated the industry, including Rupert Murdoch (STAR TV), Sir Run Run Shaw (TVB), and Por-yen Lim (ATV).

During this time, television served as a central cultural space. Almost all of the approximately 6 million inhabitants of Hong Kong in the early 1990s had at least one television in their homes and turned to television as their central source of information (Chan and Lee 1992). On average, Hong Kong residents watched more than three hours of television each day, making this a more popular leisure activity than playing computer games, seeing films, or even singing karaoke.

The two terrestrial television stations, Television Broadcasts Limited (TVB) and Asia Television Limited (ATV), were the most widely accessible and most frequently viewed. Each of the terrestrial stations transmitted two channels, in order to cater to Cantonese-speaking and English-speaking audiences. Under British rule, the Hong Kong government required these stations to provide this English-language service as a condition of licensing. Because most of the Hong Kong communities speak Cantonese but not English, the two English-language channels were not as popular, and therefore not as profitable, as their Cantonese-language counterparts. While maintaining an English-language channel allowed stations to meet their political obligations, broadcasting other channels enabled them to earn high profits.

Most of the programs, particularly on the Cantonese-language channels, offered entertainment. Some programs were imported into Hong Kong, although a significant proportion of the television programming was produced within the territory. Some of the imported programs were dubbed into Cantonese, the dialect of Chinese spoken in the region, or subtitled in Chinese characters. News, entertainment series, and films were imported from the West, but most animated programs were imported from Japan, and several popular fictional series were imported from Taiwan. In 1983, Varis (1984) found that Hong Kong television imported roughly between one-quarter (24%) and two-thirds (64%) of its programming hours, depending on the channel. Waterman and Rogers's subsequent analysis (1994) of the number of television program hours on four terrestrial channels in Hong Kong in 1989 confirmed this pattern: across all terrestrial channels in Cantonese and English, about one-third (34%) of program hours were produced in the United States, while almost two-thirds (61%) were produced domestically. Subsequent data indicate a similar trend, demonstrating little change through the mid-1990s (Wilkins 1998).

A variety of factors may explain the importation of television programs, including political, cultural, and economic considerations. Television programming in Hong Kong had been imported, mostly from the United States, to meet British regulatory requirements, rather than for economic gain. This importation marks an interdependence between British political power and multi-national corporate economic power.

Economic considerations also affected television programming. For instance, Waterman and Rogers (1994) focus primarily on domestic economic conditions to predict the extent of importation in nine East Asian countries: they conclude that a territory's wealth and its tendency to invest in broadcast media are positively associated with its likelihood of producing domestic dramatic programs for television. Regional and local television and film production centers in Asia, particularly in Japan and Hong Kong, have expanded, as they have in other regions around the world. Although not as wealthy as Japan, Hong Kong had achieved one of the highest per capita incomes in the region (Waterman and Rogers 1994: 92). Yet even Hong Kong's comparative wealth did not preclude its television industry from importing foreign commercial television programming, spurred by the political mandates of colonial rule.

Up to the time of the transition, the television services available to the community had been steadily increasing. Satellite television was first offered in 1991. Two years later Wharf Cable Limited (Wharf) initiated a cable television system. By 1993, approximately one-fifth of the households in Hong Kong could receive satellite television services through connection with STAR TV (broadcasting regional programming from Hong Kong, Taiwan, the PRC, and Japan, along with Western sports and entertainment programs and a local music video

channel), and approximately 15 percent of Hong Kong households had sub-
scribed to cable television services.

The growth of television services capitalized on potentially profitable investment decisions, occasionally constrained by British regulations that attempted to
limit concentration of ownership. The British administration stipulated that television stations not own more than 15 percent of other stations. Murdoch was unable to buy into TVB before investing in STAR TV because he encountered a
local regulation, supported by the PRC, that no foreigner should own more than
15 percent of a local terrestrial television station. These regulations also disquali-
fied political and religious groups from acquiring local television licenses, thus
emphasizing the depoliticized nature of the industry. Indeed, some refer to the
liberal nature of the media system during this colonial era.

In keeping with this attempt to portray media systems as separate from
ideological interests, the colonial government did not administer its own television station, but instead required the two terrestrial stations to carry programming and advertisements in the public interest (APIs) that its agency, Radio-
Television Hong Kong (RTHK), produced.

The government maintained its control of the industry through the work
of the Broadcasting Authority (BA), established in 1987. This body reviewed
broadcasting license proposals, as well as issuing warnings and imposing fines
for violations of license conditions (HKBA 1993). Programming standards set by
the BA dictated how subjects such as crime, family life, and violence could be
depicted, as well as appropriate presentations of cigarettes and alcohol. Regulations also defined permissible commercial advertising and sponsorship of programs; for example, tobacco companies were not authorized to advertise on
television but could sponsor programs, such as sporting events and music videos. As a condition of licensing, terrestrial television stations were required to
produce certain types of programs (public affairs and children's programs
among them) in defined quantities.

The emergence of satellite broadcasting in Hong Kong exemplified a con-
gruence of political and economic interests, in which political needs were ap-
peased in order for the industry to earn a profit. STAR TV began broadcasting
in Hong Kong in 1991, despite initial objections from TVB that STAR would
dominate the market for Cantonese-language programming (White 2005). Following his failed attempt to purchase 22 percent of TVB, attractive for its large
collection of Chinese-language programming available for distribution, Rupert
Murdoch purchased 63.6 percent of STAR TV in 1993.

At this time, just a few years prior to the impending transition, Murdoch
remarked that television had the capacity to threaten totalitarian regimes. Subsequently, the PRC banned the use of satellite dishes, even though many homes
in the southern area of China's Guangzhou province had access to cable televi-

sion services. At that time, the PRC also strictly limited the importation of foreign programs, particularly music video programs produced in Hong Kong and Taiwan.

In the remaining years prior to the transition, Murdoch steadily changed his tune, privileging the political interests of the PRC in order to maximize his ability to reach a larger share of the mainland Chinese audience. In 1995, Murdoch's News Corporation invested in the PRC's main newspaper.

Murdoch's decision to exclude British Broadcasting Corporation (BBC) World News Service programming from the array of potential services on STAR TV could also be seen as an attempt to respond to the PRC's objections directly, as well as to make more room for entertainment programming at the expense of potentially controversial news and information programming, thus indirectly also appeasing particular political interests. The BBC controversy originated with the documentary *Chairman Mao: The Last Emperor*, produced and broadcast in 1993 in Britain to commemorate the hundredth anniversary of Mao Zedong's birth. This documentary critiqued Mao's economic policies as well as his alleged relations with young girls. The PRC government argued strongly against its distribution, denouncing its portrayal of Mao, and retaliated against its showing in Britain by imposing new restrictions on BBC operations in China. It was not broadcast on television in Hong Kong, despite being purchased by TVB and approved by public censors representing the Hong Kong Film Censorship Ordinance (even though this ordinance prohibits screening films that might damage relations with other countries). Instead, private organizations showed it to community groups within the territory.

The handover from British colonial to Chinese communist rule in 1997 was met with more ritual pomp and circumstance than substantive change. The entry of the PLA into Hong Kong prompted dramatic statements by news anchors covering the events, but represented more of a symbolic assertion of national identity and strength than an immediate assertion of military power. Yet the change from Western colonial to Chinese communist rule meant a major shift in governance for the territory. So how did this affect the television industry?

Same as It Ever Was?

First, let's review what has changed within the television industry. Access to a variety of services and channels has increased dramatically, as a result of technological developments as well as a nurturing regulatory environment. Currently, Hong Kong viewers have access to more than 230 television channels across a variety of services (HKBA 2006). Wharf Cable, transformed into Hong Kong Cable Television Limited (HKCTV), grew from a domestic pay service of eight channels in

1993 to about ninety-one channels. A second domestic pay television station was licensed to PCCW Media Limited (PCCW Media, formerly PCCW VOD Limited), offering pay-on-demand programming. Interactive services included educational, shopping, and banking services, which were subsequently replaced by television and radio services broadcast through telephone technologies. Also in the post-1997 era, TVB's Galaxy Satellite Broadcasting Limited obtained a domestic pay television license and began broadcasting thirty-five channels in 2004.

Thirteen non-domestic licenses have been granted to satellite television stations in the region. Building on its non-domestic service, initiated prior to the transition, STAR TV increased its number of channels to about twenty-seven. Other non-domestic television services have been operated by Galaxy APT Satellite TV Development Limited, Starbucks (HK) Limited, Asia Plus Broadcasting Limited, MATV Limited, Turner International Asia Pacific Limited, China Entertainment Television Broadcast Limited, i-CABLE Satellite Television Limited, Sun Television Cybernetworks Enterprise Limited, Pacific Century Matrix (HK) Limited, Skywave TV Company Limited, and ATV.

Murdoch's News Corporation launched the Phoenix satellite television station just one year prior to the transition. Phoenix focused on Chinese programming, competing with China Central Television (CCTV) news services, and attracted 42 million households by 2000 (White 2005). Phoenix's rival, TVB Galaxy, suffered financially when local cable groups in southern China recorded TVB's programming, deleted the original advertisements, and resold the slots to local advertisers. Cultivating more advantageous relationships with local cable companies, Phoenix was able to maintain its economic edge over TVB until recent years, when the terrestrial stations have established more profitable political connections and the satellite station has borne significant start-up costs for new channels devoted to film and news.

The technological advancements in communication technologies that led to a proliferation of television channels may have threatened the profitability and survival of the original players. However, TVB and ATV have continued to prosper, in part by securing the right to have their programs carried by cable systems in some cities in China. These stations have been required to include digital terrestrial television (DTT) by 2007, marking yet another technological change in the landscape.

Yet even with substantial changes in communications technologies and access to services, the television industry remains remarkably similar to what it was. The central terrestrial stations, TVB and ATV, continue to broadcast one channel mostly in Cantonese and the other mostly in English. All four channels continue to focus on entertainment programs, particularly movies and dramas imported from the U.S. (such as *Grey's Anatomy*, *Alias*, and *Nip/Tuck*) on TVB and children's programming on ATV (Rothrock 2005). Post-1997 American series are still used to meet programming requirements on these terrestrial stations' English-language channels, whereas regionally produced series from China, Taiwan, Japan, and South Korea are carried on the other channels (Kan 2003).

The BA continues to review license proposals (and will do so when TVB and ATV apply for license renewal in 2015), to establish programming and advertising policies for the industry, and to review audience concerns (HKBA 2006). Domestic free and pay station licenses are granted through the Chief Executive in Council, while the other non-domestic services fall under the jurisdiction of the BA.

Hong Kong continues to be a central player within the region, exporting television programs. Policy objectives recently articulated by the government focus on economic conditions, attempting to broaden programming choices and diversity through promoting competition and investment, in order to "enhance Hong Kong as a regional broadcasting hub" (HKBA 2006). When in 1998 Hong Kong began to lose television channels, such as Disney, ESPN, and Discovery, to other regional centers, such as Singapore, regulatory policies became more supportive of satellite services.

Another essential feature of the industry, the integration of political interests with profit incentives, has also endured. Murdoch continues to try to ingratiate himself with the PRC to win its support. Phoenix satellite services support the Chinese Communist Party in both their content and their structure. The coverage of the 1997 ceremonies in Hong Kong was linked directly with CCTV for broadcast in the PRC. In 2002, STAR launched Xingkong Weishi, a Mandarin channel in mainland China catering to a young, wealthy, urban elite (Kan 2002). While news services cover controversial topics in other regions, local opposition to the authorities, such as by the Falun Gong movement and the Dalai Lama, attracts more scrutiny than sympathy. Murdoch also facilitated the publication of a book by Deng Xiaoping's daughter about her father, the broadcast of a CCTV documentary on Deng, and the quashing of a book chronicling former British governor Chris Patten's memoirs of Hong Kong. By 2002, when STAR TV began to earn a clear profit, Murdoch's political strategies seemed to have paid off in economic terms.

Whether the explicit ideological content of television has changed over time may be a matter of debate. At the time of the transition the PRC Preparatory Committee decided to maintain existing broadcasting laws, which limited political authority over licensing; for example, the government had been prohibited from revoking a television license for "broadcasting unfavorable news" (Eliason 1997: A3). However, the committee also moved to restrict peaceful protests and to control civic organizations' ties with foreign groups. Others (Lee and Chu 1998) noted the PRC's interest in keeping news coverage from supporting independent political interests within Hong Kong and Taiwan, potential subversion of Chinese communist authority, and personal attacks on Chinese political figures.

Lee (2001) suggests that these political concerns are managed within Hong Kong journalism through strategic rituals (such as offering opposing points of view, both critical and supportive of Beijing); distinguishing editorials, which must not critique Beijing, from freelance columns, which may; and utilizing narrative forms that use conditional language and assert fact over opinion. Privileging economic imperatives, television stations offer little political critique, and their failure to do so threatens democratic possibilities as well as journalistic integrity (Lee 2001).

But is critique truly more lacking today than in the past? One could point to several instances prior to the transition in which stations avoided political controversy. What constitutes appropriate controversy may also be contingent upon contextual conditions: potential controversies may involve sexual or violent content as well, distracting us from more substantive concerns with political critique. Curtin's description of TVB as "generally agnostic about program content" (1998: 288) seems particularly apt, not only for this station but also for the industry.

Governmental authorities before and after the transition engaged in similar processes of political control: both governments wished to help corporate interests turn an economic profit. Advances in technological distribution have changed the television industry in some ways, but the underlying political-economic structure and ideological content appear consistent. On the political front, the Hong Kong television stations continue to maintain an "insulated" approach, trying to avoid politically sensitive matters in their programming. Cultural content, meaning fictional programming as well as news and informational services, has been confined to the parameters dictated by the cultural politics of the region. This restriction may not be particular to Hong Kong, however; the constraints on substantive critique of dominant ruling parties, as well as of the potential consequences of global capitalism, remain pervasive in other territories as well.

The year 1997 marked a critical stage of transition within Hong Kong. Speculations over Hong Kong's future raised fears about the political situation of the territory, yet thus far economic concerns, in the form of both the regional economic crisis and the continuing economic imperatives of the industry, appear to have dominated other issues. So if colonial British and communist Chinese governance of television industries have both resulted in programming that has remained fairly consistent in its composition, language, and lack of strong ideological critique, what does this say about the power dynamics within Hong Kong? The elite, based in global capitalist structures, continue to dominate and prosper, strengthening a clique of profit-driven industrialists at the expense of substantive political debate and critique. In essence, the economic conditions of the industry, coupled with restrictive political agencies, limit the potential for more participatory, democratic engagement.

References

Chan, Joseph Man. 1994. "National Responses and Accessibility to Star TV in Asia." *Journal of Communication* 44, no. 3:112–131.

Chan, Joseph M., and Paul S. N. Lee. 1992. "Mass Communication: Consumption and Evaluation." In *Indicators of Social Development: Hong Kong 1990*, ed. Siu-Kai Lau, Hsin-chi Kuan, and Po-sun Wan. Hong Kong: Hong Kong Institute of Asia-Pacific Studies, Chinese University of Hong Kong.

Curran, James. 2002. *Media and Power*. London: Routledge.

Curtin, Michael. 1998. "Images of Trust, Economies of Suspicion: Hong Kong Media after 1997." *Historical Journal of Film, Radio, and Television* 18, no. 2:281–294.

Downing, John. 1996. *Internationalizing Media Theory: Transition, Power, and Culture*. London: Sage.

Eliason, Marcus. 1997. "China's Move to Repeal Rights Raises Fears in Hong Kong." *Austin-American Statesman*, 21 January, p. A3.

Good, Leslie. 1989. "Power, Hegemony and Communication Theory." In *Cultural Politics in Contemporary America*, ed. Ian Angus and Sut Jhally, 51–64. New York: Routledge.

Gramsci, Antonio. 1971. *Selections from the Prison Notebooks of Antonio Gramsci*. Ed. and trans. Quintin Hoare and Geoffrey Nowell Smith. New York: International Publishers.

HKBA (Hong Kong Broadcasting Authority). 1993. *Report of the Broadcasting Authority: September 1992–August 1993*. Hong Kong: Government Printer.

———. 2006. *The Hong Kong Broadcasting Scene*. http://www.info.gov.hk/info/hkin/broadcasting.pdf (accessed 25 January 2006).

Kan, Wendy. 2002. "B'casters Spice Skeds for Young Demo." *Variety* 386, no. 1, p. A4.

———. 2003. "Slow Ad Growth Keeps Budget Down." http://www.variety.com/index.asp?layout=mipcom2003&content=story&nav=territory&articleID=VR1117893496 (accessed 28 February 2006).

Lee, Chin-Chuan. 2001. "Rethinking the Political Economy: Implications for Media and Democracy in Greater China." *The Public* 8, no. 3:1–22.

Lee, Chin-Chuan, Joseph M. Chan, Zhongdang Pan, and Clement So. 2002. *Global Media Spectacle: News War over Hong Kong*. Albany: State University of New York Press.

Lee, Paul, and Leonard Chu. 1998. "Inherent Dependence on Power: The Hong Kong Press in Political Transition." *Media, Culture, and Society* 20, no. 1:59–77.

Ma, Eric Kit-wai. 2000. "Re-nationalization and Me: My Hong Kong Story after 1997." *Inter-Asia Cultural Studies* 1, no. 1:173–179.

McAnany, Emile G., and Kent T. Wilkinson. 1992. "From Cultural Imperialists to Takeover Victims." *Communication Research* 19, no. 6:724–748.

Nordenstreng, Kaarle, and Tapio Varis. 1974. "Television Traffic: A One-Way Street? A Survey Analysis of the International Flow of Television Program Material." Reports and Papers on Mass Communications, no. 70. Paris: UNESCO.

Rothrock, Vicki. 2005. "Hong Kong: ATV's Dramatic Intentions Help Fill Pipeline." http://www.variety.com/index.asp?layout=mipcom2005&content=jump&jump=territory&articleID=VR1117930292 (accessed 28 February 2006).

Schiller, Herbert I. 1971. *Mass Communications and American Empire*. Boston: Beacon.

———. 1993. "Transnational Media: Creating Consumers." *Journal of International Affairs* 47, no. 1:47–58.

Tomlinson, John. 1991. *Cultural Imperialism*. London: Pinter.

Tunstall, Jeremy. 1977. *The Media Are American: Anglo-American Media in the World*. New York: Columbia University Press.

Varis, Tapio. 1984. "The International Flow of Television Programs." *Journal of Communication* 34, no. 1:143–152.

Waterman, David, and Everett Rogers. 1994. "The Economics of Television Program Production and Trade in Far East Asia." *Journal of Communication* 44, no. 3:89–111.

White, James D. 2005. *Global Media: The Television Revolution in Asia*. New York: Routledge.

Wilkins, Karin Gwinn. 1998. "Hong Kong Television at the End of the British Empire." In *Mass Media in the Asian Pacific*, ed. Bryce T. McIntyre, 14–28. Clevedon, UK: Multilingual Matters.

———. 2004. "Communication and Transition in the Middle East: A Critical Analysis of U.S. Intervention and Academic Literature." *Gazette: The International Journal for Communication Studies* 66, no. 6:483–496.

2

Programming

Shanghai Television's
Documentary Channel:
Chinese Television as Public Space

CHRIS BERRY

In the 1990s, the transformation of news and documentary programming electrified Chinese television audiences. Gone were the "mouthpiece of the Party" lectures on the latest political line. In their place, news magazine shows like *Focus* and *Oriental Horizon* pursued investigative reporting, on-the-street interviews, and other, more spontaneous techniques. The popularity of these shows led Shanghai Television (STV) to launch China's first specialized channel for documentary programming, the Documentary Channel (Jishi Pindao), on 1 January 2002. This essay considers the arrival of the Documentary Channel as symbolic of a shift in Chinese television away from being a pedagogical tool of the party-state apparatus to interacting more complexly with the market economy and ideas of public participation. Seeing the creation of the Documentary Channel as an example of this shift, it examines it as a specific kind of public space in the culture of Shanghai and the People's Republic.

The development of a mainland Chinese market economy and a corresponding rollback of the state-led command economy—exemplified in television today by almost total financial dependence on commercials—has led scholars to consider ideas like "civil society" and "the public sphere" in the Chinese context. However, these ideas are based on a model in which "freedom" is understood as the absence of state "power." From this binary perspective, a country either has civil society and a public sphere, or it does not. Instead, drawing on Foucault's idea of power as productive, I argue in the second section of this essay that public space is produced by power and takes multiple forms, with differences and changes in such spaces corresponding to reconfigurations of power. Were it to be judged by the idealized and either/or standards of civil society and the public sphere, the Documentary Channel would have to be seen as a failure. Approached in this way, the changes from the pre–market economy era are erased within an Orientalist ideological perspective that only exists to reaffirm the alleged superiority of liberal capitalism and the West. But if the Documentary Channel is approached as a public space, the question changes. Where the "public sphere" concept imagines a space of idealized free debate waiting to emerge once the forces of the state are removed, the concept of "public space," informed by Foucault's ideas, understands areas of public debate as produced and regulated by power and appearing in a variety of forms. (The privately owned shopping mall might be a relatively straightforward example.) Instead of the binary question of whether it is a success or failure—whether China has civil society and a public sphere or not—this essay goes on to ask what sort of public space the Documentary Channel produces, by examining the forces that shape it and regulate what activities occur in that public space.

From this perspective, it is clear that the new public space of STV's Documentary Channel is shaped to meet the needs of "marketized" (*shichanghua*) socialist China. In this new post-1989 environment, the state and the market complement rather than contradict each other, and they exercise hegemony through their new alliance. However, their control is not exclusive. A multiple power structure has replaced the monopoly of the state that produced the old "mouthpiece of the party" model. Television stations' need for both good ratings and party-state approval determines the type of material that they primarily broadcast. However, journalists also have a certain power of their own—programming cannot be produced without their work. And so does the public—unless they watch, television has no product to be sold to advertisers and no viewer-pupils to be taught the lesson the party and state wish them to learn. Within this multiply determined structure, journalists and the public can attempt to carve out a space in which to produce Shanghai public culture, but only as long as they operate within the protocols established by the hegemony of the party-state apparatus and the marketplace. In this way, the Documentary Channel reveals the complex specificity of public space in China today.

New Television, New Documentary

This essay uses "documentary programming" as a general term to cover factual programming representing real life. In other words, it includes both magazine programs that package various short documentary pieces and longer, stand-alone documentary programs. But it excludes reality television, in which situations and events are designed and scripted, as well as news and talk shows. Documentary programming has, of course, been an important constituent of Chinese television from the first broadcasts in 1958. However, as Junhao Hong and his colleagues detail in their essay in this book, the nature of television in China has changed in recent years. Television documentary has played a crucial role in these changes.

There are two main aspects to the transformation of Chinese television in the 1990s. The first is television's ascension to a position of dominance amongst the media. Film and radio were the dominant media of the socialist heyday. To give just a few statistics, only 925,000 television receivers were manufactured between 1958 and Mao's death in 1976, but annual output had reached 27.67 million as early as 1989 (Huang 1994: 217). In 1978 there was less than one television receiver per hundred people, and only 10 million out of a population of nearly one billion, or less than 1 percent, had access to television. By 1996, there was a television receiver for every four people, and one billion had access (Hazelbarth 1997: 1). By 2000, this figure had risen to 1.19 billion, representing 92 percent of the population, and cable television was bringing a wider range of channels to 85.3 percent of the population in the relatively wealthy ten largest cities (Li 2001).

Second, television has been transformed from a medium owned and funded entirely by the state to one owned by the state but funded by advertising. This is part of the general "marketization" (*shichanghua*) of the economy of the People's Republic. Now advertising supplies as much as 99 percent of income for Chinese television, and only 0.5 percent of the income of national broadcaster China Central Television (CCTV) still comes from the government—less than it pays back in tax (Li 2001). Ratings are provided by ACNeilsen and CVSC-Sofres Media Peoplemeters, and the proportion of advertising money spent on television rose from 27.7 percent at the beginning of the 1990s to 72.9 percent in 1997 (*Broadcasting and Cable's TV International* 1999).

Documentary programming in various forms has played an important role in this transformation. According to Li Xiaoping, the show that powered the take-off in advertising was a daytime documentary news magazine show on CCTV called *Oriental Horizon* (*Dongfang shikong*) (Li 2001). Modeled somewhat on the investigative segments forming CBS's *60 Minutes* and debuting in 1993, *Oriental Horizon* combined factual materials with an exposure of social issues not usually aired on Chinese television, and in this it represented something very new in Chinese television and in Chinese documentary in general. *Oriental Horizon* was an experiment. After its huge success with the public and acceptance by the political establishment, CCTV went on to launch the even more successful evening show *Focus* (*Jiaodian*) in 1994. Airing for thirteen minutes every weekday after the evening news, the program regularly gets a 20 to 25 percent rating, that is, between 200 and 250 million viewers, and is popular with national leaders (Li 2002: 22–23). This huge success has inspired many copies: by the end of the 1990s there were already more than sixty similar television programs around the country as well as numerous "watchdog journalism" newspaper columns inspired by it (Chan 2002: 39).¹ As well as news magazine shows, Chinese television also has a wide range of longer documentary programming. Although beyond the scope of this essay, another new genre that has attracted the attention of those interested in civil society is the talk show, which debuted in 1996 with *Tell It Like It Is* (*Shi hua shi shuo*), modeled on *The Oprah Winfrey Show* (Bian 2001)

These programs are quite different from the documentaries of the socialist heyday. The format for documentary programming then was the *zhuanti pian*, or "special topic program," which resembled an illustrated lecture. A mixture of voiceover narration, on-the-spot interviews, and recording of events as they happen has replaced the old lecture style. This spontaneous realist rhetorical mode in television is known in Chinese as *jishizhuyi* (as opposed to the old socialist realist mode of *xianshizhuyi*). The Chinese name of STV's Documentary Channel, Jishi Pindao, was derived from this term. The new look has been facilitated by new lightweight technology and can be recognized both by the profilmic event—what happens in front of the camera—and by the style of program making. The spontaneous quality of the profilmic is signified by the sometimes stumbling delivery of thoughts in interviews, along with tears and other expressions of emotion, uncontrolled and unrehearsed. Spontaneity in program style is signified by the use of handheld cameras, the inclusion of moments of what might be considered technically unacceptable lighting and sound (but only in ways that do not detract from viewers' understanding), and the movement of characters in and out of frame or acting in other ways that signify the unexpected or contingent.

By the turn of the century, the on-the-spot style of *jishizhuyi* had become a new norm in documentary-style programming on Chinese television. The "special topic programs" are largely a thing of the past. Now a range of other styles, many of which do not meet the usual norms of on-the-spot realism, are also becoming popular. These are mostly learned from Western documentary-style programming with high ratings. They include reenactment, use of music, MTV-style editing, and so forth.

Shanghai Television's Documentary Channel

The establishment and characteristics of STV's Documentary Channel can be understood as part of the general transformation of Chinese television and of documentary on television in particular, as described above. The decision to set up the station can be understood as part of the chase for market share in a rapidly emerging multi-channel and "marketized" environment. However, a more complex web of determinations has shaped the development of the channel's programming. First, channel-originated programming itself may exist partly as a result of protectionist regulations. Second, the party-state apparatus no longer sets the agenda for programming, but it continues to guide in a reactive manner, suggesting amendments or blocking programs. The programs are initiated by the channel's journalists themselves. Initially, the agenda of the Documentary Channel program makers appears to have been the promotion of a participatory Shanghai public culture in the media space constituted by the channel, as this section will demonstrate. However, the increasing importance of commercial priorities in the television industry and the inability of this participatory culture to deliver in those terms led to restructuring of the channel in late 2005, with a shift from the local and the participatory toward the national and the entertaining. This shift will be detailed and analyzed in the final section of the essay.

In the command economy era, television operated under a pedagogical model of the media. Television in general was not prioritized, but the resources that were devoted to documentary programming were supplied in the name of educating the public. In the current market economy era, television has become a multi-channel medium. Indeed, the growth in the number of channels has been explosive. Where Shanghai Television (STV) had only one channel when it began, by 2007 it had been integrated into the Shanghai Media Group (Shanghai Wenguang Xinwen Chuanmei Jituan, SMG), which was operating thirteen television channels (Shanghai Media Group n.d.). With cable and satellite bringing television channels from all over China and even Hong Kong, a typical Chinese television viewer today has at least dozens and often more than a hundred channels to choose from. In an environment where income is dictated by advertising, an organization like SMG works to maximize its share of the audience within this multi-channel environment by trying to control as many of the available channels as possible as well as pursuing popular programming.

SMG was founded in 2001 as part of a nationwide process of conglomeratization in anticipation of the challenge posed by imports after China's entry

Table 4.1. The Documentary Channel's
Programming Production and Income

Year	Hours of Programming Produced	Advertising Income (million RMB)
2002	77	2.2
2003	156	2.2
2004	147	2.5
2005	206	4.76
2006	580 (anticipated)	7.20
2007	N/A	10 (anticipated)

Note: Figures are from Wang 2006, with the exception of the 2006 and 2007 advertising income figures, which are drawn from "SMG's Documentary Channel Grows Strong through Professionalism," 2007.

into the WTO, which took place in 2002.[2] It combined the former Shanghai Television and Oriental Television (Dongfang Dianshi), along with various other broadcasting operations. SMG is itself one of nine subsidiaries of the Shanghai Media and Entertainment Group (Shanghai Wenhua Guangbo Yingshi Jituan), also founded in 2001 as part of the same process.

Having moved almost overnight from relative channel scarcity to a multichannel environment and control of a number of channels, including many new ones, SMG was faced with the challenge of filling the channels and attracting audience. It is possible that if SMG were allowed to operate in a completely unregulated environment, it could fill the Documentary Channel with imported programming of the Discovery Channel and National Geographic Channel variety. It is always cheaper to buy programming than to originate it. However, this is where a gap opens up between the specific interests of SMG and the larger interests of the Chinese media industry and culture as perceived by the government. To protect the Chinese media industry and also Chinese media culture, all programming in the so-called "golden hours" of Chinese prime time must be Chinese-originated.[3]

Furthermore, channel-originated programming has the greatest potential to generate income. Ying Qiming, executive director of the Documentary Channel since 2005, has shown that there is a clear correlation between the amount of programming the channel originates and the income it generates, as indicated by the figures in table 4.1 (Wang 2006).

The Documentary Channel is on the air every day from about 6 AM until after 2 AM. However, it is only during the evening that it broadcasts its five and a half hours of new programming. Of that, an average of more than an hour per night was produced by the channel itself when it was established at the beginning of 2002. The high rate of repeats and use of bought programming attested to the difficulty of finding enough programming in the new multi-channel environment.[4] The correlation of channel-originated programming with income that Ying Qiming demonstrated makes efforts to originate new programming a primary concern for the channel today.

As already indicated, documentary-style programming was one of the success stories of Chinese television in the 1990s. In Shanghai itself, Shanghai Television's series *Documentary Editing Room* (*Jilupian Bianjishi*), launched in 1993, was very popular in the 1990s, sometimes commanding an audience share of more than 30 percent ("2002 Documentary Forum" 2003). This series consisted of locally produced documentaries on current Shanghai topics, no doubt contributing to its appeal. The most memorable productions from the years before the Documentary Channel's founding include "The Last Tricycle on Shanghai's Bund" ("Shanghai tan zhuihou de sanlunche"); "Inexpressible Feelings about the Black Earth" ("Nanyan heituqing"), which documented the educated youths from Shanghai sent to the communes of Heilongjiang in the far northeast during the Cultural Revolution; and "The Maomao Case" ("Maomao gaozhuang").

"The Maomao Case" seems to have been particularly popular, touching many viewers. It is cited as one of STV's most successful programs in almost every article of any length about the station. The program followed a young woman from the countryside who had come to Shanghai with her baby boy—only a few months old at the time—in search of his father, who refused to admit paternity. In addition to its obvious melodramatic appeal, the program dealt with the floating population from the countryside in the city and the question of the rule of law, two issues that are important to every Chinese city dweller today. The program begins with the narrating journalist reporting to the audience that *Documentary Editing Room* heard about the situation when a viewer called in and told them about it. This sense of viewer participation is common in the series. Not only do many of the initial ideas come from Shanghai viewers and most of the programs depict Shanghai citizens and issues in their daily lives or their histories, but also the series frequently asks for comments from bystanders and other Shanghai residents. In this sense, it can be said to have built up the program as a Shanghai public culture together with its viewers.[5] China's leading documentary scholar, Xinyu Lu, has claimed that this relationship it built with its audience was one of the most important reasons for its success ("2002 Documentary Forum" 2003).

With this history of success behind *Documentary Editing Room*, the Documentary Channel was built up around the program. It was the most important and popular of the locally originated programs on the new channel when it began airing in 2002. According to the main editor of the program, Wang Xiaolong, who had been working on it since 1994, *Documentary Editing Room* had the largest staff allocated to any single program, and included sixteen program makers. It filled an hour of the broadcast schedule every weekday.[6]

If *Documentary Editing Room* was the jewel in the Documentary Channel's crown on its establishment, it was surrounded by a series of other locally produced programs. Each of these was intended to build on certain aspects of the appeal of local documentary. *Friday Night Files* (*Xingxiwu Dang'an*) was a weekly show screening at 9:00 in the evening. Its specialty was documentaries with a historical element, and it focused on Shanghai people and Shanghai stories. It was launched in February 1998 on the Oriental Television station, which was folded into the SMG along with STV, and then it was transferred across to the new Documentary Channel. In 2005, the word "Friday" was dropped from the program's title, and it was rescheduled for broadcast on Saturday and Sunday evenings ("*Friday Night Files*" n.d.).

A new show launched with the Documentary Channel was *New Wave* (*Xin Shengdai*), which aired amateur twenty-minute documentaries beginning twenty-five minutes before *Friday Night Files* every Friday evening. It encouraged the Shanghai audience to participate not just by suggesting program ideas or being interviewed, but also by making the programs themselves. In practice, this meant mostly programs by local film, media, and journalism students or other young people. The opening sequence of *New Wave* emphasizes youth and individual expression with three slogans: "A Series from Young People Themselves" ("Yidang xin shengdai ziji de lanmu"), "A Window on Individuality ("Yishan zhanshi gexing de chuangkou"), and "Youth Topics" ("Qingnianren de ticai"). Judging by the four-VCD set 2002 *Award-Winning Works* put out by the channel, its programming style is not necessarily unconventional. Most (but not all) of the award-winning works focus on interesting personalities and are narrated. More important, however, nearly all the award-winning programs are focused on events in and people of Shanghai itself, with little attention to other parts of China.

For those with a particular interest in documentary, a weekly show known in English as *Documentary Talk Show* (original Chinese title: *Jingdian Chongfang*) brought documentary filmmakers to meet studio audiences. Each week, the show broadcast segments of "classic" documentary films introduced by the filmmaker and the host, and then followed them up with an in-studio question-and-answer session. Some of the films had been shot by and already screened on other Chinese television stations; the show's Chinese title implies "repeat screening." However, others were made by independent filmmakers. The screening of segments rather than whole films enabled the program editors to avoid any particularly sensitive segments of the original film that would normally make it impossible to broadcast. The films and filmmakers came from all over China, although the program was shot with a Shanghai studio audience.

Finally, the channel rounded out its range of locally originated programming with another daily program. Where *Documentary Editing Room* focused on relatively long documentaries, *Insight (Kanjian)* ran ten-minute pieces. In this, it seems to have been modeled on CCTV's phenomenally successful *Oriental Horizon*. The short format allows for a quicker production time and therefore more topical programming than does the longer format of *Documentary Editing Room*. However, for the most part *Insight* steered away from controversy and did not engage in investigative reporting. Like so much of the rest of the Documentary Channel's local programming, it emphasized Shanghai people, topics, and events. This can be discerned from the synopses of sixty-six programs from the first four years of the series (Shanghai Television Documentary Channel 2004).

In addition to originating and airing programming, the Documentary Channel tried in other ways not only to promote itself to its potential Shanghai audience but also to involve that audience in the channel's culture. It engaged professional audience research companies to not only measure ratings but also find out audience reaction to programming. However, the channel's journalists felt they needed contact with the public and the audience themselves. Most of them are local, and therefore they held neighborhood meetings and other informal focus group activities. Their aim was to get to know their audience, to get suggestions for programming, and to get direct responses to recently aired material.[7]

Chinese Documentaries, Chinese Publics

The movement away from the old "special topic" film toward a range of more spontaneous and locally initiated documentary television programming on local topics at STV's Documentary Channel is part of the general rollback of the centralized economy and society of the Maoist heyday. In place of a system in which—after consultation—the state initiated, guided, and judged all activity, a society and economy have emerged in which the citizenry can and do initiate many activities by themselves. In the context of these exciting developments, scholars and commentators inside and outside China have turned repeatedly to the social model that celebrates the separation of state and society—liberal capitalist democracy—in their search for appropriate concepts. "Civil society," "the public sphere," and "freedom of the press" are all invoked frequently in discussions of general social change and transformation of the media and culture. I have discussed these debates in more detail elsewhere (Berry, forthcoming). He Baogang (1997) provides an excellent and detailed discussion of the many debates that developed in the 1990s. Terms like "civil society," "the public sphere," and "freedom of the press" could also be advanced to understand the initial efforts of the Documentary Channel to produce and proliferate Shanghai public culture on Shanghai

Television. But what are the risks of using such foreign ideas in a contemporary Chinese context? How appropriate and effective are these concepts for understanding the Documentary Channel?

However historically circumscribed such concepts as "civil society" and the "public sphere" might have been in their original delineation, their contemporary invocation shares an opposition between state and society, according to which freedom is believed to prosper as the separation between the two grows and the role of the state is minimized. Amidst the numerous debates on the subject, three main positions have emerged. First, some believe that China is moving toward these models. For example, Li Xiaoping, the former executive producer of the CCTV news magazine shows *Focus* and *Oriental Horizon*, argues that "Chinese television has gained much more freedom and independence," and *Focus* "helps galvanize more public debate and subsequently pressure on government to tackle the problem. . . . media plays the role of a campaigner for social justice" (Li 2002: 18, 26; see also Xu 2000; Graham 2003: 1). Generally speaking, this position is more often held by journalists and other public commentators. The remaining two positions are more often held by scholars.

A second group believes that nothing has really changed and that "the Chinese propaganda authorities have not relinquished their control over television," as Yong Zhong puts it. In his essay on the apparent public sphere of debating contests on CCTV, he finds numerous ideological controls (2002: 27; see also Zhong 1998, 2001; Zhao 1998). In contrast to Li Xiaoping (2001), Alex Chan (2002) sees new television documentary as a mere safety valve. A third group argues that China is too different for these foreign ideas to be applied. Michael Keane's scholarship on Chinese television policy is exemplary in this regard. Keane points out that "[w]hereas citizens in liberal democracies seek to influence the formulation of policy by force of ideas, by interest group activities and ultimately through the ballot box . . . [u]nder the Chinese socialist tradition, we find . . . the balance shifts towards interpretation of policy" (Keane 2001: 783; see also Keane 2003). As Keane explains, in Western societies policy is manifested and enforced as law, which is inflexible. In China, the tendency is for regulation, which is not ironclad law but subject to negotiation.

Insights such as Keane's into the inadequacies of models like civil society, the public sphere, and freedom of expression in the Chinese context are worth pursuing further. What are the implications and consequences of accepting such a model as a standard against which to measure developments in China? First, using these models assumes an East-West binarism that almost automatically perpetuates Orientalism, because they measure China against a Western standard that is assumed to be ideal, find it lacking, and therefore affirm Western superiority.

Furthermore, the consideration of such concepts usually rests on the dubious assumption that they exist (or once existed) in the West. In fact, the Habermasian bourgeois public sphere was only open to a limited segment of the population; it excluded those without property, women (Fraser 1992), people of color (Morley 2000: 118–124), the illiterate, and others. Others have spoken of the formation of "counter-publics" where proletarians and others come together to organize and strategize (Negt and Kluge 1993). Important though these critiques unquestionably are, they are largely reformist in spirit, implying that the notion of the public sphere itself as a zone of free discourse defined by separation from the state is still useful.

A more fundamental problem lies in the concept of freedom at work here. Underlying this concept is a negative concept of power as solely oppressive and exclusively possessed by the state. Therefore, if the state is removed, power is removed, and freedom results. Foucault's work has been central to the project of rethinking the concept of power as productive as well as repressive. Foucault differentiates the productive power of modernity from the repressive power of the ancien regime in Europe (1976, 1977). He distinguishes between external forms of productive power, or disciplines, and the internalization of productive power in such forms as identity. This idea of productiveness means not necessarily that power is good, but that it is active and shapes activities and conditions. If we transfer such an understanding of power to ideas of the public and civil society, how does it change our understanding of them?

If public space is theorized, in contrast to the public sphere, as produced by power relationships amongst multiple social actors and as multiple in its variations, then we may have a more subtle way of describing different types of public space and public activity than is allowed by the impossible either/or standard of the public sphere. Instead of asking if we do or do not have a public sphere, we can try to ask what kind of a public space we are looking at. Who are the actors in that public space? What protocols govern what they do in that space, including the discourse they can produce? What is the scope of the space produced?

The Documentary Channel as Public Space

The consequences of using concepts like the public sphere and civil society, on the one hand, or public space on the other, become clearer if we consider more recent developments at the Documentary Channel. Promoting local culture with local stories and local participation had resulted in very good ratings for *Documentary Editing Room* in the 1990s. However, when the Documentary Channel itself pursued a similar strategy after its establishment at the beginning of 2002, it did not achieve similar ratings. Indeed, it struggled to break even in its initial years. When I interviewed Yuan Yemin, its executive director, in 2002, he claimed the channel was at least breaking even. But articles covering its restructuring (such as

Wang 2006) often claim that it did not turn a profit until 2005. At the end of 2005, a shake-up took place and a raft of new programs were introduced. I will discuss this in more detail below, but the basic trend was away from Shanghai-oriented programming that emphasized local participation and toward more national and international programming that emphasized entertainment.

How might we understand this history using the concepts of the public sphere and civil society? We might conclude simply that the journalists of the Documentary Channel tried to use their programming to make the channel a public space where Shanghai participatory public culture could flourish, but that this effort failed. Within this explanatory framework, the creation of a public sphere or a civil society is understood as the consequence of minimizing state power. Therefore, an attempt to explain this failure will look toward questions of censorship and control.

The Discovery Channel carefully avoids controversy in its programming, and this avoidance cannot have helped it attract high ratings. All programs are vetted by people in authority at every stage, from concept to broadcast. In December 2002, I spoke to Wang Xiaolong, the editor of *Documentary Editing Room*, Wang Mingyuan of *New Wave*, Yu Yongjing of *Insight*, Liu Jia of *Documentary Talk Show*, and channel chief executive Yuan Yemin. All of them were completely frank about the vetting, making clear that it is normal and taken for granted in Chinese broadcasting. However, Wang Xiaolong and Yuan Yemin also pointed out that almost all of this vetting was done internally. Yuan and his colleagues in charge of the channel only turned to outside authorities in cases where they had doubts. Furthermore, all the people I spoke to indicated that problem programs were much fewer than they had been in the 1990s, because the journalists had a better understanding of the boundaries. In other words, they had internalized the standards for what is and is not acceptable to the party-state apparatus that owns and operates the television stations.

These are important characteristics of the Chinese television environment in general. The party-state apparatus remains the ultimate power. If it deems that a program presents an ideological problem, its decision trumps both the economic interests of the station—which will not receive any return on its investment if the program does not air—and the journalist's belief in the worth of the story.

However, there are problems with an analysis based on these ideas of the public sphere and civil society. The party-state apparatus has held ultimate power from the very beginning of Chinese television, and this power has never wavered. The concepts of the public sphere and civil society are therefore not adequate to account for either the emergence of the participatory Shanghai culture around the Documentary Channel on its establishment or its more recent eclipse.

Furthermore, such an analysis runs the risk of making it seem as though nothing at all has changed in the politics of Chinese television. While the supreme power of the party-state apparatus should not be overlooked, the complexities of changing economics must also be considered, together with their impact both on how the television audience is envisioned and produced and on how it can respond. If we try to think about Chinese television and the Documentary Channel as public space, on the other hand, we can produce a more complex picture. Among the variables that we can take into account are the size of the space, the powers that create and maintain it, and the values and goals they bring to regulating what can and cannot happen in that space.

From such a perspective, one of the first points that needs to be made clear is that the behavior of the party-state apparatus has changed. Although it retains the power of ultimate sanction, as already noted, it exercises that power reactively rather than proactively. It does not set the agenda or fund the programs anymore. A public space analysis of the Documentary Channel must note that the party-state apparatus is no longer the only factor producing and maintaining the public space that the channel can be understood as constituting.

The analysis of the establishment of the Documentary Channel already given above reveals various actors at work in the production of the channel and its public space. This variety supersedes the old monopoly of the party-state apparatus. Each of these actors has its own interests and its own corresponding ideas of what the public space of the channel is for and what should be going on in that space.

For the party-state apparatus, the public space of television is a classroom and the viewers are the pupils. For the commercial interests of the station and for the advertisers who pay for the programming, the viewers are a product to be sold to the advertisers, a potential market assembled to be advertised to via the public space of the channel.

The third set of actors is the journalists. Their behavior around the establishment of the Documentary Channel indicates that they have developed their own values, which are autonomous from those of the state. They see themselves not just as the state's mouthpiece but as operating autonomously, with the public as their potential partners participating in the space of the channel. However, precisely how they can operate together and what kind of public culture they may produce is shaped by other factors. These include the power structure or relationships among the various sets of actors.

As long as the party-state apparatus has ultimate control over what gets aired, the collaboration between the journalists and viewers must fit in with its values. In other words, the journalists and viewers can create a public culture around being from Shanghai, documenting Shanghai culture today, and addressing those issues in Shanghai that have been acknowledged by the party-state apparatus as worthy of airing. But they cannot engage in activities that challenge the pedagogical model, either by straying too far away from the educational values preferred by the party-state apparatus or by challenging the legitimacy of that apparatus.

However, the success of *Documentary Editing Room* in the 1990s and the characteristics of the Documentary Channel in its early days reveal that the party-state apparatus's pedagogical model and the journalists' idea of participatory public culture are not necessarily at absolute loggerheads, as the public sphere or civil society model implies. What the changes after 2005 reveal is that that the economic interests of the channel and the advertisers, who are operating with a market model, also trump those of the journalists. As long as the public culture that the journalists were pursuing delivered the ratings, there was no problem, but once they did not things had to change. Again, this reveals the inadequacy of the public sphere or civil society model by showing that growth of the market economy does not necessarily happen at the expense of the power of the state, and does not necessarily lead to a growth in public culture.

However, to understand why the Documentary Channel did not deliver economically, we need to turn to another variable in the analysis of public spaces: not the players in television, but its scope. The shift to a multi-channel television environment reconfigured the public space of the Documentary Channel. In the 1990s, the limited number of channels available to most Chinese viewers created a clear division between two cultures produced by programming—a national public space associated with the CCTV channels available all over the country, and a local public space associated with the local television station, in this case STV. With satellite and cable, that distinction has become blurred. Local stations such as STV can be accessed nationally and even internationally. Increasingly, they perceive themselves as locally based stations that are playing to a potential national audience. Indeed, the "President's words" on the SMG website identify two key tasks. One is commercialization, and "the other is to step by step transfer the role of the group from a local broadcasting organization of broadcasting and TV programs to a content provider and conductor facing to the country as a whole and even overseas Chinese speaking world. *Furthermore, our market is not only Shanghai but also the entire Chinese world and global market.*" (Shanghai Media Group n.d., emphasis added). In these circumstances, developing Shanghai programs for Shanghai audiences was disconnected from the reality of the channel's potential viewership and the scope of its new public space.

Moreover, in the Chinese multi-channel environment, there is little if any possibility of a mass audience. Instead of choosing between a handful of stations, viewers are using their remote controls to flit among a plethora of channels from all over China. Only the most exceptional of circumstances could turn a documentary series into must-see viewing for the whole audience. Perhaps only national media events like the announcement that Beijing had been awarded the

2008 Olympics or the annual CCTV New Year gala, discussed in Xinyu Lu's essay in this volume, could achieve such a status. However, as Lu notes, even the New Year gala is no longer guaranteed the ratings it used to get.

Within the new environment, new strategies were required to try and win ratings and improve the channel's financial health. The discourse that emerged around the late 2005 restructuring is dominated by the values of profit and loss, revealing the high priority placed on market values. The changes that took place are manifestations of this. First, it was announced that the channel intended to change its Chinese name from Jishi Pindao to Zhenshi Pindao (literally "Truth Channel"). The English name was to remain unchanged. (So far, the channel remains Jishi Pindao, however, indicating that the name change has not yet been approved at the higher levels of the party-state structure. Why it has not remains unclear.)

In 2002, Wang Xiaolong, the editor of *Documentary Editing Room*, explained the choice of the word *jishi* to name the channel by saying that it symbolized the desire to avoid drama or quasi-dramatic documentary, of which there was too much on television already.[8] By 2005, the connotations of *jishi* were a minus rather than a plus. The channel's new executive director, Ying Qiming, explained that *jishi* did indeed suggest on-the-spot documentaries, but that this was now seen as excluding more contemporary forms of documentary programming, such as archive-based documentaries and docudramas. Furthermore, he declared that *jishi* was a genre—on-the-spot documentaries—whereas *zhenshi*, truth, was more of a brand, something he compared with the Discovery Channel (Qian 2006).

This invocation of the idea of a brand and the use of the Discovery Channel as a model indicates the new power of the market model of public space within the channel itself. Indeed, reports from around the time of the late 2005 shake-up underlined this by their frequent emphasis that the channel attracted viewers that were of value to advertisers. Their demographics were characterized by the "three highs"—high income, high education, and high age (Cui 2005). At least the first two are considered highly attractive by many advertisers.

As part of its new strategy, described as "growing strong through professionalism," the channel also instituted "daily shows," replacing weekly shows with a consistent evening line-up every weekday ("SMG's Documentary Channel Grows Strong through Professionalism" 2007). In 2007, this evening lineup begins at seven with a new program called *Cultural China* (*Wenhua Zhongguo*), devoted to Chinese cultural traditions, followed at half past seven by a slot devoted to law documentaries, running under different series titles each day of the week. At five minutes before eight, a new series called *DV365* screens very short digital video pieces, replacing *New Wave* with a faster-paced series. Then, at eight, *Was* (*Wangshi*) presents archive-based historical documentary, followed at half past eight by *Documentary Editing Room*, which remains the channel's signature series ("Introduction to the Documentary Channel's Series" 2006). At nine o'clock, an hour is given over to Discovery Channel programming, followed by another hour-long series called *Legend* (*Chuanqi*), which broadcasts documentary from around the world. Finally, at eleven, the channel airs an hour-long talk show, already established on Hong Kong's Phoenix Television, that focuses on individuals. Its title is *Tell Your Story—An Appointment with Luyu* (*Shuochu Ni de Gushi—Luyu You Yue*) ("Moving Every Viewer with Her Wise Beauty" 2005).

The figures in table 4.1 show that this new line-up resulted in increased income. However, from the perspective of this essay, its most crucial characteristic is its move away from the local and toward a greater proportion of nationally oriented and internationally sourced programming, in accordance with the new national (and potentially international) scope of the channel's public space. As the title *Cultural China* implies, the new shows focus on national stories rather than Shanghai stories. Given the national reach of SMG's shows today, this makes commercial sense. But it also means the waning of a programming logic based on the idea of participatory Shanghai culture.

With this history of the Documentary Channel in mind, rather than concluding that "they" do not have a televisual public sphere in Shanghai (and, by implication, that "we" do in the West), we can see this analysis as laying the groundwork for a comparative analysis of televisual public space under conditions of global marketization. There are certainly important differences between televisual public space in China and in, say, the United Kingdom or the United States. The state has a greater role in the UK than in the U.S., but in neither country does it have the direct interest in content that it does in China. On the other hand, there are also important similarities. These include the reconfigurations pursuant upon the new multi-channel environment, the increased emphasis on market dynamics, and the trading in audience-as-product. It may well be that in both China and the West these factors are at least as important as the state in shaping the ways in which both journalists and viewers can participate in televisual public space.

Notes

I would like to thank the Faculty of Humanities at the University of California, Berkeley for a Faculty Research Grant that initiated the research for this project, and also the University of California Pacific Rim Research Program, whose grant to me and Professor Lisa Rofel of the University of California, Santa Cruz enabled me to extend and widen my initial research project. In addition to the help and cooperation of all the interviewees quoted in this essay, I would like to express my gratitude to Professor Xinyu Lu of Fudan University, who introduced me to her friends and colleagues at the Documentary Chan-

nel, and also to Zhang Shujuan, who helped me to record programs over a period of months when I could not be in Shanghai.

1. Synopses of a year's worth of programming can be found in Liang 2002.
2. Interview with Yuan Yemin, executive director of the Documentary Channel, 27 December 2002.
3. Interview with Wang Xiaolong, editor of *Documentary Editing Room*, 27 December 2002.
4. Interview with Yuan Yemin.
5. The scripts of the programs mentioned here, along with comments from their makers, can be found in *Documentary Editing Room* series group 2001.
6. Interview with Wang Xiaolong.
7. Interview with Wang Xiaolong.
8. Interview with Wang Xiaolong.

References

"The 2002 Documentary Forum, Report No. 3: The Serialization of Chinese Documentaries" [2002 Nian jilupian luntan zhi san: Zhongguo jilupian lanmuhua]. 16 January 2003. http://www.filmsea.com.cn/newsreel/commentator/200301160017.html (accessed 31 August 2007).

Berry, Chris. Forthcoming. "New Documentary in China: *Public Space*, Public Television." In *Electronic Elsewheres: Media, Technology, and Social Space*, ed. Lynn Spigel, Kim Soyoung, and Chris Berry. Minneapolis: University of Minnesota Press.

Bian, Yi. 2001. "Talk Shows 'Tell It as It Is.'" *China Daily*, 8 March. http://www.chinadaily.com.cn/cndydb/2001/03/d9-1show.309.html (accessed 10 March 2001).

Broadcasting and Cable's TV International 7, no. 21 (1 November 1999): 5.

Chan, Alex. 2002. "From Propaganda to Hegemony: *Jiaodian Fangtan* and China's Media Policy." *Journal of Contemporary China* 11, no. 30:35–51.

Cui, Yufang. 2005. "STV Confidently Promotes the Documentary Channel on the Basis of Its 'Three High Demographics'" [Dingwei "Sangao renshi" Shanghai dianshi xinxin shizu tuichu Zhenshi pindao]. http://61/135/142/194/news/2005/2005-12-24/8/669516.shtml (accessed 31 August 2007).

Documentary Editing Room Series Group [Jilupian bianjishi Lanmu Zu], ed. 2001. *Eye-Witness: Documentary Editing Room—Telling You True Stories* [Muji: Jilupian bianjishi—Gaosu ni zhenshi de gushi]. Shanghai: Dongfang Chuban Zhongxin.

Foucault, Michel. 1976. *The History of Sexuality, Volume 1: An Introduction*. Trans. Robert Hurley. Harmondsworth: Penguin.

———. 1977. *Discipline and Punish: The Birth of the Prison*. Trans. Alan Sheridan. Harmondsworth: Penguin.

Fraser, Nancy. 1992. "Rethinking the Public Sphere: A Contribution to the Critique of Actually Existing Democracy." In *Habermas and the Public Sphere*, ed. Craig Calhoun, 109–142. Cambridge, Mass.: MIT Press.

"Friday Night Files" [Xingxiwu dang'an]. N.d. http://tv.orinno.com/v2/programinfo_853_.html (accessed 28 August 2007).

Graham, Terence. 2003. "The Future of TV in China." Hong Kong: Telecommunications Research Project, Centre for Asian Studies, University of Hong Kong. http://www.trp.hku.hk/papers/2003/tv_china_wp.pdf (accessed 8 August 2005).

Hazelbarth, Todd. 1997. *The Chinese Media: More Autonomous and Diverse—Within Limits; An Intelligence Monograph.* Washington, D.C.: Central Intelligence Agency, Center for the Study of Intelligence.

He Baogang. 1997. *The Democratic Implications of Civil Society in China.* New York: St. Martin's.

Huang, Yu. 1994. "Peaceful Evolution: The Case of Television Reform in Post-Mao China." *Media, Culture, and Society* 16, no. 2:217–241.

"Introduction to the Documentary Channel's Series" [Jishi pindao lanmu jieshao]. 2006. http://video.sina.com.cn/doc/2006-12-28/175331703.html (accessed 31 August 2007).

Keane, Michael. 2001. "Broadcasting Policy, Creative Compliance, and the Myth of Civil Society in China." *Media, Culture, and Society* 23, no. 6:783–798.

———. 2003. "Civil Society, Regulatory Space, and Cultural Authority in China's Television Industry." In *Television, Regulation, and Civil Society in Asia,* ed. Philip Kitley, 69–187. London: Routledge.

Li, Xiaoping. 2001. "Significant Changes in the Chinese Television Industry and Their Impact in the PRC: An Insider's Perspective." Washington, D.C.: Working Paper of the Center for Northeast Asian Policy Studies, the Brookings Institution. Columbia International Affairs Online, http://www.ciaonet.org/wps/lix01 (accessed 10 September 2002).

———. 2002. "'Focus' (*Jiaodian Fangtan*) and the Changes in the Chinese Television Industry." *Journal of Contemporary China* 11, no. 30:17–34.

Liang, Jianzeng, ed. 2002. *Jiaodian Dang'an 2002* [*Focus Cases,* 2002]. Beijing: Wenhua Yishu Chubanshe.

Morley, David. 2000. *Home Territories: Media, Mobility, and Identity.* London: Routledge.

"Moving Every Viewer with Her Wise Beauty: *An Appointment with Luyu* Tells Your Story" [Yong zhixingmei dadong eiwei guanzhong *Luyu you yue* shuochu ni de gushi]. 15 July 2005. http://ent.tom.com/1323/1587/2005715-143198.html (accessed 8 August 2007).

Negt, Oskar, and Alexander Kluge. 1993. *Public Sphere and Experience: Toward an Analysis of the Bourgeois and Proletarian Public Sphere.* Trans. Peter Labanyi et al. Minneapolis: University of Minnesota Press.

Qian, Yijiao. 2006. "From *Jishi* to 'Zhenshi'" [Cong *jishi* dao "zhenshi"]. 4 January. http://news.sina.com.cn/c/2006-01-04/15148771644.shtml (accessed 28 August 2007). Originally published in *Xinmin Zhoubao.*

Shanghai Media Group. N.d. "Shanghai Media Group." http://www.smg.sh.cn/english/index.html (accessed 20 August 2007).

Shanghai Television Documentary Channel. 2004. *Insight: Detailing Shanghai* [*Kanjian: Shanghai Xijie*]. Shanghai: Xuelin Chubanshe.

"SMG's Documentary Channel Grows Strong through Professionalism" [SMG Jishi Pindao You Zhuan Er Qiang]. 2 August 2007. http://www.oursee.com/jiao/jz/200782/24475302.html (accessed 15 August 2007).

Wang, Xiaoyi. 2006. "Qinggan yu lizhi: Shanghai Jishi pindao de shangyehua juece zhi lu" [Emotion and Reason: The Shanghai Documentary Channel's Commercialization Policy]. http://news.xinhuanet.com/newmedia/2006-07/18/content_4850210.htm (accessed 26 September 2007). Originally published in *Diyi Caijing Ribao* (*No. 1 Finance Daily*).

Xu, Hua. 2000. "Morality Discourse in the Marketplace: Narratives in the Chinese Television News Magazine *Oriental Horizon*." *Journalism Studies* 1, no. 4:637–647.

Zhao, Bin. 1998. "Popular Family Television and Party Ideology: The Spring Festival Eve Happy Gathering." *Media, Culture, and Society* 20, no. 1:43–58.

Zhong, Yong. 1998. "Mass of Master's Medium? A Case Study of Chinese Talk Shows." *Asia Pacific Media Educator*, no. 5:92–102.

———. 2001. "The Other Edge of Commercialisation: Enhancing CCTV's Propaganda." *Media International Australia*, no. 100:167–180.

———. 2002. "Debating with Muzzled Mouths: A Case Analysis of How Control Works in a Chinese Television Debate Used for Educating Youths." *Media, Culture, and Society* 24, no. 1:27–47.

Made in Taiwan: An Analysis of *Meteor Garden* as an East Asian Idol Drama

The rise of the boy band F4 from the trend-setting television show *Meteor Garden* (2001) has drastically changed the landscape of TV drama programming in Taiwan and across Asia. Accelerating a frenzied consumption of idol dramas (*ou xiang ju*), the show has enthralled a target audience aged 10 to 35 and raised important questions about international marketing and cultural politics: how did the story of four boys and one girl in an affluent college in Taipei captivate followers across East Asia and China? What aesthetic and commercial strategies enabled producer Angie Chai to market these beautiful, troubled youths so successfully? And most importantly, what are the economic, cultural, and political implications when a local TV program compellingly reimagines something as global as a twenty-first-century East Asian identity?

In my view, *Meteor Garden* owes its broad appeal to three main factors. First, it is an exciting intertextual experiment. An adaptation of the popular Japanese *manga Hana yori dango* (*Boys over Flowers*), *Meteor Garden* is a modern Cinderella story, a make-believe romance bridging the gap between haves and have-nots. The winning combination of comic book, TV drama, and fairytale makes *Meteor Garden* an important case study of narrative in popular culture, for it merges the romantic appeal of comics' transgressive fantasy world with the realist poetics of TV drama's everyday urban experience.

Second, the images of *Meteor Garden* are seductive because they not only gratify a young audience's desires to look at sex and violence but also boldly visualize a new exhibitionism of male sexuality, one that fashions and fetishizes a masculine body over and against plot and character. Angie Chai suggests that in idol drama "acting skills are subordinate to star-like charisma and presence." Her emphasis on the supremacy of image makes the actors the bearers of new physical standards in East Asia. More controversial, perhaps, is the way this visuality is put to use in a narrative that seduces viewers through aestheticized violence. To unfold the cultural logic of the images driving *Meteor Garden*, I will turn later in the essay to Laura Mulvey's theory of visual pleasures in the global economy.

Finally, the transregional success of a locally produced Taiwanese TV drama compels us to revisit current theories of "cultural proximity" (Iwabuchi 2001, 2002, 2004). Koichi Iwabuchi argues that it is insufficient to assume "that the existence of some essential cultural similarities automatically urges the audience to be attracted to media texts of culturally proximate regions" (Iwabuchi 2001: 57). Instead, he suggests, one needs to recognize the active agency of the local audience in identifying the "culturally proximate" pleasure produced by popular TV programs. This argument is compelling, and represents an advance over other cross-cultural media theories, but it also reaffirms a mimetic hierarchy in which the distinction between the primary culture and its emulators remains ineffaceable.

One might argue that the phenomenal success of *Meteor Garden* challenges the stability of this hierarchy. The show not only originates in Japanese comics but is mediated through once-colonized and marginalized Taiwanese production and marketing. These derivative and peripheral origins de-nationalize the TV program by abolishing the paradigm of primary and secondary cultures—a yardstick of differentiation for theories of "cultural proximity." And unlike many Japanese and Korean cultural products, which are produced and received *as* nationalist representations, *Meteor Garden* does not significantly communicate any concept or image of the nation-state. In fact, my study ultimately demonstrates that the show's various local audiences envision a democracy of cultural alignment that includes, on equal terms, East Asian viewers from Tokyo, Seoul, Taipei, Singapore, Jakarta, Beijing, Hanoi, and Kuala Lumpur. As this list indicates, it is the city as much as the nation that ties together the shared experience of the show's new, egalitarian, transnational form of East Asian community.

Some Background

Meteor Garden's success can be partly explained on aesthetic grounds, for the TV drama integrates and magnifies two very popular forms of storytelling: Japanese comic books and Japanese idol dramas, both of which have dominated Asian markets for years (Iwabuchi 2002). In fact, Taiwanese idol dramas like *Meteor Garden* combine two interrelated genres in Japanese TV programming: "trendy dramas" and "post-trendy dramas." The former focus on the "depictions of stylish urban lifestyles and trendy nightspots abundant with extravagant designer clothes and accessories, sets with chic interior designs, and the latest pop music, all of which clearly reflected the then prevailing highly materialistic consumerism Japanese young people enjoyed under the so-called bubble-economy" (Iwabuchi 2004: 9). The "post-trendy dramas," on the other hand, give more weight to plot development, "sympathetically depicting young people's yearnings for love, friendship, work, and dreams" (Iwabuchi 2004: 10), even though trendy consumerism is still vital to the sub-genre's success. Taiwan, as many critics have noted, is especially receptive to Japanese culture as a result of its colonial history (it was occupied by Japan between 1895 and 1945), "cultural proximity" to Japan (Straubhaar 1997: 291), active social networks, and regional geopolitics (Lam and Ja 2004). Moreover, the island's media deregulation in the late 1980s facilitated the importation and circulation of Japanese TV dramas; these were "first broadcast in Taiwan on the Star TV Chinese Channel in May 1992 and immediately became very popular with the young generation" (M.-t. Lee 2004: 132). From *Tokyo Love Story* (1991) and Fuji TV's *Love 2000* to the latest record-breaking South Korean TV drama *Daejanggeum* (*Jewel in the Palace*, 2003), these shows created the *ha-ri* (Japanese fever) and *han-liu* (Korean wave) that today dominate young Taiwanese consumers' taste in fashion, architecture, food, and entertainment.

Taiwan's embrace of Japan's trendy postmodern culture is not without controversy. Critics, Yu-fen Ko notes (2004: 110), are particularly sensitive to the ways in which "Japanization" may signal a new form of colonization and might trigger national or cultural identity crises among Taiwan's impressionable youths. Iwabuchi's study of the issue is especially informative (2002: 122–130). However, others note that the critiques of Japanese neo-imperialism mythologize a simplistic binary opposition between local/Taiwanese/native and foreign/Japanese/imperialist. As Yufen Ko points out, such nationalistic discourses often romanticize "the local" as both resistant to cultural invasion by the Other and unified in its search for a self-determined identity. In other words, "'the local' is perceived as an originally self-contained, passive and innocent victimized subject to aggression from *outside*" (Ko 2004: 113). But careful analysis of Taiwan's complex cultural contexts shows that "the local"—heterogeneous and diversified—is often complicit in promoting, marketing, and consuming rather than resisting other cultures (Iwabuchi 2002). As a result, the critical discourse of binarism reveals a nationalist anxiety about making "Taiwan" a coherent and independent political and cultural entity.

Nowhere is Taiwan's problematization of the self-other boundary more apparent than in its strategic courtship of political enemies and allies. Thus, to understand the island's reception of Japanese culture, it is important to take into account the role that China plays in Taiwan's interactions with other superpowers. Since abolishing martial law in 1987, Taiwan has accelerated its democratization and promoted itself as the "free China" (as opposed to the communist China) that encourages freer media flow and an ever more internationalizing market. The island's embrace of the first Asian satellite network, STAR TV, for example, has quickly expanded the viewing experience of its residents and opened up new windows on the culture of its Asian neighbors. For Taiwan, however, a part of Japan's cultural attraction may have derived from the Taiwanese public's willingness to undertake a calculated political risk: by consuming the culture of its past colonial master, Taiwan implicitly challenges China's tactic of military intimidation and diplomatic isolation, strategies that seek to put the "renegade province" in its place. During Taiwan's presidential elections in 1996, 2000, and 2004, for instance, China intensified its threat of military invasion in (ultimately unsuccessful) attempts to silence those voices supporting independence. And the ongoing China-Taiwan political crisis has been and continues to be affected by larger political algebras involving the U.S., South and North Korea, China, and Japan. Thus, taking into account the historical antagonism and recently intensified rivalry between Japan and China in particular, I would suggest that Taiwan's Japanizing cultural trend both reflects and responds to the whole region's volatile political conditions.

The Melodramatic Model

Despite this complex political subtext, the main attractions of idol dramas are on the surface. These stories constitute a "relationship" genre devoid of postmodern Western cynicism, and many of them validate young viewers' desire for love and romance and present to them an alternative vision of East Asian modernity, one that seems to reconcile traditional values (i.e., filial piety, respect for authority, and civic duty) with ideals of progress (sexual freedom, gender and racial equality, democracy, romance, and civil liberty). More significantly, perhaps, are idol dramas' trend-setting representations of how young East Asian urbanites skillfully consume, fashion, and capitalize on the materiality of their new "glocal" culture.

To a large extent, idol dramas tend to generate these three attractions through melodrama. Although originally a Western narrative genre (*melos* is Greek for "song" or "a piece of melody"), melodrama has evolved in the past century from an art form generally considered "inferior" to a powerful, global narrative tool in film and TV series. Conventionally, melodrama is often characterized by "sensationalism, emotional intensity, hyperbole, strong action, violence, rhetorical excesses, moral polarities, brutal villainy and its ultimate elimination, and the triumph of good" (Dissanayake 1993: 1). Exaggerated action manipulates the audience's emotions and hence is often seen as hyperbolically disingenuous. However, Ien Ang argues that in popular soap operas, "melodramas have a myth-making function" because the emotional appeal of the characters derives not from their verisimilitude but from "the metaphorical role they play in the popular imagination" (Ang 1985: 64). Ang defends melodrama's symbolic importance with a groundbreaking analysis of the 1980s American TV series *Dallas*. In particular, she shows how the viewer's melodramatic imagination produces identification and pleasure. Concurring with this analysis, Dissanayake argues that the audience's complex attraction to melodrama reveals that the genre contains a "subversive potential for exposing bourgeois ideology and an enabling vision to map the dialectic between ideology and desire" (Dissanayake 1993: 1).

In the context of Chinese generic categorization, it is important to note with Chris Berry that the standard Chinese translation of "melodrama" into *jiating lunlipian* ("family ethics film") prioritizes "ethically defined social and kinship roles" over and against European and American melodrama's focus on individual psychology and its expression. Of course, these different emphases are not mutually exclusive. "In so far as the emergence of the modern Chinese melodrama is coincident with the Chinese experience of modernity as a European import," Berry further suggests, "we may therefore hypothesise that the Chinese family *lunlipian* is itself a modern and hybrid form that stages the tension between 'tradition' and 'modernity' as a tension between different models of subjectivity, with competing value systems for judging behaviour" (2003: 186). Berry's paradigm applies especially well to Taiwan's TV drama, which illustrates a profound struggle between personal passion and social constraints in a time of change. We might even suggest that the "sinologized" melodrama is a genre of *becoming* that showcases destabilized postmodern configurations of the relation between self and family.

Following Ang, Dissanayake, and Berry, I would also add that in the case of idol dramas we must be sensitive not only to the symbolic but also to the *ironic* meanings of *Meteor Garden* as a transregional TV sensation. Its popularity reveals both social aspirations and the gender and class paradoxes that shape them in contemporary East Asian societies.

Locating Idol Dramas

According to critics, idol dramas combine a "feel-good" optimism and a "realistic" representation of young people's everyday urban experience (Iwabuchi 2002; Ko 2004; M.-t. Lee 2004). This optimism, however, is consistently offset by what Ang characterizes as "the tragic structure of feeling" (1985: 61) or what Dissanayake describes as recognition of the "ineluctability of human suffering" (1993: 4) in Asian melodramatic narrative traditions. The paradoxical combination of hope and resignation seems to have guided the audience's eclectic interpretations of "realism" as a representation of emotional and spatial reality, complemented by fictional scenarios and cultural sensationalism. Discussing *Tokyo Love Story*, for example, young urbanites enthuse that "it is not a story about somebody else. It is a story about our generation, about us, about myself" (Kevin 2005). By the same token, *Meteor Garden* also connects with the viewers on the cultural logic of "here, now, me, and us," which gives voice to a fear of transient human existence and an urgent desire for instant gratification.

The emotional realism of the idol dramas is thus firmly grounded in realistic urban settings. As Yufen Ko comments, the "realism arguments are often based on the Japanese dramas' elaborate settings, lighting, quantity of outdoor scenes including tall buildings, subway stations, and busy streets, and the overall urban ambience" (Ko 2004: 108). It is the ambience of the destined city that helps identify Tokyo, in Ien Ang's words, as "the symbol for East Asian cultural modernity, the idealized location for 'trendy' modern life, characterized by material affluence, consumerism, female emancipation, and individualism" (Ang 2004: 307). Ang's characterization aptly captures the spirit of "movement" in Japanese idol dramas, which use Tokyo's attractive urban cityscape to stage a swinging modern lifestyle and to market progressive changes in society. This image of Tokyo, in all of its televised affectation and glory, seems to map out a trajectory for other Asian cities and citizens to follow in order to become global, unique, modern, symbolic, and significant.

Many examples support the audience's transference of their emotional investment in the characters' lives to an infatuation with the *lived* urban space. One of the most celebrated instances is A Tong's *Cinderella's Tour in Tokyo* (1999), a bestseller in Taiwan. A Tong, then a twenty-three-year-old enthusiast of Japanese TV dramas, traveled to Japan to trace and *experience* the paths undertaken by her beloved characters in several Japanese TV series. Juxtaposing her personal photos and narration of the scenes with stills and dialogue excerpted from the TV shows, A Tong "successfully mixes media consumption and travel practice, reality and fiction, memory and presence" (M.-t. Lee 2004: 139). The author's personal triumph instantly inspired the marketing of packaged "Japanese TV drama tours," which include not only trendy scenic spots and popular shopping districts (O-

Figure 5.1. Gang of Four in Kamio Yoko's *Boys over Flowers* (Taipei: Dong Li, 2004).

Daiba, for example) but also such ordinary places as apartments and telephone booths, which are being transformed into symbolic sites (M.-t. Lee 2004: 140). These popular tours hence fully capitalize on and testify to idol dramas' ability to initiate and commercialize the viewers' own performance fantasy: by retracing the stars' footsteps, the travelers seek to incorporate stories depicted on the TV shows into their own experiences and stories.

Under the aegis of such an imitation fantasy, Kamio Yoko's *Boys over Flowers* becomes an ideal script for Taipei to promote and elevate itself as a glamorous city of the future, able to provide touring fans of *Meteor Garden* an important dramatic space in which their mediated relationship with the show's stars can be traced step by step and place by place.

The Origin of Meteor Garden: Boys over Flowers

Meteor Garden owes its iconicity to Kamio Yoko's manga comic series *Boys over Flowers* (*Hana yori dango*), which ran in *Margaret Comics Magazine* from 1992 to 2004, a total of thirty-six volumes. Angie Chai produced thirty episodes of *Meteor Garden I*, but the show ended abruptly in the middle of volume 29 while the comic book was still being published in Japan. *Meteor Garden II*, with thirty-one episodes, was no longer based on the comic. Thus, *Meteor Garden* is half rather faithful adaptation and half invention.

The comic and television series have important plot differences. The high schoolers in the comic books become college students in the TV drama. This

Figure 5.2. Gang of Four in *Meteor Garden* (dir. Yueh-Hsun Tsai, CTS [Chinese Television System], 2002).

change caters to a broader cultural concern about the story's sexual content, which might make the teenagers' involvement seem inappropriate. And as we'll see, their different endings—one ends with a conjugal kiss in a Catholic church and the other ends with an image of a loner on an abandoned field—mark the distinctive ways the two stories resolve problems of class relations, love, and personal character.

These differences notwithstanding, Chai's adaptation reveals studious attention to the style, language, and content of Kamio Yoko's work. Stylistically, the comics suit the narrative form of the TV drama in that each volume evokes strong emotive response, staging conflict, suspense, and resolution in ways that can be reproduced in episodes.

This structural resemblance—a form of Sergei Eisenstein's "calculated pressures on the audience's psyche" (1988: 39)—is complemented by the way each theatrically manipulates images. If, with Larry Gonick (1993, 33–44), we understand the "language" of comics to be a combination of three critical concepts, kinesthetic, iconic, and symbolic, we find that *Meteor Garden* is especially skilled at presenting the iconic representation of the characters. This is apparent in the fetishistic construction of each star's unique hairstyle (figures 5.1 and 5.2). Shancai's braids give her the look of the pure, unspoiled country bumpkin who is marginalized in the wealthy community that valorizes excess, sophistication, and artificiality (figures 5.3 and 5.4). Dao Mingshi's short curly hair creates a sense of abrasive unruliness and manifests his arrogance and indomitable rage. Hua Zelei's slightly feminine hairdo, flow-

Figure 5.3. Shancai's braid in Kamio Yoko's *Boys over Flowers* (Taipei: Dong Li, 2004).

ing and undulating, attests to his compassion and sensitivity. Ximen's well-groomed appearance underscores his reputation as a polished playboy. Finally, Meizuo's shoulder-length straight hair gives him a balance between masculinity and femininity and calls attention to his role as a diplomatic mediator of conflicts.

Chai's iconic translation of the characters' appearance constitutes both a fashion statement and an ambivalent socio-cultural critique of class antagonism. Combining appearance and class consciousness makes visuality become both an expression of and an agent for ideology. In fact, two of the most important issues in *Meteor Garden* are class and gender relations.

Class Romance

Thematically, in addition to marketing the aspirations and conflicts of young people's daily life, *Meteor Garden* is about a new-millennium class war, materialized in the combative relationship between Shancai and Dao Mingshi. Shancai,

Figure 5.4. Shancai's braids in *Meteor Garden* (Barbie Hsu as Shancai, CTS, 2002).

the daughter of a lower-middle-class family, attends Yingde, an expensive private college founded by Dao Mingshi's family. As her name indicates—*shancai* is a kind of weed that grows, endures, and prospers even under adverse circumstances—she challenges and survives the abusive and stratified culture on campus.

More intriguing, perhaps, is Dao Mingshi's attraction to Shancai's righteous defiance. She embodies a social conscience that speaks for the weak and stands up to bullies. The melodramatic structure of suffering, comical as it seems in the show's cartoonish depiction, is embedded within the resistance to Shancai's challenge to the fundamental injustice of a capitalist society.

As the story evolves, the class conflict is compounded with sexual tension to produce the show's romantic appeal. Yet considering Dao Mingshi's violent, abusive behavior, one might ask why the audience is attracted to a fantasy world of disruptive and disdainful social elites? What is there in the characterization of Dao Mingshi—a good-for-nothing rich teenager—that makes the viewer sympathize with his love-struck frustration? Moreover, what are the larger cultural implications for class relations of East Asian viewers' acceptance and even embrace of Dao Mingshi's hierarchized view of the world?

In interviews, Kamio Yoko acknowledged that the wealthy bully (named Domyoji Tsukasa in the comic) was not her first choice for male lead. She had intended to make Hanazawa Rui, the bon vivant (who became the television show's Hua Zelei), the central figure; however, the overwhelming amount of fan mail for Domyoji Tsukasa forced her to change focus. His colorful and distinctive personality seems to exercise a stronger hold on the reader's imagination than Hanazawa Rui's peaceful and sensitive demeanor. The narrative emphasis on the negative as well as positive features of a main character creates an ambivalent composite of a "hero" whom both readers of the comic and viewers of the television show "love to hate." This love-hate relationship with a postmodern figure echoes the audience's own ambiguous judgment of the elite class in Taiwanese and broader East Asian society: the Yingde campus is a microcosm of a society in which the F4—these two youths and their two friends, the rich and powerful bullies who dominate the school—create a hegemonic discourse of exclusion and control, which instills not only fear and anxiety but also order and envy in the general populace, as the ingratiating kowtowing of Shancai's parents attests.

But Dao Mingshi's claim on viewers goes beyond the cultural logic of class envy in East Asia. He also exemplifies a spectacle of exhibitionist male sexuality that unleashes the audience's scopophilic imagination; his sadistic outbursts gratify a male fantasy of possession and control. Moreover, his unbridled passion also appeals to the young female audience because it demonstrates a commitment to love and romance.

In fact, one key to *Meteor Garden*'s popularity is the show's more explicit attention to female sexual desire. As the producer Angie Chai explained at the outset of the project, her show aimed to fill a gap in Taiwan's TV programming, which, according to marketing research, had not paid enough attention to adolescent viewers or to the need for a new *male* teen idol group "to gratify people's fantasies." "As a result, devising a program for Taiwan youth and creating a new teen idol group became the twin focal points of Chai's new production" (Chai 2002b). Working with this twin focus, Chai highlighted F4's "to-be-looked-at-ness" to market the sexual attraction of the lead characters. Her strategy worked. The Walt Disney Company signed F4 to be its spokesmen in Asia in 2002.

In garnering the young female audience's passion for *watching*, the show ventures into a new territory that gives women a certain freedom of sexual expression. Departing from the conventional dramas that tend to eroticize the female body, *Meteor Garden* shifts its attention to the female characters' own sexual fantasization of the lead characters. Dao Mingshi, in particular, corresponds to what Richard Dyer (2004) would characterize as the classic image of a star, constructed through the visual relations between characters within the diegetic space and between the camera apparatus and the actor.

Working against the conventions of Taiwan's television dramas, which focus on family issues and social changes (Iwabuchi 2002; Ko 2004), Chai's show not only valorizes individual passion but also validates women's scopophilic desire. Thus it raises the same questions that Miriam Hansen asks about women's spectatorial pleasure: "If a man is made to occupy the place of erotic object, how does this af-

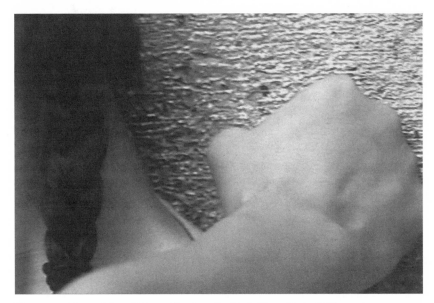

Figure 5.5. Fist and fury (*Meteor Garden*, dir. Yueh-Hsun Tsai, CTS, 2002).

fect the organization of vision? If the desiring look is aligned with the position of a female viewer, does this open up a space for female subjectivity and, by the same token, an alternative conception of visual pleasure?" (Hansen 2000: 231).

Hansen qualifies these questions by citing other feminists who worry that connecting the female desiring look to subjectivity merely confirms "the patriarchal logic of vision" (Hansen 2000: 231). However this may be, Chai, a female producer, has clearly paid tribute to young women's economic power as consumers and to their increasingly active role in the search for romantic partners.

In addition to marketing Dao's desirability, Chai further encourages the audience's identification with the lead female character, Shancai. When Shancai challenges F4's Machiavellian rule of the campus, the reactions to her bravery are curiously mixed: she is treated as a public enemy who disrupts the stability of the ordered community on the one hand and as a socialist hero who speaks for the oppressed and champions social and gender equality on the other. Considering her moral courage, why isn't her self-sacrifice hailed as a form of heroism? The answer seems to be that she bears the ethical burden of being a progressive but threatening female figure who needs to be contained and castigated. As a result, her social activism, along with her famed unruliness, make her an ideal target for Dao Mingshi's sadistic spying, which not only acts out viewers' own anxiety about Shancai's class and gender transgression, but also evokes their voyeuristic pleasure in monitoring the characters' stormy relationship.

Figure 5.6. Sexual violence (*Meteor Garden*, dir. Yueh-Hsun Tsai, CTS, 2002).

The vindictive pleasure of "objectifying" Shancai climaxes in a scene of near-rape. Shancai's jealous classmates secretly videotape her rendezvous with Hua Zelei and present the evidence to Dao Mingshi, who then suspects Shancai of betraying his affection by carrying on a clandestine relationship with his rival. He angrily confronts her, first on the rooftop and then in the staircase, and, in a fit of anger, violently attacks her and tears open her shirt. In this particular scene Dao Mingshi tightens his muscles to intimidate Shancai. His fist on the wall next to her neck and braids shows a phallic control of her image and life (figure 5.5). His subsequent tearing of her shirt further reveals a furious outburst of sexual rage, a brutal act of violation that reduces her to an object of erotic fantasy (figure 5.6).

From voyeurism to retribution, the whole community conspires to control the story and punish the girl. Unsurprisingly, then, Laura Mulvey's famous analysis of visual pleasure and spectatorial sadism applies well here. Mulvey (2000) suggests that there are two forms of pleasure associated with this kind of dominance:

> Voyeurism . . . has association with sadism: pleasure lies in ascertaining guilt . . . asserting control and subjugating the guilty person through punishment or forgiveness. This sadistic side fits in well with narrative. Sadism demands a story, depends on making something happen, forcing a change in another person, a battle of will and strength, victory/defeat, all occurring in a linear time with a beginning and an end. Fetishistic scopophilia, on the other hand, can exist outside linear time as the erotic instinct is focused on the look alone. (43)

Mulvey's comment illustrates the ways the director/artist anticipates the viewer's narrative desire to oversee the story's dramatic development by making the characters perform what the audience might have hoped to act upon—be it a gaze, a punishment, or an erotic instinct.

This logic explains the narrative agency of Dao Mingshi, who channels the viewer's possessive desire to control Shancai's image, objectify her body, and re-write her story. This incident further transforms their platonic courtship into a sadistic form of sexual possession; moreover, the subsequent return of the scene in flashbacks underscores Shancai's confused mixture of fear and excitement at having unleashed Dao Mingshi's passion. Is he a prince or a beast or both? Shancai reveals herself to have ambivalent fetishistic, scopophilic desires, which she partially satisfies by reliving and re-seeing herself as a victim and an image.

The recurrence of Shancai's flashbacks is very significant. It transforms her from the prey of others into a witness of her own physical and psychological suffering. Her shift from a spectacle to a spectator, however, generates both textual and visual ambiguities. First of all, these flashbacks are perceived as *her* memories and hence reconstructed from *her* viewpoint, which fixates on an erotic interplay between violence and romance. Reliving the traumatic moment seems to convince Shancai (and the audience) that Dao's violence is less a confirmation of his bigotry than a forceful expression of his frustrated love. Shancai's flashbacks hence make her a voyeur of Dao's emotional "truth."

Furthermore, by revisiting the self in crisis, Shancai also asserts a position that Miriam Hansen characterizes as "a narcissistic doubling, [in which] the subject of the look constitutes itself as object, graphically illustrating Freud's formulation of the autoerotic dilemma: 'Too bad that I cannot kiss myself'" (2000: 233). In fact, the self-love created by these flashbacks undermines Shancai's earlier socialist struggle to eliminate class hierarchy and compromises her idealistic vision of renegotiating the power dynamic between center and periphery. Thus her narcissism shows the limits of her transgression: her anger at Dao's abuse of class privilege is displaced by her acceptance of Dao's fetishistic obsession with her image.

Meteor Garden sends a mixed message about social equality and the direction of women's movement in Taiwan specifically and in East Asia generally. The show's mockery of the social elites' class snobbism, though successful in caricaturing the imprudence of a materialistic society, nevertheless glorifies the luxury of leisure and idolizes the class of the idle. Even Shancai's bourgeois moral outrage validates an institutionalized respect for money more than it does a socialist ethic of equality. Throughout the narrative, the lifestyle and luxuries of the rich are used to tempt Shancai and break down her resistance. From Dao's gratuitous "goodwill" kidnapping (which forces Shancai into experiencing the lavish lifestyle of the upper class) to his generous gift giving, the show philanthropizes him in such a way that Shancai's class antagonism is slowly dissolved. All these special treatments suggest a fairytale narrative structure, one that, to the delight of the aspiring young female audience, foregrounds a grand resolution to the protagonist's struggle with poverty and injustice.

The pleasure of watching idol dramas such as *Meteor Garden* therefore derives from the (perhaps ethically ambiguous) mixture of realist identification and romantic escapism. It is easy for the audience to recognize Shancai's everyday problems: work, making ends meet, familial relations, friendships, and unrequited love. In the larger context of a globalizing economy, these problems call attention to East Asian women's evolving positions in their marriages and families and at work. Shancai's down-to-earth quality gives her emotional credibility as a modern woman living through changes.

On the other hand, her Cinderella experience paints the escapist prospect of a toil-free future with the security of love and material comfort. In her analysis of "melodramatic identifications," Ien Ang suggests that "the pleasure of fantasy lies in its offering the subject an opportunity to take up positions which she could not do in real life: through fantasy she can move beyond the structural constraints of everyday life and explore other situations, other identities, other lives" (Ang 1997: 162). I would suggest that Shancai cleaves rather closely to reality, that the audience is likely to fantasize her not simply as one of those "other lives," but as one of the extraordinary "dream-come-true" romantics.

Although Shancai starts out as a progressive female character who symbolizes an open-minded inquiry into the role of women and the meaning of class in contemporary East Asian societies, her challenge to the existing structure falls short of what might be expected. I would even argue that her ascent to the top of the social ladder all but predetermines the destruction of her idealism. As the series evolves, her aspiration to upward mobility and obsession with romance erode her commitment to equality, autonomy, and self-determination.

Revisiting "Cultural Proximity"

Shancai's limitations as a trailblazer on gender and class issues confirm the pragmatism of the show, which maximizes the attractions of a modern, democratic, and capitalist society without disrupting the existing social order. Reading Shancai's experience allegorically in a transnational context, one might also see an interesting parallel between Taiwan's self-effacing humility as a cultural exporter and Shancai's unassuming role as an evolving middle-class model.

As many studies have noted, concerns about media imperialism often focus on "the imbalances of power and media flow" (Straubhaar 1991: 40). The dependence theorists especially like to use the U.S. media influence on other developing countries as an example of how an economic superpower determines and disseminates expressions of ideology. However, other studies have underscored the dynamic process of cultural approximation that complicates the power relations between cultural importers and exporters (Iwabuchi 2002).

In the case of Taiwan, most critics agree that Japanese idol dramas (and most recently Korean TV dramas) have become more popular than American TV shows in the island as a result of East Asian producers' sensitivity to the region-specific cultural predicaments of urban East Asian audiences. Iwabuchi argues that "cultural proximity" should therefore be understood as an issue of both time and space.

> The emerging dialectic of comfortable distance and cultural similarity between Japan and Taiwan seems to be based upon a consciousness that Taiwan and Japan live in the same time, thanks to ever-narrowing gaps between Taiwan and Japan in terms of material conditions; the urban consumerism of an expanding middle class; the changing role of women in society; the development of communication technologies and media industries; the reworking of local cultural values; and the re-territorialization of images diffused by American popular culture. (2002: 156)

According to this model, Japan and Taiwan have been able to synchronize their metaphorical times—their industrial pace and socio-historical progress—and thereby generate a comprehensible "contemporaneity" for viewers in both countries. But it should be said that Taiwan's cultural vision of the world is essentially different from Japan's. An island of limited resources and uncertain political future, Taiwan's survival strategy is not to become one of the standard-bearers, but to imitate, negotiate with, and integrate with other trendsetters. This is especially apparent, for instance, in Taiwan's delicate efforts to join Tokyo and Washington under the umbrella of the Theater Missile Defense (TMD) system, which, much to China's displeasure, promises to strengthen the security ties among Taiwan, Japan, and the U.S. (Lam and Ja 2004: 259). Spawned from this cooperative political strategy is Taiwan's cultural tendency toward self-effacing practicality, which derives from an awareness of its own political marginalization and insecurity.

In the case of *Meteor Garden*, the show's ingenuity is hence not its claim to be a new cultural model, but its recognition of a need to synthesize and appropriate other cultural models. The transparency of this self-consciousness—an acknowledgment of and a reflection upon the interdependence of global media exchange—in effect contributes to other East Asian nations' wide acceptance of Taiwanese idol dramas. To understand the full extent of the Taiwanese cultural industry's pragmatism, it is especially useful to compare the different conclusions of the TV show and the comics.

Shancai in the idol drama exemplifies the "honest" virtues of the middle class, working within the system and climbing the social ladder. Her perfor-

Figure 5.7. Conjugal kiss (*Meteor Garden*, dir. Yueh-Hsun Tsai, CTS, 2002).

mance in the travel agency, for instance, demonstrates her gradual success as a good employee and a valuable community member. Shancai in the comic, on the other hand, struggles with poverty and continues to challenge the hierarchy of a capitalist class system.

In Chai's final TV episode, Shancai reunites with the long-lost Dao Mingshi in Barcelona, Spain, where they join hands on a symbolic visit to a local Catholic church (figure 5.7). Their reconciliation outside of Taiwan seems to announce their status as world citizens whose romantic adventure *must* extend beyond the island. Shancai's economic productivity also enables her to assert a certain masculine power, one that Dao Mingshi seems to have lost because of his disease-riddled idleness (he has amnesia and other ailments). Yet the seductive power of the show is manifest in Shancai's (and Taiwan's) integration into a global economy in which the romantic partnership is built upon cultural tolerance.

In comparison, Kamio Yoko's story ends on a note of defiant uncertainty that gives voice to her strong critique of phallocentric capitalism. Tsukushi (the Shancai character) turns down Domyoji Tsukasa's marriage proposal to give herself space and time to explore the world. In the concluding chapter, she is invited to the graduation ball at which F4 wave farewell to their school. Her magical carriage—her father's aging vehicle—breaks down on the road and she cannot reach the party on time. Carrying her expensive, beautiful evening gown, she arrives at the ball with her face sweaty and her shirt and pants stained. Standing among the

Figure 5.8. Shancai's independence in the comic *Boys over Flowers*.

formally attired crowd, she remains a lone figure of dissension. She evokes disgust
from her detractors and admiration from her friends and continues to be a controversial figure, one who chooses to stay outside the system. In fact, our last view of
Kamio Yoko's heroine shows her standing under the vast sky—taking up more
than three-quarters of the frame—far away from the skyscrapers, those symbols of
vertical social structure and male power (figure 5.8). Her elevated image is firmly
grounded in nature; her smile echoes her liberated mind, which is neither controlled by greed nor ruled by fear. She is by herself but happy and engaged with
life and the world, more self-sufficient than solipsistic.

The symbolic resonance of both final images, indeed of the whole Japanese
comic and Taiwanese TV series, depends upon the East Asian audience's attraction to a transitional modern lifestyle, one that comprises a comic fantasy of exaggerated personalities, threatening sexual violence, reconciled class relations, and
progressive gender and economic outlooks. Although the two conclusions seem
very different, they navigate the same paradigmatic contemporary possibilities.
They applaud a girl's progressive but limited challenge to the culture of coercion,
on the one hand, and yet remain ambivalent about deconstructing the power hierarchy, on the other. While Kamio's post-fairytale comic resists the temptation of

turning the ugly duckling into a beautiful but submissive swan, Chai's show allows the emerging democratic system to expand and absorb dissension.

Ultimately, the comic's uncompromising vision emphasizes an ethic of self-preservation, which not only illustrates a progressive feminist viewpoint but also implicates, to some extent, Japan's above-the-fray political and cultural position in Asia. As Iwabuchi's analysis of Japanese transnationalism indicates, the "cultural proximity" theorists recognize Japan as the model to be "caught up to" and approximated by other Asian nations (Iwabuchi 2002: 156–157). Hence Kamio's socialist break from the capitalist community inevitably idolizes the path of a pioneer whose idealism attracts followers (as the numerous fan clubs for *Boys over Flowers* attest).

Angie Chai's drama series, however, captures the transitional moment of Taiwan's political and cultural reality, one that accepts negotiation (whether between the advocates of independence and the nationalists who support reunification, or between first-world and developing countries, or between classes and sexes) as the most viable strategy. Chai's indigenization of Kamio's narrative therefore makes visible Taiwan's transformative philosophy of *becoming*, an approach that sees the constant fluctuation of its identity politics as a diplomatic necessity. In the end, the TV show's ideological pragmatism is precisely what facilitates its acceptance by other Asian cultures, for they, too, are struggling with these challenges.

Notes

I wish to thank the editors, Chris Berry and Ying Zhu, for their insightful comments on an earlier draft of this essay.

References

A-Tong. 1999. *Cinderella's Tour in Tokyo.* [In Chinese.] Taipei: Ching-hsin.
Ang, Ien. 1985. *Watching Dallas: Soap Opera and the Melodramatic Imagination.* London: Routledge.
———. 1997. "Melodramatic Identifications: Television Fiction and Women's Fantasy." In *Feminist Television Criticism: A Reader,* ed. Charlotte Brunsdon, Julie D'Acci, and Lynn Spigel, 155–166. Oxford: Oxford University Press.
———. 2004. "The Cultural Intimacy of TV Drama." In *Feeling Asian Modernities: Transnational Consumption of Japanese TV Dramas,* ed. Koichi Iwabuchi, 303–310. Hong Kong: Hong Kong University Press.
Berry, Chris. 2003. "*Wedding Banquet*: A Family (Melodrama) Affair." In *Chinese Films in Focus: 25 New Takes,* ed. Chris Berry, 183–190. London: British Film Institute Publishing.
Boyd-Barrett, Oliver. 1998. "Media Imperialism Reformulated." In *Electronic Empires:*

Global Media and Local Resistance, ed. Daya Kishan Thussu, 157–176. London: Arnold.

Chai, Angie. 2002a. "The Stars of Asia—Innovators." *BusinessWeek*, 2 July. http://www .businessweek.com/magazine/content/02_27/b3790631.htm.

———. 2002b. "You've Got to Have Beauty." *Taiwan Panorama*, September. http://www .sinorama.com.tw (accessed 11 March 2008).

———. 2004. *Meteor Garden I & II*. Taipei: Hua Shi.

Cheng, Chun-yun. 1998. *Consumer Behavior of Teenagers toward Japanese Fashion Goods*. Master's thesis, The Graduate Institute of International Business, National Taiwan University.

Dines, Gail, and Jean M. Humez, eds. 2003. *Gender, Race, and Class in Media*. London: Sage.

Dissanayake, Wimal. 1993. Introduction to *Melodrama and Asian Cinema*, 1–8. Cambridge: Cambridge University Press.

Dyer, Richard. 2004. *Heavenly Bodies: Film Stars and Society*. New York: Routledge.

Eisenstein, Sergei. 1988. *S. M. Eisenstein: Selected Writings*, vol. 1, 1922–1934. Bloomington: Indiana University Press.

Gonick, Larry. 1993. *The Cartoon Guide to (Non) Communication*. New York: Harper Perennial.

Gwenllian-Jones, Sara, and Roberta Pearson, eds. 2004. *Cult Television*. Minneapolis: University of Minnesota Press.

Hall, Stuart. 1997. "The Local and the Global: Globalization and Ethnicity." In *Culture, Globalization and the World System: Contemporary Conditions for the Representation of Identity*, ed. Anthony King, 41–68. Minneapolis: University of Minnesota Press.

Hansen, Miriam. 2000. "Pleasure, Ambivalence, Identification: Valentino and Female Spectatorship." In *Feminism and Film*, ed. E. Ann Kaplan, 226–252. Oxford: Oxford University Press.

Iwabuchi, Koichi. 2001. "Becoming 'Culturally Proximate': The A/Scent of Japanese Idol Dramas in Taiwan." In *Asian Media Productions*, ed. Brian Moeran, 54–74. Honolulu: University of Hawai'i Press.

———. 2002. *Recentering Globalization: Popular Culture and Japanese Transnationalism*. Durham, N.C.: Duke University Press.

———. 2004. "Cultural Globalization and Asian Media Connections." Introduction to *Feeling Asian Modernities: Transnational Consumption of Japanese TV Dramas*, ed. Koichi Iwabuchi, 1–22. Hong Kong: Hong Kong University Press.

Kamio Yoko. 2001. *Liu Xing Hua Yuan*. Trans. Lin Yiting. Taipei: Dongli Chubanshe.

Kevin. 2005. "Kevin's Home." http://home.ust.nk/ukwtse (accessed 21 January 2006).

Ko, Yu-fen. 2004. "The Desired Form: Japanese Idol Dramas in Taiwan." In *Feeling Asian Modernities: Transnational Consumption of Japanese TV Dramas*, ed. Koichi Iwabuchi, 107–128. Hong Kong: Hong Kong University Press.

Lam, Peng-Er, and Ian-Chong Ja. 2004. "Japan-Taiwan Relations: Between Affinity and Reality." *Asian Affairs* 30, no. 4:249–267.

Lee, Chin-Chuan. 1980. *Media Imperialism Reconsidered: The Homogenizing of Television Culture*. London: Sage.

Lee, Ming-tsung. 2004. "Traveling with Japanese TV Dramas: Cross-cultural Orientation and Flowing Identification of Contemporary Taiwanese Youth." In *Feeling Asian Modernities: Transnational Consumption of Japanese TV Dramas*, ed. Koichi Iwabuchi, 129–154. Hong Kong: Hong Kong University Press.

Lin, Szu-Ping. 2003. "The Woman with Broken Palm Lines: Subject, Agency, Fortune-Telling, and Women in Taiwanese Television Drama." In *Multiple Modernities: Cinemas and Popular Media in Transcultural East Asia*, ed. Jenny Kwok Wah Lau, 222–237. Philadelphia, Penn.: Temple University Press.

Martinez, D. P., ed. 1998. *The Worlds of Japanese Popular Culture: Gender, Shifting Boundaries, and Global Cultures*. Cambridge: Cambridge University Press.

Moeran, Brian, ed. 2001. *Asian Media Productions*. Honolulu: University of Hawai'i Press.

Mulvey, Laura. 2000. "Visual Pleasure and Narrative Cinema." In *Feminism and Film*, ed. E. Ann Kaplan, 34–47. Oxford: Oxford University Press.

Rubinstein, Murray, ed. 1994. *The Other Taiwan: 1945 to the Present*. New York: M. E. Sharpe.

Storey, John, ed. 1998. *Cultural Theory and Popular Culture*. London: Pearson Prentice Hall.

Straubhaar, Joseph. 1991. "Beyond Media Imperialism: Asymmetrical Interdependence and Cultural Proximity." *Critical Studies in Mass Communication* 8, no. 1:39–59.

———. 1997. "Distinguishing the Global, Regional, and National Levels of World Television." In *Media in Global Context: A Reader*, ed. Annabelle Sreberny-Mohammadi, Dwayne Winseck, Jim McKenna, and Oliver Boyd-Barrett, 284–298. London: Arnold.

Su, Heng. 1995. *The Cultural Impact under the Open Sky: Reports on the Viewing Habits of Taiwanese Audiences*. [In Chinese.] Taipei: Cultural Council.

Thussu, Daya Kishan, ed. 1998. *Electronic Empires: Global Media and Local Resistance*. London: Arnold.

Williams, Raymond. 2003. *Television: Technology and Cultural Form*. London: Routledge.

Ritual, Television, and State Ideology: Rereading CCTV's 2006 *Spring Festival Gala*

XINYU LU

CCTV's *Spring Festival Gala* program has run on Chinese New Year's Eve since 1983, throughout the very important period since the beginning of China's policy of economic reform and opening up to the outside world. Whole families gather to watch it, making it a unique television event in China, and even, perhaps, a new folk custom. This is a topic worthy of attention, whether in Chinese cultural studies or media studies.

Part One

In "Popular Family Television and Party Ideology: The Spring Festival Eve Happy Gathering," Zhao Bin analyzes the dominant power of state political ideology in CCTV's 1997 *Spring Festival Gala* (Zhao 1998). In that politically sensitive year,

Hong Kong was returned to China. Mainly relying on textual analysis, Zhao teases out the relationship between state and family from the perspective of the nationalist "main melody" themes. Although she perceives the impact of marketization and commercialism on the program, she places greater stress on the transformation of ways to produce consensus via propaganda and state ideology. She believes the program is a modern version of the ancient Confucian ideal of "great oneness." She writes,

> If subjected to the strict law of the market, the institution would probably have either petered out or taken on a very different form. The imperative of the party-state, however, has kept it going. In it the party has simply found the best opportunity to convey social and ideological messages simultaneously to the widest audience possible. The Spring Festival Eve can thus be seen as a unique situation in which families are wired via television to the central state. The ancient Confucian "great oneness" ideal of the state governed like one family suddenly appears more real than ever. (Zhao 1998: 46)

Therefore, television, invented in the West, fulfils a particular social function in Chinese society: it helps to strengthen traditional ideology, centered on the family, and to unite families into the "imagined community" of the nation. Here, Zhao ignores the integration of capital and power that follows cooperation between market and state. Together, they shape the *Spring Festival Gala*, which is based on borrowing from tradition. Furthermore, the ideology of the state governed like one family that she sees as a peculiarly Chinese combination of tradition and the party-state might be better seen as a wider link between television, media, and the nation-state. Dave Morley (1992) provides a detailed analysis of television's ritual function in Western society as a symbolic model for building family life and participating in national community. He points out that broadcasting plays an important role in integrating the state and blood family into one national family. What must be emphasized here is that traditional China cannot simply be equated with the modern nation-state. Furthermore, the complicated relationships between feudalism and the administrative system of prefectures and counties and between an understanding of common humanity and discrimination between Chinese and foreigners, all of which were part of the Confucian conceptualization of "great oneness," cannot simply be equated with the modern nation-state's claims to territorial sovereignty. "Great oneness" and "national unity" have different historical connotations. Furthermore, the notion of "family" in the patriarchal clan system is not the same as the multiple forms of the modern family, which is typified by the nuclear family. In brief, "state," "family," "great oneness," and "unity" must all be discussed in the context of specific historical changes. The concepts of "family" and "state" in modern society and Confucian thought are very different. Behind this difference lie the complex transformations of modernity in Chinese society over the past one hundred years, the historical drive behind which should be the focus of attention and explanation. Rather than saying that the television program *Spring Festival Gala* has entered Chinese people's homes because they identify with the traditional concept of the family, it would be better to say that it has become one of the most important television programs for Chinese people precisely because the concepts of heaven, earth, God, and human connected to traditional Han Chinese rites have waned in modern society, leaving a structural lack to be filled. The show thus replaces the sacred time that used to be offered to God and the ancestors. The decline of the complicated clan sacrificial rites and their symbolic significance undermines the *Spring Festival Gala*'s meaning. This is why the media echoes with criticism immediately after the *Gala*, even though its ratings keep going up. In this society, the expectation and hope that the *Spring Festival Gala* will be a structural rite are necessary if television is to serve as a rite of the modern nation-state. The "imagined community" itself is a product of modernity. Benedict Anderson believes that with the retreat of religion, "what was required was a secular transformation of fatality into continuity, contingency into meaning. . . . few things were (are) better suited to this end than an idea of nation" (Anderson 1991: 11).

I recognize the value of textual analysis. However, I emphasize that a text is not merely the author's but also the reader's or audience's. Therefore, audience research can be an important aspect of textual analysis. In the era of the mass media, audiences play an integral role in the production of texts. Coming from different positions, with different understandings and perspectives, audiences and television producers come together and meet. However, behind them are the common culture, history, and politics of a single society, determining the possibility of dialogue between them and also foreshadowing conflicts of interest. James Carey (1975) believes there are two kinds of media research, the transmission and the ritual views of communication, which have shaped the scopes of empirical and cultural studies research, respectively. Social science empirical research based on the idea of transmission or transportation is in the mainstream. It focuses on the transmission and receipt of information. This is a spatial and geographical concept, seeking speedy and effective transmission of information through space, placing distance under human control. Therefore, information is not neutral or objective. Such ideas of transportation have always developed alongside religious concepts, as European Christianity and the culture of the white man spread across the globe. The encounter between white Christians and the indigenous "heathens and savages" of America was, under the general rubric of transportation, a spatial movement with the aim of establishing God's kingdom on earth. Therefore, transportation has self-evident moral significance. Following the invention of modern broadcasting technology in the nineteenth century, Americans first used it as a means of disseminating the Christian gospel more quickly and efficiently.

The ritual concept of communication has even earlier origins. Unlike the focus on intensified transmission of information in space, it operates within a temporal concept and is concerned with the maintenance and development of society, that is, the expression of shared beliefs. According to Carey (writing in the 1970s), mainstream communications research in America was only interested in behavior and functions and overlooked the cultural meaning of human behavior. Social science had cut itself off from culture, isolating facts from culture, which in this thinking was reduced to ethnocentrism, meaning that in fact ethnocentrism was isolated. He contends that seeing communication as ritual did not exclude the process of dissemination and the resulting behavioral changes. In fact, he believed that the significance of those elements can only be comprehended within a framework of ritual and the social order.

On this basis, Horace Newcomb and Paul Hirsch (1994) developed the concept of "television as a cultural forum," according to which ritual should be seen as a process and not a product, with television functioning to restore consensus. Television throws out more questions than it answers, although it operates within the framework of mainstream ideology. For example, in the United States television has become a public forum testing the functions and boundaries of political pluralism. Television is a complete system, providing the audience with an ideological system within culture. It is a flexible text—for example, television program genres have common models, but within these genres the most successful are often the most challenging and the most individual. Television is a stream of consciousness, supplying a cornucopia of changes and not a map of fixed and dominant ideology. Therefore, audiences have the power that is produced by multiple choices, through which they participate in the discussions of the texts.

In the context of debates in the larger Chinese discursive sphere, this article focuses on the ritual significance of the dual spatial and temporal transformation of broadcasting in the social discourses of the contemporary nation and market. The annual debates following the *Spring Festival Gala* demonstrate the significance of television as a forum. Twenty years of the *Spring Festival Gala* constitutes a lineage of changes in mainstream ideology, but what are the social forces behind these changes? This is the crux of the matter. The idea that the public votes by means of the remote control cannot explain the peculiar phenomenon of audiences simultaneously watching and criticizing the *Gala*. Newcomb and Hirsch's concept of "television as a cultural forum" emphasizes the peaceful co-existence of social differences through negotiation, which overlooks the different powers and stances of the media, producers, and audiences and the conflicts of interest among them. Audience criticism certainly does affect the *Spring Festival Gala*, but it does so within a dominant structural framework. The concept also overlooks the way in which the marketization of the media is shaping television texts, which is a particularly important factor to bear in mind in interpreting contemporary Chinese television.

Here, I hope to grasp the significance of the *Spring Festival Gala* from a number of perspectives. These include state ideology's appropriation of traditional customs, including folk drama and art forms; the delicate and complex representations of social crises and conflicts within the state ideological system; and also the shaping of the *Gala* by the marketization of Chinese television and the ideology of consumerism. All of this structures the *Gala*'s appearing to be in crisis, amongst a diverse range of contested discourses, and is the main concern of this essay.

Part Two

In an essay interpreting the 2002 *Spring Festival Gala*, I pointed to the shift from popular to national significance in the production of "Beijing time" as "universal time" (Lu 2003). Zhao Bin's article also emphasizes the significance of "Beijing time" for the *Spring Festival Gala*. China has only one time zone, and therefore what Beijing time essentially embodies is the consciousness of national territorial sovereignty. It is the realization of space through time. The 1997 *Spring Festival Gala* was the first to make Beijing time a theme. Because it was the heartbeat and pulse of the motherland, the program's presenters proclaimed it three times. Beijing time has become a structuring element of the *Spring Festival Gala*. Particularly important is the countdown to midnight. But even more significant is that Beijing time is clearly becoming the most valuable time for advertising. The 2006 *Spring Festival Gala* had two countdowns: the one to midnight and one to the beginning of the program at eight o'clock. Advertising slots were sold during both. According to media reports, the eight o'clock and midnight slots raised RMB 5.39 million (approximately US$670,000) and RMB 9.66 million (approximately US$1.2 million) respectively. In 2005, the midnight slot had fetched RMB 6.8 million (approximately US$822,000).

In today's globalization, the *Gala* has also begun to target ethnic Chinese living outside the People's Republic in an effort to build a new "audio-visual territory." The 2006 *Spring Festival Gala* was broadcast live around the world via the internet and CCTV's international channels, in multiple languages, maximizing the deterritorialization of Beijing time. This broadcast illustrates the importance of what Anderson (1991: 24) calls "homogenous, empty time" to the nation-state, except that Anderson's print capitalism is superseded by electronic and Internet capitalism. The latter can provide a more direct simultaneity, which is a necessary precondition for ritual. Along with the *Gala's* spotlight on the Internet and "netizens," this simultaneity has become a feature of the program. The 2006 *Gala* invited a young internet singing star to perform. On 22 December 2005, CCTV IPTV, a wholly owned subsidary of CCTV and the Chinese International Television Company, launched "The 2006 CCTV IPTV Cyber Spring Festival for Chinese All Over the World," the first large-scale internet television event in the history of the Chinese internet, promoting the "Cyber Spring Festival" as a brand. "IPTV" stands for "internet protocol television," and CCTV IPTV acts as an agent negotiating the global webcasting of programming owned by CCTV. Its goal is to serve the "Chinese global community," a concept spun out of the nation-state and also the beginnings of a marketing concept.

Cross-talk two-man comedy (*xiangsheng*) and small sketches are crucial structuring elements of the *Spring Festival Gala*. They are so important because they originated in the world of the north Chinese dialect, which is the precursor of Mandarin, the unified national language. However, the monopoly of northern and northeastern sketches was broken in 2006 by southern programming items. Sketches from Sichuan, Hunan, and Hubei appeared in 2006, along with cross-talk from Taiwan, amounting to four of the ten cross-talk and sketch events. However, they were only in southern-accented Mandarin, not in full southern dialect. This was expressed in the theme of the Taiwanese cross-talk piece, "Learning Mandarin," which used dialect-accented Mandarin but did not replace Mandarin directly with dialect. In this way, it confirmed the dominance of Mandarin, into the environment of which it brought dialects. The rise of dialect programming on local television stations in 2004 and 2005 has led the State Administration of Radio, Film, and Television (SARFT) to issue three sets of regulations suppressing such material and emphasizing that dialects and non-standard Mandarin may not be used. The *Spring Festival Gala* has contravened these regulations. The link between dialects and Mandarin today is a reflection of the link between the state and localities. This link became a hot topic in broadcasting circles in 2005. It is also a result of marketization. Local television stations need to develop their dialect audiences to compete with CCTV's monopoly. The SARFT bans are designed to protect not only the state's nationalism, but also CCTV's monopoly position in the market.

In an era when the principle that a state media system should perform public service is being progressively weakened, Dave Morley and Kevin Robins (1995: 2) argue that there is a growing tension between globalism and localism. In China, dialect programs have appeared as a result of the shift from a state-owned media system that performs public service to a marketized system in which products must be developed. A conflict of interest results between CCTV and local television stations. The effort to develop minority audiences for dialect programming is an effort to divide the target audience for advertising—to wrest a handful of rice from CCTV's plate and the national advertising market. It cannot be seen as simply a growth in the media's awareness of the grassroots audience, because all these dialect areas are economically developed. Behind the development of local consciousness is the media's advertising business strategy, which is known as market segmentation. This has been acclaimed as one of the most influential business strategies of the twentieth century, and in this case it uses local dialects as the basis for drawing lines between territories. However, the numerous dialects and minority nationality languages distributed across the vast countryside have not seen the spontaneous development of programming in those dialects and minority nationality languages, because the farmers deeply mired in economic difficulty are not the targets of the advertising business.

The situation becomes clearer if we compare the development of such programming with the evolution of operatic melodies in Chinese traditional drama. China's diversity of dialects is the wellspring of its colorful range of local opera melodies. However, these melodies are not confined to certain areas and isolated from each other. In other words, their territories are shifting, and the melodies themselves are fluid, so that southern and northern dialects mix. An example is the *pi huang* or Beijing opera. Zhou Yibai (2004: 608) has explained, "This is a mixture of two melodies from two different sources." The *xi pi* melody came from the Shaanxi provincial opera. Mixing with the *xiang yang* melody from the Han River area of Hubei Province, it developed into the *chu* melody and then the Hubei *xi pi*. The source of the *er huang* melody was Anhui provincial opera, which evolved through the *yi yang* melody into the *si ping* melody. In turn, with the infusion of the *chui* tune, this became the *si ping* opera, and then this became the *er huang* found in Anhui. These two kinds of opera mixed in the Han River basin and spread to Beijing, where they joined Anhui opera, the Kun music, and varieties of clapper-based opera to form the Beijing opera. The Beijing opera has continued to absorb all manner of local opera modes of singing, instrument playing, performance, and gesture (Zhou 2004: 608–612). Furthermore, the same opera materials may exist in different regional and dialect versions, which can borrow from each other and change. They share a common legacy. Zhou Yibai's "Sources and Legacy for Chinese Opera" (Zhou 2004: 614–641) shows that later generations have adopted the Yuan, Ming, and Qing dynasty Za opera and narratives, and this adoption shows the importance of Chinese traditional opera for folk and grassroots art forms. In contrast, behind today's local identities is monopoly: the aim is segmentation, not opposition. CCTV, with its ever stronger position of monopoly in the advertising market, and the local stations, with their production of regional segmentation, are mutually dependent.

Part Three

Marketization has created increasing tension between CCTV's monopoly position and the interests of the local television stations. The media are very sensitive to this tension and pay great attention to it. There are continual reports that some powerful local stations, such as Hunan Satellite TV and Dragon Satellite TV from Shanghai, want to challenge CCTV's *Spring Festival Gala*. Indeed, Hunan Satellite TV's completely commercial evening show *Super Girl* (a singing contest modeled on *American Idol*) is perceived to have taught CCTV a lesson in 2005. It was reported that the price of an advertising slot in the final episode of *Super Girl* was RMB 112,500 (approximately US$13,900). This was slightly higher than the top price paid for the 7:45 PM slot on CCTV: RMB 110,000 (approximately US$13,600). In 2006, Shanghai's Dragon Satellite TV scored a first by broadcasting its own *Spring Comes to the East* program at the same time as CCTV's *Spring Festival Gala*. However, its 2006 *Glittering Chinese All-Stars Gala* avoided Spring Festival Eve itself, and therefore did not pose a direct challenge to CCTV. Although the market share of CCTV's *Spring Festival Gala* dropped from 23.8 percent in 2005 to 17.5 percent in 2006, it continues to top the listings. The main reason for this is that the local stations do not have the political and symbolic resources of state ideology. They cannot attain the aura of national ritual that goes with this program, and therefore most of them yield and carry CCTV's *Spring Festival Gala*.

CCTV has added new elements to the *Gala* in an effort to appease and win the loyalty of the local stations. In 2006, in the name of "hanging out the lantern decorations to celebrate the New Year and harmony across the universe," presenters from thirty-five local television stations took part in a series of skits involving trying to solve traditional lantern riddles. The skits actually served as valuable advertisements for the local stations. Interestingly enough, these skits replaced scenes of hosts reading out congratulatory telegrams from overseas, as had been done in previous years.

By some coincidence, the most powerful local media, such as Shanghai Media Group and Hunan Satellite TV, also took "Chinese around the world" as their target market. Knowing that they could not match CCTV's political resources, each provincial satellite station pushed its tactics of depoliticization and delocalization as far as it could. However, this strategy, like that of localization, was intended to construct a market. Two instances are noteworthy here. First, Shanghai Media Group attempted to collaborate with transnational financial firms, and this effort has been hailed by the state as a new form of "international image building" by means of market mechanisms. Second, the impact of Hunan Satellite TV's *Super Girl* extended beyond China when the super girl Li Yuchun was chosen, rather than a more traditional hero such as

China's first astronaut, to become the image ambassador of the 2006 "China in London" events. At one time, a photo of her together with London mayor Ken Livingstone was all over China's media.

The possibility and practice of symbolizing China in the forms of "non-political" ideology challenge CCTV's advantageous position. This challenge may well be allowed and even encouraged by the state today, as it promotes the formation and export of "national culture" industries. The global strategy of the media industry is characterized by delocalization (to enable shows to be understood by wider audiences) and depoliticization, as can be clearly seen in the Chinese film industry's tendency to produce blockbusters. So there is certainly tension between politicized state nationalism domestically and "depoliticization" and marketization overseas. But they are also two sides of the same coin. This is manifested in the yearly changes in the content of the *Spring Festival Gala* as well as the endless challenges it faces. Here, the market is a new politics that appears as "non-politicization" and directly participates in the reorganization of state ideology. This is why the media not only pick over the details of the *Spring Festival Gala*'s contents but also report on its advertising revenues.

The *Gala*'s gross advertising revenue was more than RMB 400 million (approximately US$49.6 million) in 2006, an increase of 10 percent over the previous year. The exclusive right to name one of its events was sold in an auction called "My Favorite Program of the *Spring Festival Gala*"; the minimum bid was RMB 25.8 million (approximately US$3.2 million), and the auction was won by a pharmaceutical company for RMB 45.08 million (approximately US$5.6 million). Nowadays, state nationalism has to be supported by the market. On the one hand, ideology's worth must be measured in cash; on the other hand, monopoly on and pursuit of ideological discourses can be transformed directly into control of the market. Underlying the market is a map of the new and ever-changing state ideology, and control over different ideologies is a manifestation of the market economy. This is the significance of the *Spring Festival Gala*'s frequent designation as a "treasure trove," as I will demonstrate in what follows.

The Taiwan problem is always at the top of the national agenda, so Taiwanese themes always have an especially important political position in the *Gala*. Two items related to this theme stood out in 2006. One was the thought-provoking "Learning to Speak Mandarin" cross-talk comedy skit by Taiwanese performers, in which Taiwanese aboriginal-accented Mandarin was used to update traditional Beijing cross-talk. The second was the voting on names for the two pandas to be presented as a gift to Taiwan, which was simultaneously a political activity and an advertising event. Regular advertising reduces a show's ratings, can occupy only a limited amount of time, and is even subject to continual criticism from the public. Therefore, invisible forms of advertising and sponsorship have become part of the *Spring Festival Gala*. Voting on the pandas' names was organized by a telecommunications company and CCTV's Public Information Center. Numerous trailers for the event appeared before the *Gala* on many different channels, saying, "If you want to know what he's called, watch CCTV's *Spring Festival Gala*." Text-message (SMS) votes cost RMB 1 (approximately US$0.12), which is ten times the regular cost of a text message. Although subtitles warned the television audience about the charge, the presenters did not. Instead, they encouraged the audience to vote five times during the show. Just before the midnight countdown, the panda's names were announced as Tuantuan and Yuanyuan (names playing on *tuanyuan*, "unification"). More than 110 million text-message votes were received, meaning that they alone generated revenue of more than RMB 100 million (approximately US$12.4 million). A report in the *Beijing Evening News* of 31 January 2006, under the heading "SMS Upset: CCTV *Spring Festival Gala* SMS Fee Extortion," pointed out that many people voted without understanding the fees and afterward received numerous messages for which they were charged RMB 1 each.

The use of text messages to communicate with the audience and generate income originated with the 2002 *Spring Festival Gala*, for which CCTV and China Mobile cooperated on text voting. The audience was invited to answer questions posed by the presenters and to choose favorite items of programming, making this the year that sketches on the program became disguised advertising. This was a business innovation in the Chinese market, and it grew like a gathering tide until it hit a high-water mark with Hunan Satellite TV's *Super Girl* in 2005. *Super Girl* began as a copy of *American Idol* and became a wildly popular commercial entertainment program. The basic fee for text-message votes for favorite singers was RMB 1, and in 2005 text-message income accounted for approximately half of the total revenue generated by the program, amounting to RMB 30 million (approximately US$3.86 million).

However, the vote to name the pandas during the 2006 *Spring Festival Gala* was criticized widely by the press and on the internet. Many felt that charging for text-message votes was a means of extracting cash from, and destroying the trust of, the public. This is a classic example of CCTV's greedy and speedy conversion of the political resource of a monopoly over state ideology into commercial profits. CCTV has promised "transparent running of the *Spring Festival Gala*" since 2005 as a way of compromising with, adjusting to, and even appeasing the endless criticism and questioning of such things as the corruption revealed by the Zhao An case. Zhao An was the deputy head of CCTV's arts programming center and head of the arts department. He was a member of the team in charge of the CCTV *Spring Festival Gala* seven times and headed the team four times. In December 2003 he was tried for bribery in the Beijing First Intermediate People's Court and sentenced to ten years' imprisonment. However, the "transparent running of the *Spring Festival Gala*" has only reduced the opportunities for personal pursuit of profit. It has not changed the increasingly rapacious corporate pursuit of profit.

Part Four

I have argued elsewhere that the 2002 *Spring Festival Gala* assiduously avoided skits about farmers because the "three problems concerning farmers, agriculture, and the rural areas" had already become a social crisis and therefore a taboo topic (Lu 2003: 94). Since then, the central government has made solving these three problems a top priority, and many reports on them have begun to appear in the media. In 2004, CCTV announced that the "topic of the three problems" would appear in the 2005 *Spring Festival Gala*. In 2006, a large number of skits about the three problems were spotlighted. The creators of the skits tried to use mainstream ideology to bridge the rural-urban gap. Rural characters addressed their city-folk employers as "pal." But behind this fabricated "pally" feeling is the rural-urban divide, and its implausibility has led to criticism that the "*Spring Festival Gala* once again trashed rural peasants" (Guo 2006). In fact, the rupture between this kind of "politically correct" ideology and grim reality is beyond repair. As a result, almost all the sketches with a political task are attacked, because they are not permitted to touch on real social divisions and wounds, and they are therefore incapable of satire and parody. Reduced to a footnote in state ideology, they cannot produce carnivalesque resistance and have lost their ability to be a source of pleasure for the audience.

Creating sketches for the *Spring Festival Gala* each year is more difficult than walking a tightrope. They are subject to not only repeated censorship and revision by the state authorities, but also social pressure to be "politically correct." In 2006, the sketch "A Small Matter" was voted the audience favorite. However, a line in the skit was solemnly criticized: "You old idiot, you must have forgotten to take your medicine!" This was discussed in an article entitled "A Wave of Insults, Discrimination, and Moral Collapse—On the 2006 CCTV *Spring Festival Gala* sketch 'A Small Matter'" (Zhu 2006). Its author stated, "I know that if this line were said in the Western media, it would attract a wave of reproaches, and if the actor were not sued, the television station would at least receive all kinds of lobbying." Several million elderly people become senile every year, and therefore, concludes the author, this line expressed the collapse of "national morality." But it was merely a line of dialogue spoken by the female actor Song Dandan in a sketch. To demand that every line by every character be politically irreproachable goes beyond political censorship, because the actor is also at risk of being sued! In these circumstances, sketches are impossible. We are far removed here from the spirit of folk carnival. The author of this article needs to read Bakhtin and then return to tell us about the West again.

In Bakhtin's eyes (1984), festival is a primal and indestructible category of human culture. It may wane, but it cannot become extinct, and it is capable of taking humans temporarily into a utopia. In contemporary society, the meaning of festival is already fractured. However, substitutes are still being sought, and the ritual form of mass media is just such a substitute. But there are crucial differences. The CCTV *Spring Festival Gala* is dominated by the thirst for this kind of ritual, which then gets transformed into state ideology. Then the stage occupied by state ideology yields monopoly profits. However, in a time when nation-states are under attack from globalization, the *Gala* is under ever greater pressure. First, globalization is a challenge to the concept of the nation-state, leading to attacks from outside and internal fractures. Second, the marketization of the Chinese media is strengthening the conflict of interest between central and local media. The media's pursuit of consumerist ideology and the generation of profits out of it ceaselessly threaten CCTV's monopoly. The national carnival stirred up around Hunan Satellite TV's *Super Girl* is seen as a challenge to the politicized *Spring Festival Gala*. It is not the aim of this essay to analyze in detail the complex debates about markets, politics, democracy, and national essence generated by this perception of *Super Girl*. Here, I only wish to point out the current and ongoing power of the fragmentation of state ideology. In China today, the market is the source of the nation's new identity but also drives it to tear itself apart. The developments and difficulties of the CCTV *Spring Festival Gala* over the last twenty years and more epitomize this society's political, economic, and ideological contradictions and conflicts.

With the waning of traditional political ideology, it seems that only the market can hold society together. A notable newspaper from the south of the country published a series of extraordinary editorials about *Super Girl*. The author of one remarkable piece wrote, "*Super Girl* is an exotic bloom in the garden of socialist spiritual civilization. Its blossoming has revolutionary significance, as history will prove. Some so-called experts are conservative. They turn their noses up at everything the *popular masses* like, and treasure everything that should be swept away by the tide of history. Time will show that those people are on the way out" (Dai 2005). This author got one thing right: the entertainment industry developed under "depoliticized" marketization is increasingly the core of "socialist spiritual civilization." The market has become the mouthpiece of the "people." The appropriation of the "people" by the market is very significant, and the issue needs to be further addressed by scholars of Chinese mass culture. What exactly is the relationship between the "masses" addressed by the cultural industries and the politically sovereign "people"? Is it really as the literary critic Wu Liang (2005) so forcefully asserts: "The 'people' are the 'masses'"? Why does the market today insist on flying the flag of the "people"? The transformation of the "masses" addressed by the cultural industries into the "people" in Chinese discourse indicates the market's demand for the right to speak in an era when it is has an ideological function on the political and state levels. However, unless you can demonstrate that the globally popular Hollywood cinema is a symbol of "entertainment democracy," we cannot safely label the selection of the "super girl" a gold standard for "democracy," "equality," and "freedom." Therefore, the term "market 'depoliticization'" is not correct at all, and behind the debate about *Super Girl* is a profound political issue.

The market is politics, and it is precisely this hidden political quality that propels the market success of *Super Girl*. It is no exaggeration to say that nearly all the media in China took part in this debate in 2005, fanning the flames and acting as free advertising for the show, and what lies behind all these debates are in fact Chinese political issues. This is why so many "public intellectuals" scrambled to participate in the debate over a commercial program. Whether for or against the program, all the debaters took it for granted that marketplace success meant the triumph of democracy. But neither applauding the market as the victory of the grass roots nor opposing it as populist democracy gets to the roots of its victory in China. If critics ignore the pleasure the audience derives from participating, all their analysis will be empty. With this in mind, it can be seen that *Super Girl* could not have been as successful as it was without the CCTV *Spring Festival Gala*. The *Gala*'s refusal to feature *Super Girl* in 2006 hit the headlines precisely because much of the pleasure of *Super Girl* derives from its challenge to the CCTV *Spring Festival Gala*'s monopoly and privilege. This challenge derives from the political and national bankruptcy of the *Gala*'s imagination of utopia and the vacuum created by it. Imaginings of the market as a victory over the state are why such a commercial program wins so much political attention, and this kind of excessive interpretation is also why it is such a success in the marketplace. In the short article "Exposing the Myth of *Super Girl* Democracy," the scholar Xu Jiling (2005) says, "The so-called '*Super Girl* Democracy' is only a populist democracy. History has already proved and will continue to prove that populist democracy is the best disguise for power to achieve its aim." Although there are clear differences in the positions taken in the debate discussed above, they share a common rhetoric in that they all make claims in the name of history. The blogger Anti's rebuttal of Xu's argument is typical:

> Professor Xu alerts us to the dangers of populist democracy, because "populist democracy is the best disguise for power to achieve its aim." So why do I feel like he's telling a joke? Damn it! Does power need a disguise to achieve its aim? Isn't it managing perfectly well right now? We like *Super Girl* because she gives the Chinese *people* an opportunity to experience the joy of free choice and the hatefulness of power and its aims. How can Professor Xu see

this as a disguise for power to achieve its aim? Isn't this a case of getting things completely back to front? (Anti 2005)

Here, *Super Girl* and the *Spring Festival Gala* are imagined as symbols respectively of civil society and authority; of democracy and authority; and of the market and the state. From this is produced the pleasure of imagining "resistance." As far as the audience of mass culture is concerned, television is filling the structuring absence produced by the loss of significant ritual and a sense of identity in contemporary society. These are the preconditions for the manufacture of the space filled by the pop idol Li Yuchun. Pop idols are worshiped because the "populist democracy" that Xu Jiling is so disgusted by and warns us against is already in decline, not because it is on the rise. In an era of ever more fragmented interests and increased stratification, politics has lost its ability to bridge the gaps and create consensus. This has created an opening for the mass media, which unify the audience and manufacture consensus. This utopia of shared "love" where people are equal and united motivates fan groups to spontaneously organize to experience their share of the "love." It is not enthusiasm for democracy that drives fan mania. Instead, fan mania is an outlet in an era of "non-political" individualism in which the need for social ritual has been suppressed. Here "democracy" has, ironically, been utilized by a market equipped with modern communication technologies and has become the catchphrase for media firms' push for profits. In fact, this is an absolute travesty of democracy.

If democracy can only survive under the hegemony of the market, is it still democracy? Li Yuchun's androgyny is simply a genre of pop stardom and a fashion mode that has been on the international stage for a long time. It is irrelevant to the gender politics of feminism and contributes nothing to the radical movement for the legalization of homosexuality. It merely hints, in an ambivalent and vague manner, at issues of gender and sexuality, and is no challenge to the fundamental values of the social mainstream. It provides a gentle and commercial sense of resistance, from which men and women alike can derive a safe pleasure. Because it does so, androgyny is even more able to inspire pleasure than either traditional or radical female imagery, and therefore is also of higher commercial value. In this regard, it is worth noting that although John Fiske's theories must be questioned in many ways, he puts the production of pleasure at the center of research into popular culture (1989). The invisibility and visibility of popular carnival ritual under the conditions of the modern nation-state and the market are a crucial topic for research into popular culture.

The CCTV *Spring Festival Gala* still needs to demonstrate its ability to create carnival for the Chinese people. And if it can do it, to what extent can it manage it?

References

Anderson, Benedict. 1991. *Imagined Communities: Reflections on the Origin and Spread of Nationalism*. London: Verso.

Anti. 2005. "Open Letter to Professor Xu Jiling." [In Chinese.] *Xici hutong*, 29 August. http://www.xici.net/b159317/d29970675.htm (accessed 8 August 2007).

Bakhtin, Mikhail. 1984. *Rabelais and His World*. Trans. Hélène Iswolsky. Bloomington: Indiana University Press.

Carey, James W. 1975. "A Cultural Approach to Communication." *Communication* 2:1–22.

Dai, Xingwei. 2005. "Let's Celebrate *Super Girl*." [In Chinese.] *Nanfang Daily*, 25 August.

Fiske, John. 1989. *Understanding Popular Culture*. London: Routledge.

Guo Shongmin. 2006. "*Spring Festival Gala* Once Again Trashed Rural Peasants." [In Chinese.] *New Beijing Daily*, 20 January.

Liang, Wu. 2005. "For and Against Mobile Phones." [In Chinese.] *Haishang wentan*, no. 6. http://www.zydg.net/magazine/article/1005-7536/2005/06/162071.html and http://www.8181.net.cn/magazine/html/172/172875.htm (accessed 21 March 2008).

Lu, Xinyu. 2003. "Reading the 2002 Spring Festival Gala." [In Chinese.] *Dushu*, no. 1:90–96.

Morley, David. 1992. *Television, Audiences, and Cultural Studies*. London: Routledge.

Morley, David, and Kevin Robins. 1995. *Spaces of Identity: Global Media, Electronic Landscapes, and Cultural Boundaries*. London: Routledge.

Newcomb, Horace, and Paul M. Hirsch. 1994. "Television as a Cultural Forum." In *Television: The Critical View*, 4th ed., ed. Horace Newcomb, 503–515. New York: Oxford University Press.

Xu Jiling. 2005. "Exposing the Myth of *Super Girl* Democracy." [In Chinese.] *Xinjing News*, 29 August.

Zhao Bin. 1998. "Popular Family Television and Party Ideology: The Spring Festival Eve Happy Gathering." *Media, Culture, and Society* 20, no. 1:43–58.

Zhou Yibai. 2004. *The History of the Chinese Opera*. [In Chinese.] Shanghai: Shanghai Bookstore Press.

Zhu, Tao. 2006. "A Wave of Insults, Discrimination, and Moral Collapse—On the 2006 CCTV *Spring Festival Gala* Sketch 'A Small Matter.'" [In Chinese.] http://www.xschina.org/show.php?id=6047 (accessed 12 March 2008).

3

Reception

Mediation Journalism in Chinese Television: Double-Time Narrations of SARS

HAIQING YU

On 2 May 2003, a television interview on China Central Television (CCTV) attracted the attention of millions of Chinese television viewers, as well as people from academic and journalistic circles. In the program, Wang Zhi, a famous investigative journalist with CCTV who was awarded the title of "Anti-SARS Hero" by the Chinese government later that year, interviewed Wang Qishan, the newly appointed mayor of Beijing. The mayor had issued two news releases in the previous ten days, announcing that he would lead the capital in the war on Severe Acute Respiratory Syndrome (SARS). The interview, characterized by pointedness and straightforwardness, was called "a surgical strike" by Wang's colleagues (Tai 2003). Wang's questions to the mayor included, "When you first took up your post [as mayor], the number [of SARS cases] was between 300 and 400. . . . But the number jumped to 2705 yesterday. . . . This is contradictory to what you described concerning implementing strict measures [to control SARS]. What does that tell us? . . . Can we trust you in the fight against SARS? . . . Beijing's spring has been vividly described as a 'masked spring.' Summer is coming; will it, too, be masked?" (*Face to Face* 2003).

Wang Zhi's interview of the Beijing mayor has been hailed as "a milestone in Chinese journalism ideology" (Zhang 2003). The milestone is characterized by open, yet tentative and reserved, journalistic independence, as manifested in Wang Zhi's role as an investigator and inquisitor facing a high-ranking state official. Rather than assuming the usual role as the Communist Party's "tongue and throat" (*hou she*), the Chinese journalist repositions himself between the state and society. As a mediator, or third party, the journalist uses his intellect and conscience to serve both the state and the nation, satisfies both "party logic" and "people logic," and in doing so meets the market's requirement of high ratings.[1] Wang and his investigative program *Face to Face* (*Mian dui mian*), on which he conducted the in-depth interview, have hence enjoyed increasing popularity among television audiences. Wang and his colleagues have also become champions of a new face of Chinese professional journalism.

This chapter aims to examine the new face of Chinese professional journalism through case studies of SARS reportage on Chinese television. I argue that Chinese journalists are becoming mediators between the state and society in reporting (presenting) discordant social dramas in contemporary China. As mediators, journalists, while representing themselves as professionals, resort to non-professional means to articulate an intellectual interpretation of contemporary Chinese political culture. The professional journalism they represent is a mediation journalism built on a strategy I will call "double-time narration."

Barbie Zelizer applies the concept of "double time" in reframing journalists as an interpretive community in the American context (Zelizer 1993). She draws the notion from Homi Bhabha (1994: 145) but applies it to journalism, seeing it as the interpretive framework and narrative practice of American professional journalists. Zelizer argues that journalists constitute themselves, on the one hand, as the objects of news accounts through a *local mode* of interpreting history, and, on the other hand, as subjects of reflexive accounts of the earlier reportage through a *durational mode* of interpreting history. Double time guarantees journalists a double authority as both eyewitnesses of history and historians. Double time, for both Bhabha and Zelizer, encompasses narrations in and of the past and the present, and renders the agents of history (postcolonial people in Bhabha's work, and American journalists in Zelizer's) both objects and subjects of the narrations of the nation.

I agree with Zelizer that the notion of professionalism alone is inadequate for examining the operational and behavioral patterns of journalists and that journalists use more elaborate mechanisms than professional ethics to construct reality. The notion of local and durational modes of interpretation, which is implied in the double temporal positions of journalistic productions, is also useful in the Chinese context. The double-time narrations that I use in this chapter build on Zelizer's contribution to journalism studies. I view "double time" as an inherent quality of journalistic productions within any single mode of interpretation. It is realized through a doubly temporal and spatial arrangement. Double-time narrations incorporate a narration as events unfold and another when they are retold, and a narration of the official time and another of the unofficial time, both through double spaces—the official space (the mainstream media, such as television) and the unofficial space (the Internet, for example). Double-time narrations are therefore doubly spatio-temporal.

Through the double spatial modes of narrations in both traditional and new media, double-time narrations help Chinese journalists open a field of mediation among the different logics they need to follow, and in the process consolidate into a mediation community. As a mediation community, journalists function as an organic part of a complex of relationships, and produce and use knowledge in the service of change. Mediation journalism can thus also be used as a new paradigm to explain Chinese media culture and Chinese modernity at the turn of the twenty-first century.

The chapter intends to locate the everyday practices of Chinese journalists (represented by investigative journalists at CCTV) within the big picture of the Chinese politico-cultural context and to view Chinese journalism from a historical perspective. It is composed of four parts. The first is a review of the literature on Chinese journalism and a historical contextualization of the evolving concept of professionalism in the Chinese media in the twentieth century. The second problematizes the current use of professional journalism in the Chinese media from insiders' perspectives.[2] It focuses on professional ethics as understood by investigative journalists and views investigative journalism as exemplary of the "*yin-yang* face" of Chinese journalists. This understanding underpins and heralds the central concept of double-time narrations. The third part explores the concept of double-time narrations, using SARS reportage as a case study, to bring Chinese journalists' *yin-yang* face into a theoretical framework. The theorization of the double-time framework continues in the fourth, which explores the concept of mediation journalism. Situated in multiple relationships that can be problematized, modified, and readjusted, Chinese journalists are perfecting their craft as mediators between the state, society, and the market. Mediation journalism signifies a synthesized consciousness in Chinese journalists of their different historical roles. And the conclusion offers a critical evaluation of mediation journalism in contemporary intellectual politics.

The Many Faces of Chinese Journalists

Like the concept of objectivity in modern journalism, that of professionalism (*zhiye xing* or *zhuanye xing*) is elusive and open to different interpretations at different historical stages. Professional codes, such as objectivity and balance, which are recognized universally, may be used by journalists to conceal the constructed nature of their news productions (Gans 1980; Tuchman 1978) and by the Chinese Communist Party to promote the "party character" (*dang xing*) in Chinese journalism (Gan 1994: 40; Cao 2000: 674). Professionalism, therefore, better serves as a theoretical foil, rather than a guide, in examining the intellectual politics of Chinese journalists. It can be politicized and historicized by different political players in the making of Chinese journalism, during which Chinese journalists have been variably portrayed as enlighteners, propagandists, and professionals, or as all of these at once.

The portrayal of Chinese journalists as enlighteners can be traced back to the Chinese Enlightenment movement at the opening of the twentieth century. Modern Chinese journalism was introduced by "new-learning" (*xin xue*) scholars in their efforts to create a new-style press for China in the last years of the Qing Dynasty, and promoted by "Enlightenment scholars" (*qimeng xuezhe*) in the "New Cultural Movement" (*xin wenhua yundong*) in the years around 1919. Prominent figures such as Liang Qichao, Sun Yatsen, and Chen Duxiu were all known as essayists, publicists, and enlighteners. They either copied and domesticated the foreign press (Mittler 2004) or created their own press to propagate Enlightenment ideologies and disseminate their visions of a modern China (Judge 1996). Liang Qichao, a forerunner of the Chinese enlightenment movement and doyen of modern Chinese journalism, for example, used the power of the press to enlighten the masses and fight against feudalism and imperialism. Using political commentaries (and sometimes literary supplements) to debate and promulgate issues of national importance, Liang and his successors (mainly the New Cultural intellectuals of the May Fourth generation) initiated a tradition in Chinese intellectual politics that emphasizes active engagement with the media (Judge 1996; de Burgh 2003a: 96–102; Schwarcz 1986).

As enlighteners, the new Chinese journalists were engaged intellectuals who used journalism to challenge the authorities, express popular grievances, and educate the people about enlightenment ideas and the need for reform. They were committed to national politics as insiders, who "seize[d] upon the media of the day as their means" to engage with the future of their country (de Burgh 2000: 556).

This enlightener-insider trait of Chinese journalists echoes the cultural tradition of Chinese intellectual politics, which emphasizes active engagement with state affairs and moral, political, and social commitments to national lives as "historical-cultural actors" (Ko 2001: 539). Like Liang himself, those men of learning are self-conscious political agents who feel they have a historical mission and a moral obligation to the nation-state as both counselors or advisors of the leaders and educators of the people. This intellectual tradition emphasizes commitment to and engagement with the establishment rather than critical detachment (and hence intellectual independence) from it. It generates two concurrent tides in modern Chinese intellectual politics: an aspiration to become a state official and a sense of social mission. One is a manifestation of a statist tendency, and the other of an elitist tendency. The elitist tendency manifests in modern journalists' self-assigned role as the people's representatives, spokespeople, educators, and enlighteners. Professionalism means using the press as an intellectual means to a political end. The statist tendency manifests in the journalists' role as propagandists or ideologues of the ruling party. Under such a media ideology, the mass media are propaganda machines and journalists propagandists of the party. This is clearly shown in the period of the civil war between the communists and nationalists, when journalists functioned as conduits and secondary definers of the Communist Party line in both camps, albeit more so in the communist camp (Nathan 1985: 133–151; de Burgh 2003a: chapter 4). After the founding of the People's Republic in 1949, Chinese journalists were further institutionalized as the "tongue and throat" of the party, and as a result obtained the social-political status of "state cadres" (*guojia ganbu*) and propagandists or propaganda workers (*xuanchan gongzuo zhe*). Professionalism is thus equated with clientelism.

By "clientelism" I mean here the patronage relationship between journalists and the party-state.[3] In this relationship, journalists are employed by and speak for their political patrons in return for protection and sponsorship. As state employees, journalists and intellectuals consider party membership and official patronage to be an effective way to influence policymaking and assert their intellectual power. Remonstrance with the leadership and limited criticism within the system are considered not dissident and confrontational, but "an expression of service to the state" (Ko 2001: 545). Chinese intellectuals continue to enter client-patron relationships that subject them to the establishment. John Israel has even commented that one is not "a legitimate intellectual" in China if one is not some kind of establishment intellectual (Israel 1986: x).

As establishment intellectuals, Chinese journalists are considered conduits and secondary definers of the party line. Serving the party and its enlightened leaders becomes the professional paradigm even among the leftist journalists who advocate freedom of the press. Establishment journalists and intellectuals such as Su Shaozhi, Sun Xupei, and Hu Jiwei, the chief advocates of freedom of the press in the 1980s, believed that the media should be both the flagship of the vanguard of the party and the mouthpiece of the party and the people (Ruan 1990). As a result of being ideologues and collaborators with power, Chinese journalists have constantly found themselves caught in factional warfare within party leadership. Journalists' professionalism is constantly abused by the leaders they serve (Goldman 1994; Hood 1994). Because of this, their "intellectual autonomy" is "severely limited by the orthodoxy of the state which they help[ed] to maintain" (Ko 2001: 548).

The pairing of the people with the party, however, is a sign of journalistic independence from the omnipotent party-state. Using "the people" to balance the "the party," Chinese journalists are in effect looking back at their tradition of being enlighteners and publicists and drawing from it the power and wisdom required by the present. Though limited in scope and practice, the call for professional autonomy and "objective reporting" has started to erode party journalism from within (Polumbaum 1990; L. Li 1994).

Media reforms in the post-Tiananmen era have seen the commercialization and conglomeration of Chinese media, a gradual institutionalization of media management that entails formalized and regularized control and censorship (Polumbaum 1994), and a transformation of China's media policy from propaganda to hegemony and from domination to compromise (Chan 2002). Since the 1990s, the "ambiguities and contradictions" arising from party logic and people logic have been further complicated by market logic, which has subjected Chinese media to a tug of war between the party line and the bottom line (Lee 1990; He 2003; Zhao 1998).

Chinese media, though having been gradually weaned from government subsidies and pushed into the global media market, are still required to provide "three satisfactions" (*san ge manyi*): they must satisfy the party, the audience, and the market. Consequently, Chinese journalism has been transformed from a solely propagandist model to "a propagandist/commercial model" (Zhao 1997), or, more precisely, to a propagandist/commercial/populist model. Journalists are increasingly assuming triple roles as ideologists/propagandists, news brokers, and enlighteners, in the name of professional journalism. They are not simply serving two masters and toeing two lines (Zhao 1998; Pan 2000); they are serving *three* masters and toeing *three* lines.

Under such circumstances, Chinese media organizations have been pushed to devise strategies to reduce the cognitive dissonance resulting from the tension between the three logics. These have ranged from "living with dissonance in the public discourse universe to radically reducing dissonance by aligning with an alternative ideology and expressing deviant ideas in a different public discourse universe" (He 2003: 198). Chinese journalists have been forced to devise localized and situational practices to deal with ideological and conceptual dissonances and contradictions arising from the tensions among the lines they serve (He 2000).

Amid the tensions and ambiguities, Chinese journalists have started to call themselves "professionals" (*zhiye renshi*) or "media people" (*meiti ren*) in order to differentiate themselves from those who act as the "tongue and throat" of the party, and from those media brokers who sell journalism for personal profit. The emergence of media brokers is a result of the accelerated commercialization of Chinese media in the 1990s. In a rush for profit, and sometimes in a violent reaction to the entrenched party logic, these media brokers equate people logic with market logic. But they do not use market logic to balance or check party logic, as their predecessors did in the 1980s. Rather, they misuse market logic to increase media corruption (Zhao 1998: 72–93). Market logic thus contributes to the erosion of professional ethics envisioned by the old and new "professionals" and fails to prevent political infringement on professional autonomy and freedom of the media.

Rather, it is the professionals or media people who stand for (limited) intellectual independence and represent a new professionalism in Chinese media. As the following section will demonstrate, this new professionalism combines technical excellence, efficiency, and competitiveness (in the media market) with commitment to social missions as the nation's conscience, loyalty to the party line as the state's elite and establishment intellectuals, and intellectual aspirations to dissect, analyze, and reflect. This redefined professionalism becomes essential to their efforts to represent, interpret, and dissect history.

Professionalism Revisited

The above analysis has shown that professionalism can be historicized and situated. For enlightenment intellectuals, professional journalism means being the voice of the people and the conscience of society; for establishment intellectuals, professional journalism means being the propagandist of the state and the eye, ear, and mouth of the party; for the new media people, professional journalism means gathering, disseminating, and analyzing information according to the principles of objectivity, efficiency, and intellectual autonomy. The coexistence of different interpretations of professional journalism has complicated the working lives of Chinese journalists, who have to take situated actions and develop tactics on the basis of opportunistic calculations and specificities (Pan 2000; Pan and Lu 2003). It has led Xu Yu to refer to Chinese journalism as "professionalism without guarantees" (X. Yu 1994).

Investigative journalism best exemplifies the situated, fragmented, and truncated nature of professionalism in the Chinese media today (H. Yu 2006). Investigative journalists, represented in this essay by those of CCTV's *News Focus* (*Jiaodian fangtan*) and *News Probe* (*Xinwen diaocha*), two of the most famous investigative programs in Chinese television, have been accused of only targeting "flies" (low-ranking officials and low-level corruption) and "dead tigers" (high-level corruption the state has already determined to crack down on). If they are watchdogs, they are not only "on the Party's leashes" but also wearing "an indisputable official jacket" (Zhou 2000, 588). As self-proclaimed "kings without crowns," investigative journalists strive to maintain the professional standards practiced by their counterparts in the West, such as impartiality, objectivity, and truth. But despite their best efforts, they are known as "birds in a cage" and "fish" swimming in an "economic pond" contained in the "political jar" (de Burgh 2003b; Zhou 2000; X. Yu 1994).

Although investigative journalists themselves generally do not contest outsiders' criticisms, they offer an insider's point of view to explain and justify their situated, fragmented, and truncated professionalism. They believe that they should stop being simply "policy footnotes" (Lin 1994: 79) and become instruments for social change, since they can be "at once within the system and at odds with it" (Mufson 1998: A1). Bai Yansong, a leading professional journalist with CCTV, for example, confesses, "Living with obstacles does not mean a loss or lack of intellectual ideals and enthusiasms. . . . If sarcasm, indignation, and radical words and actions could solve all the problems [that China has], I would resort to them instead of suffering [as I am] as a media professional" (Bai 2000: 9).

The generation of Liu Binyan, as Hugo de Burgh observes, is perhaps "the last to see itself as working totally within the system for Party and government" (de Burgh 2000: 556). Most intellectuals (including journalists) have chosen to function in the system, but with an outsider's spirit. The single-minded individuals who have voiced dissent and fought for journalistic independence and intellectual autonomy—such as Liu Binyan and Dai Qing, the Chinese journalists most known in the West—are either ousted or supervised closely by state authorities to ensure their voices are not heard by the majority of Chinese society (Link 2003; C. Li 1997: 279–299). Rather, it is the professional establishment journalists, "criticizing the system within the system," who are shaping the contours of Chinese journalism in the twenty-first century (J. Wang 1999). Pragmatism rather than idealism dominates their professional ethics.

As insiders, investigative journalists believe that they should produce positive social effects by redressing social wrongs on behalf of the weak, while collaborating with the government to secure social stability and implement state policies (X. Li 2002). Instead of reporting from the perspective of the officials and speaking as representatives of the government, investigative journalists pride themselves on giving voice to popular concerns. Concepts like "equal-level perspective" (*pingdeng shijiao*) and "zero-distance reporting" (*ling juli baodao*) have gained currency. *News Probe*, for example, specifies four guidelines for its investigative journalists: they should have a spirit of questioning, a perspective of equality, a sense of balance, and an attitude of equilibrium (*News Probe* 2003).

The spirit of questioning (*zhiyi de jingshen*) is exemplified by Wang Zhi's "surgical strike" on the Beijing mayor, which was broadcast nationwide within forty-eight hours after the interview was conducted. Wang Zhi regards questioning as laying a path toward truth, "the ultimate purpose that an interview aims at" (Tai 2003). In the interview, he does not allow the state official to dominate the discursive sphere, but occupies a position equal to his by treating him as his equal. In other interviews with doctors and nurses, Wang again demonstrates such a perspective of equality (*pingdeng de shijiao*). The perspective of equality appeals to the civic conscience of media professionals and prompts them to treat both ordinary individuals and the powerful and privileged as their equals. The journalist is no longer a "lap dog" to the state and a "barking dog" to the people, but a mediator between the party line and the bottom line. In this way, Wang has achieved a sense of balance (*pingheng de yishi*) between party logic and people logic, between promoting the official ideology (*zhu xuanlü*, "keynote melody") and the unofficial ideology, the interests of ordinary people. As a late-1990s version of the "people character" (*renmin xin*) advocated by journalists in the 1980s, the perspective of equality is used not to pit the nation against the state, but to recuperate and mobilize the nation to balance the state's power.

Wang Zhi's questioning is not strong enough to challenge the mayor. Instead, the mayor's image as a strong leader is reinforced when he demonstrates his government's determination to win the war on SARS. Both the mayor's popularity and Wang Zhi's soared after the interview was broadcast nationwide: the mayor was hailed as a representative of a new enlightened leadership led by Hu Jintao and Wen Jiabao, and Wang as presenting a new face of professionalism in Chinese media. *Face to Face*, which had been on the air for only four months, became one of the most-watched programs on Chinese television. Investigative journalism, represented by *Face to Face* and *News Probe*, has become an area where "the Party line meets the media's bottom line, the legitimacy imperative of the Party leadership overlaps the credibility imperative of the commercialized news media and the professional and social imperative of journalists" (Zhou 2000: 585).

Wang Zhi and his colleagues demonstrated admirable courage, energy, and wisdom in the anti-SARS media campaign between April and June 2003. They challenged state officials on issues of popular concern and gave expression to popular reflections on Chinese political and social systems. However, their highly cherished professionalism had a very short lifespan—"the door slam[med] shut" as SARS faded from world headlines after July 2003 (Bezlova 2003). As the state once again tightened its control over the media, Chinese journalists retreated to their familiar roles as accomplices of party and market logics.

Therefore, investigative journalists require an attitude of equilibrium (*pingjing de xintai*) in order to live with and resist setbacks from political forces and temptations from market forces—both are corrupting professionalism in

Chinese journalism. The attitude of equilibrium has been a key component of Chinese professional journalism, and it played a central role in justifying the "*yin-yang* face" of Chinese journalists in the media campaigns on SARS.

The concept of *yin-yang* face (*yin-yang lian*) is rooted in ancient Chinese culture. It refers to the pairing, mixing, and compromising of two different and opposing faces: *yin*, which is dark, passive, downward, negative, contracting, and weak; and *yang*, which is bright, active, upward, positive, expanding, and strong. I use the phrase figuratively here to point to the contradictory manifestations of professionalism in Chinese journalism. In a broad sense, *yin* and *yang* mean inaction and action. The inaction of *yin* was evidenced in Chinese journalists' collaboration with the state in covering up the SARS outbreak in early 2003. The action of *yang* was evidenced in their bold and open SARS reportage, known as "media frenzy" (*chao zuo*, literally "stir-fry"), from late April to June 2003.

The switch between *yin* and *yang* is a salient feature of Chinese journalism. Professionals like Bai Yansong have to adapt to and live with such a switch between faces and maintain an attitude of equilibrium in order to facilitate the formation of an informed citizenry at convenient times and in convenient venues. While *News Probe's* first three professional guidelines have counterparts in Western journalism, the fourth, the attitude of equilibrium, is uniquely Chinese. It is promulgated in an authoritarian state where journalism is still an institutional force in policing the populace and where propaganda is far from dead. Among the first three, the spirit of questioning functions more as a technique and means to an end than as a professional code of conduct. It is through questioning that equality and balance, or impartiality, fairness, wholeness, and accuracy—qualities universally understood as crucial for journalists—can be achieved and truths uncovered.

Professionalism, embodied in the four professional guidelines for *News Probe* investigative journalists, is punctuated by journalists' *yin-yang* faces. As the following section will show, it serves as a code word for journalists' experimentation with professional boundaries through doubly articulated narratives. The *yin-yang* face of Chinese journalists in SARS reportage and their doubly articulated narratives of SARS embody their dilemma, caught between the party line, the people line, the market line, and the intellectual line, as well as their strategies for mediating between these different lines.

Double-Time Narrations of SARS

Manifested as the inaction of *yin* and action of *yang*, SARS reportage was doubly articulated over time. Such double articulation creates what Zelizer has called local and durational modes of interpretation of history—hence the narrations of

SARS were double-timed. It involves a doubly spatial mode of news production: official space and non-official space. These different modes allow journalists to insert an encoded *yin* message in the *yang* articulations of news productions. A typical strategy is slanted objective reporting, or objective reporting with a twist.[4]

In *The Battle of Guiwei* (*Guiwei zhi zhan*), a celebrated five-part documentary produced by CCTV in June 2003 and broadcast in July, for instance, the editor skillfully uses *yin-yang* techniques through slanted objective reporting. The first episode starts with an official chronology of the SARS outbreak—where and when it started and how the government responded to the epidemic, leading the whole nation in a glorious and victorious war against it. However, small details gleaned from interviews are interjected throughout. In one interview, Zhong Nanshan, an outspoken medical expert, divulges that SARS was first reported by local health departments to epidemic and disease prevention authorities at both provincial and national levels in late 2002, after the deaths of several patients and medical practitioners. Neither Zhong nor the narrator comments on the discrepancy between this statement and the official narrative, which claims that such reports were not made until the spring of 2003. Viewers may wonder why, if the epidemic was reported in late 2002, effective action was not taken until April 2003, and whether the former mayor of Beijing and the former minister of health (both sacked for negligence) were scapegoats caught up in some kind of conspiracy.

The interview thus contains a hidden script that challenges the authority of the open script. The encoding of the hidden script shapes its decoding by the audience. The slanted objective reporting makes it possible for the audience to read between the lines.[5] I watched the documentary with the chief editor in his Beijing home in September 2003. When I commented on the discrepancy, he replied, with a knowing smile, "I'm happy you've got it." He took pleasure in successfully playing such an "edge ball" (*ca bian qiu*).[6]

The small pleasure he achieved, however, came at a cost: much valuable footage was not used in the final edit because it was too politically sensitive, including an interview by Wang Zhi of Jiang Yanyong, the "whistle blower" and the real anti-SARS hero (Jakes 2003). Pointing at the piles of digital videotapes, the editor said, "Look at those tapes. They are the true history. It was so empowering to drive around Beijing without any traffic jam or political jam for a whole month [between April and May 2003]." After a little pause, he continued, "I don't know when the public will be able to watch them. I know they will—sooner or later. That's why I've recorded and kept them."

This kind of private and offstage talk is not limited to conversations with friends. Chinese journalists also use newsletters, journals, and new media, especially the internet, to articulate a *yin* version of news stories that is in contrast to the *yang* version sanctioned by the state censors. *Yin* and *yang* hence not only imply different stages and modes of media production, but also suggest different kinds of news production. The indirect, coded or suppressed, and offstage articulations (the hidden script), together with (and in contrast to) the open, direct, and onstage expressions (the open script), form a second dimension of Chinese journalists' *yin-yang* face. Double-time narrations do not simply mean different phases or stages of media production, but also incorporate different venues for and kinds of news production. Double-time narrations are inherently doubly tempo-spatial. And internal newsletters and the internet are integral to this doubly articulated professionalism in Chinese media.

In CCTV's News Commentary Department, two internal publications, *News Probe Monthly* (*Xinwen diaocha yuekan*) and *Empty Talk* (*Kong tan*), have become an offstage arena for "intellectual and emotional catharsis" among investigative journalists (personal communication, 2003). These journals or pamphlets feature background stories of news production, lamentations for a topic or a program "shot dead" by the censors, complaints about policy intervention in news productions, and reflections on personal and local experiences. Many media reform policies, such as the call for people logic in investigative journalism, the commercialization of non-news production in the mass media, and the call for journalists (rather than leaders) to play a central role in news investigation and production, are said to have stemmed from such offstage "catharsis" (personal communication, 2003).

The internet is another space for journalists' intellectual and emotional catharsis, as well as a tool for finding, gathering, and disseminating information. Chinese journalists habitually visit popular Chinese-language websites for news sources, including Chinese-language websites based overseas, such as those of the Singapore-based *Lianhe Zaobao* and the Hong Kong–based *South China Morning Post.*[7] Many journalists use electronic bulletin boards (BBSes) to make complaints, confessions, and reflections to exchange ideas, and to publicize stories that cannot be published or broadcast officially. One popular BBS is Journalists' Home (Jizhe de jia), at www.xici.net (based in Nanjing and Beijing) Many journalists visit Journalists' Home regularly because, as one commented, it offers the least-censored space to express oneself and to find good sources of (alternative) news (personal communication, 2003).

Through the internet, Chinese journalists were already aware of the outbreak of SARS in the southern city of Guangzhou in early 2003. News of the outbreak traveled via the internet from China to Hong Kong, to the United States and the World Health Organization, and back to China. The transnational electronic flow of information alerted some (not all) journalists in Guangzhou and Beijing to the news value of the outbreak. Their eagerness to investigate and report the epidemic was quickly crushed by orders for silence issued by the propaganda departments. They were not provided with the necessary money or equipment, let alone permission, to report on SARS (personal communication, 2003). They watched the political winds closely, and broke silence just shortly before the state declared an open war on SARS on 20 April 2003.

Telecommunications has the potential to loosen "thought work" (Lynch 2000). The new media, especially, can mobilize popular opposition and resistance, particularly when information can flow globally via the internet (H. Yu 2007; McCormick and Liu 2003). The internet not only allows Chinese journalists to publicize and gather information, but also facilitates the transformation of their intellectual catharsis into social action. For instance, when a child died in June 2003 because of police inaction, an investigative journalist used the internet to expose local authorities' abuse of power and spur Chinese internet users to reflect on issues of citizenship and human rights (H. Yu 2006).

To summarize, both the broad and narrow senses of "*yin-yang* face" point to a defining feature of professional journalism in Chinese media in general and television in particular. Chinese journalists' *yin-yang* face in its broad sense reflects the macro-politics of Chinese media and the fragmented and truncated nature of professional journalism, and can be situated in the broad socio-political context that the first two sections of this chapter have examined. Their *yin-yang* face in its narrow sense mirrors the micro-politics of Chinese journalism and is a salient aspect of Chinese journalists' everyday practices, as this section has demonstrated.

Both senses of *yin-yang* face also embody an intellectual strategy that is based on doubly situated articulations or narrations of the current situation. Through different stages, modes, and spaces of media production, Chinese journalists present a kaleidoscope of *yin-yang* faces that resemble Beijing opera masks. These *yin-yang* faces create a continuum of ambiguities and contradictions that fragment the current situation that the state has carefully constructed and presented, and deconstruct any effort to write *the* national history. As such, the *yin-yang* face of Chinese journalists represents more than situational tactics; it signifies a systematic strategy or paradigm that I have called "double-time narrations" in the making of media stories about SARS.

Through different stages, lines, and spaces of production in making news stories about SARS, double-time narrations become Chinese journalists' grand strategy—or "noble hypocrisy," as some journalists lightheartedly refer to it—for mediating between different logics or lines. In the process of mediating, the professional journalists are consolidated into an interpretive community as well as a mediation community. As mediators, they excel less by removing their *yin-yang* mask than by using it to formulate a new kind of journalism. This new journalism, which I call "mediation journalism," affects both the everyday reality and the operational and behavioral patterns of Chinese journalists.

Mediation Journalism

Mediation theories in television studies tend to privilege the medium and the message as the critical sites for the construction of the audience. Television, for example, is doubly articulated in the sense that it is doubly consumed, both as technology and as meaning, as object and as content, and hence it effectively mediates between consumption and articulation or ideology. It is also doubly situated in the sense that it mediates between the private and the public, the local and the translocal, the real and the fictional, and between idea and ideology, culture and cultivation, text and context (Silverstone 1994: 134–143). For audiences, the doubly articulated and doubly situated nature of televisual mediation creates a sense of being present and yet powerless. In other words, the proximity of time and space creates a sense of displacement for audiences situated at home.

In such a theory of mediation, the journalist is often regarded as a dependent variable, a creation and product of the medium rather than the creator and producer of the mediated articulations. But as the Lasswellian formulation in journalism ("Who says what, to whom, in what channel, and with what effect?") suggests, a message depends on an agent, principally its producer, for the primary and secondary meanings that are encoded in it.

In fact, mediation has been the nodal point linking journalism and intellectual politics in Chinese media ideology. The Chinese journalism tradition that saw journalists as intellectuals and enlighteners viewed them also as an intermediate layer between ignorant masses waiting to be educated and enlightened on one hand and conservative elites in the polity on the other. Liang Qichao, the doyen of Chinese journalism, for example, saw the press as performing two major functions: communicating ideas to, and disseminating them among, the public; and supervising and mobilizing public opinion in order to influence government (de Burgh 2003a: 96–99). The new journalists in the late Qing and early Republican eras constructed a middle realm, using the print media to open a field of mediation "not only between past and present notions of society and politics but also between foreign and indigenous ideals and concepts" (Judge 1996: 12). Journalists became cultural brokers and mediators. This functionalist view of journalism still defines Chinese journalism today. In the words of one journalist,

> Journalists are the *mediators between people and government.* Their tasks are the communication of news and scrutiny. The responsibilities of the journalists are to make a news programme that keeps the interest of the people—but not all stations are the same. Impartiality is very necessary but the absolute is impossible. We can only do our best. (de Burgh 2003a: 140, my italics)

As mediators contained by the system, Chinese journalists resort to the technique of double-time narration, which allows them to comment on or criticize the system from within and to produce different narrative representations within the given ideological framework. The production of differences within official boundaries does not signify a total rejection of or revolt against the dominant ideology, nor does it suggest a complete quiescence and cooperation with it. The production of difference via double-time narrations creates an unobtrusive space in which to press, test, and negotiate the boundaries of the permissible. Mediation signals both opposition in alliance and alliance in opposition.

This kind of mediation among different lines (especially between the party line and the people line) has been characteristic of Chinese intellectual politics. Stanley Rosen, for example, gives a fascinating account of how daring *Beijing Youth Daily* reporters used "nationalism" and "patriotism" to push the envelope of reporting of and debate on controversial issues and consequently stimulated public reflection on issues of citizenship and democracy (Rosen 2000). Paul Pickowicz shows, in his study of popular Chinese cinema in the early 1980s, that the privileged filmmakers of the system could produce "official" work (funded and sanctioned by the state) with "unofficial" themes to represent alternative and minoritized political realities (Pickowicz 1989). In producing the "unofficial" and disguising it as the "official," Chinese intellectuals are perfecting their craft as mediators.

Opening a field of mediation between the different lines of the post-socialist Chinese media sphere, the new professionals or media people are able to express popular grievances, encourage debate of government politics, check power from above, and generate political, social, intellectual, and economic value in news productions, via both traditional and new media, including television, newspapers, and the internet. In mediating among the different lines, they make it possible to create multiple "regimes of truth," which, according to Foucault, signify circular dynamics through which the production of a particular truth reinforces the power structure at work (Foucault 1991: 256). As the very technology of mediation journalism, double-time narrations have reinforced the power structures involving the party-state, the nation, the market, and the intelligentsia.

As a middle realm between power structures, media people and public intellectuals in general form multiple relationships and multiple modes of mediation between various social forces and actors. Mediation journalism is therefore situated in relationships that can be problematized, modified, and readjusted. Situated in such a theoretical framework, Chinese journalists' positions as propagandists for or clients of the party, enlighteners or educators of society, and professional media workers in the global media industry signify and enhance a synthesized consciousness and organicity in Chinese intellectual politics.

Being in complex relationships with various powers and technologies, however, does not entail passivity. As Radhakrishnan says, following Gramsci's theory of organic intellectuals,

> To be located within a relationship does not mean the same thing as being condemned to that complex of relationships in a spirit of passive acceptance. Through a synthetic consciousness of these relations, knowledge can be produced as change and as a theory of change. (Radhakrishnan 1996: 49–50)

Radhakrishnan believes that intellectuals should combine the Gramscian organic intellectual with the Foucauldian specific intellectual through the concept of mediation. An effective intellectual is situated between "multiple positionings and multiple determinations and multiple alliances" (56–57). Through mediation, intellectuals function as an organic part of a multi-dimensional reality, and produce and use knowledge to generate change.

Chin-Chuan Lee once called for new discourses to "account for the role of China's journalism in the growing interpenetrating web of the local, the national and the global to maintain a dynamic equilibrium between universal principles (human rights, freedom of expression) and national narratives (sovereignty)" (Lee 2000a: 572). Mediation journalism may provide a new paradigm to explain the roles and strategies of Chinese journalists in maintaining "a dynamic equilibrium" between conflicting forces and discourses that shape Chinese journalism and Chinese modernity at the turn of the twenty-first century.

Conclusion

Chinese journalists have been "battling a confluence of ideological currents and molding a hybrid ideology ridden with conflicting identities, images, and subjectivities" (Lee 2003: 17). They try to find equilibrium between the conflicting forces of a burgeoning market economy and a strong party leadership, between the imperative for dissent and the imperative for consent, and between popular expressions and official discourses. In their struggles to mediate between the different lines or logics, Chinese journalists present a *yin-yang* face through double-time narrations. Double-time narrations on SARS revealed a new feature of Chinese professional journalism, which I have called mediation journalism. As a theory of relationship and change, as well as everyday practice, mediation journalism represents a creative intellectual breakthrough from the quagmire of "the 'dominant structure' of communist ideology (party propaganda) in relation to the 'residual structure' of Confucian ethos (intellectual ethics) and the 'emerging structure' of imported media professionalism in tandem with the market logic" (Lee 2003: 17).

As knowledge producers, journalists are conditioned by "relevance struc-tures that entail personal biography, interest, schooling, paradigmatic commit-ment, the larger politico-economic history, and the epochal worldview sur-rounding them" (Lee 2000b: 7). External forces, most notably the market-state, have continued to serve as a point of departure in studies of Chinese journalists and journalism. But, as this chapter has demonstrated, internal forces play an essential role in determining the operational and behavioral patterns of Chi-nese professional journalists.

Mediation journalism has different manifestations under different circum-stances. The SARS reportage is a special case when social forces and conflicts were brought into full play in times of national crisis. At such a time, mediation journalism demonstrates a strong intellectual and populist tendency, and Chi-nese journalists are able to initiate ideological and journalistic innovations from the periphery and the unofficial arena. At other times, especially when China is involved in international conflicts and crisis, mediation journalism exhibits a strong statist tendency, and Chinese journalists are in the vanguard of those manufacturing aggressive nationalist discourses.[8]

Chinese journalism is embedded in Chinese intellectual politics. It is an evolving process, in which journalists are both propellers and impact sites of Chi-nese modernity. Wang Guangwu's view of the modern Chinese intellectual is pertinent to the current discussion of Chinese intellectual politics: "[He] was open to change. He was master of his pluralist environment and, had the conditions continued, there is no doubt that he could have consolidated a new tradition of free, imaginative, and wide-ranging inquiry and opened up a new era of creativity for China" (G. Wang 1991: 295–296). While the pace of consolidating the new tradition of intellectual inquiry remains to be determined by the evolving cultural transformation in postsocialist China, a "new era of creativity" has started to take shape, as the SARS reportage has demonstrated. Mediation may magnify, but not erase, the contradictions within Chinese media culture. As an index of Chinese media culture, it will continue to shape the behavioral and operational patterns of Chinese journalists and to impact on the Chinese public sphere.

Notes

1. "Party logic" and "people logic," and the corresponding terms "party character" and "people character," have been widely used in Chinese media studies to refer to the party-state principle (party journalism) and the popular principle (populist journalism).
2. The "insiders" I refer to are Chinese establishment journalists, whom I quote and study in this chapter.
3. Clientelism is not just typical of Chinese journalism, but has been a defining characteristic of Chinese society; patron-client networks operate within and between

villages (Oi 1989), enterprises (Walder 1986), and local governments (McCormick 1990) and are a factor in intellectual politics (Goldman 1981; Cheek and Hamrin 1986).

4. Claiming objectivity can be a journalistic strategy in the West as well, allowing journalists to negotiate, discuss, and challenge the boundaries of what is permissible and functioning as a strategic ritual to protect them against being punished for reporting the truth. See Tuchman 1978 and Ehrlich 1996.

5. For a study of Chinese audiences as active decoders of media messages, see Friedman 1995: 295–310.

6. An "edge ball" in Ping-Pong is a ball that hits the very edge of the table; it is within bounds and therefore legal, but almost impossible for the other player to return. It has become a popular term in Chinese journalism for creative defiance in compliance (personal communication, 2003).

7. Chinese journalists are well aware of internet censorship in China. When a newsworthy event occurs, they often turn to overseas Chinese-language websites for more up-to-date and comprehensive coverage than is available from resources based in China. Those websites, though sometimes difficult to access directly, are accessible via proxy servers. Many Chinese journalists are skillful at using proxy servers to access censored websites. For internet censorship in China, see ONI 2005.

8. The aggressive nationalist discourses in Chinese journalism are evident, for example, in coverage of the collision of a Chinese Navy jet with a U.S. spy plane in 2001 (He 2003: 204–205). While I agree with He's suggestion that the Chinese media peddle nationalism because it is a safe and profitable enterprise, I would suggest using the concept of "hyper-nationalism" to explain the internal logic of the nationalism of Chinese journalists (and intellectuals generally). "Hyper-nationalism," a concept proposed by Tani Barlow, is "an ideology and politics of nation building that transform its agent or subject into an imaginary equivalent of the nation," "a highly productive and personalized nationalism" that has characterized Chinese intellectuals (and journalists) since the late nineteenth century (Barlow 1991: 214). Patriotism about the state and loyalty to the nation tend to converge in the journalistic paradigm and serve as the bottom line for Chinese journalists, amid all the other lines they mediate. The concept of hyper-nationalism among Chinese journalists in light of intellectual politics is a major topic and requires a fuller and more detailed treatment than the space of this chapter permits.

References

Bai Yansong. 2000. *Tong bing kuaile zhe* [*Painful and Cheerful*]. Beijing: Huayi chubanshe.

Barlow, Tani. 1991. "*Zhishifenzi* (Chinese Intellectuals) and Power." *Dialectical Anthropology* 16, nos. 3–4:209–232.

Bezlova, Antoaneta. 2003. "Media in China: The Door Slams Shut." *Asia Times*, 24 June. http://www.atimes.com/atimes/China/EF24Ado1.html (accessed 10 October 2004).

Bhabha, Homi. 1994. *The Location of Culture*. London: Routledge.

Cao, Qing. 2000. "Journalism as Politics: Reporting Hong Kong's Handover in the Chinese Press." *Journalism Studies* 1, no. 4:665–678.

Chan, Alex. 2002. "From Propaganda to Hegemony: Jiaodian Fangtan and China's Media Policy." *Journal of Contemporary China* 11, no. 30:35–51.

Cheek, Timothy, and Carol Lee Hamrin, eds. 1986. *China's Establishment Intellectuals.* Armonk, N.Y.: M. E. Sharpe.

de Burgh, Hugo. 2000. "Chinese Journalism and the Academy: The Politics and Pedagogy of the Media." *Journalism Studies* 1, no. 4:549–558.

———. 2003a. *The Chinese Journalist: Mediating Information in the World's Most Populous Country.* London: Routledge.

———. 2003b. "Kings without Crowns? The Re-emergence of Investigative Journalism in China." *Media, Culture & Society* 25, no. 6:801–820.

Ehrlich, Matthew C. 1996. "Using 'Ritual' to Study Journalism." *Journal of Communication Inquiry* 20, no. 2:3–17.

Face to Face [*Mian dui mian*]. 2003. "Wang Qishan: No Joke in a War" [Wang Qishan: Jun zhong wu xi yan]. Broadcast by CCTV, 2 May.

Foucault, Michel. 1991. *Discipline and Punish: The Birth of the Prison.* Trans. Alan Sheridan. London: Penguin.

Friedman, Edward. 1995. *National Identity and Democratic Prospects in Socialist China.* Armonk, N.Y.: M. E. Sharpe.

Gan, Xifen. 1994. "Debates Contribute to the Development of the Journalistic Science." *Journal of Communication* 44:38–51.

Gans, Herbert J. 1980. *Deciding What's News: A Study of CBS Evening News, NBC Nightly News, Newsweek, and Time.* London: Constable.

Goldman, Merle. 1981. *China's Intellectuals: Advise and Dissent.* Cambridge, Mass.: Harvard University Press.

———. 1994. "The Role of the Press in Post-Mao Political Struggles." In *China's Media, Media's China,* ed. Chin-Chuan Lee, 23–36. Boulder, Colo.: Westview.

He, Zhou. 2000. "Working with a Dying Ideology: Dissonance and Its Reduction in Chinese Journalism." *Journalism Studies* 1, no. 4:599–616.

———. 2003. "How Do the Chinese Media Reduce Organizational Incongruence? Bureaucratic Capitalism in the Name of Communism." In *Chinese Media, Global Contexts,* ed. Chin-Chuan Lee, 196–214. London: Routledge Curzon.

Hood, Marlowe. 1994. "The Use and Abuse of Mass Media by Chinese Leaders during the 1980s." In *China's Media, Media's China,* ed. Chin-Chuan Lee, 37–57. Boulder, Colo.: Westview.

Israel, John. 1986. Foreword to *China's Establishment Intellectuals,* ed. Carol Lee Hamrin and Timothy Cheek, ix–xix. Armonk, N.Y.: M. E. Sharpe.

Jakes, Susan. 2003. "People Who Mattered 2003: Jiang Yanyong." *Time.* http://www.time.com/time/asia/2003/poypm2003/jiang_yanyong.html (accessed 10 October 2004).

Judge, Joan. 1996. *Print and Politics: "Shibao" and the Culture of Reform in Late Qing China.* Stanford, Calif.: Stanford University Press.

Ko, Sung-Bin. 2001. "The Exploration of Historical-Cultural Perspective on Behavior Pattern of Chinese Intellectuals." *Journal of Contemporary China* 10, no. 28:533–549.

Lee, Chin-Chuan. 1990. "Mass Media: Of China, about China." In *Voices of China: Interplay of Politics and Journalism,* ed. Chin-Chuan Lee, 3–32. New York: Guilford.

———. 2000a. "China's Journalism: The Emancipatory Potential of Social Theory." *Journalism Studies* 1, no. 4:559–575.

———. 2000b. "Chinese Communication: Prisms, Trajectories, and Modes of Understanding." In *Power, Money, and Media: Communication Patterns and Bureaucratic Control in Cultural China,* ed. Chin-Chuan Lee, 3–44. Evanston, Ill.: Northwestern University Press.

———. 2003. "The Global and the National of the Chinese Media: Discourses, Market, Technology, and Ideology." In *Chinese Media, Global Contexts*, ed. Chin-Chuan Lee, 1–31. London: Routledge Curzon.

Li, Cheng. 1997. *Rediscovering China: Dynamics and Dilemmas of Reform*. Lanham, Md.: Rowman and Littlefield.

Li, Liangrong. 1994. "'Objective Reporting' in China." In *China's Media, Media's China*, ed. Chin-Chuan Lee, 227–237. Boulder, Colo.: Westview.

Li, Xiaoping. 2002. "'Focus' (Jiaodian Fangtan) and the Changes in the Chinese Television Industry." *Journal of Contemporary China* 11, no. 30:17–34.

Lin, Jing. 1994. *The Opening of the Chinese Mind: Democratic Changes in China since 1978*. Westport, Conn.: Praeger.

Link, Perry. 2003. "Liu Binyan: Fearless and Incorruptible, China's Conscience Speaks the Truth." *Time*. http://www.time.com/time/asia/2003/heroes/liu_binyan.html (accessed 26 November 2004).

Lynch, Daniel. 2000. "The Nature and Consequences of China's Unique Pattern of Telecommunications Development." In *Power, Money, and Media: Communication Patterns and Bureaucratic Control in Cultural China*, ed. Chin-Chuan Lee, 179–207. Evanston, Ill.: Northwestern University Press.

McCormick, Barrett L. 1990. *Political Reform in Post-Mao China*. Berkeley: University of California Press.

McCormick, Barrett L., and Qing Liu. 2003. "Globalization and the Chinese Media: Technologies, Content, Commerce, and the Prospects for the Public Sphere." In *Chinese Media, Global Contexts*, ed. Chin-Chuan Lee, 139–158. London: Routledge Curzon.

Mittler, Barbara. 2004. *A Newspaper for China? Power, Identity, and Change in Shanghai's News Media, 1872–1912*. Cambridge, Mass.: Harvard University Asia Center.

Mufson, Steven. 1998. "The Next Generation." *Washington Post*, 18 June.

Nathan, Andrew J. 1985. *Chinese Democracy*. Berkeley: University of California Press.

News Probe [*Xinwen diaocha*]. 2003. CCTV online publication. http://www.cctv.com/program/xwdc/20030704/100182.shtml (accessed 11 November 2004).

Oi, Jean C. 1989. *State and Peasant in Contemporary China: The Political Economy of Village Government*. Berkeley: University of California Press.

ONI (Open Net Initiative). 2005. *Internet Filtering in China in 2004–2005: A Country Study*. http://www.opennetinitiative.net/studies/china (accessed 14 May 2005).

Pan, Zhongdang. 2000. "Improvising for Reform Activities: The Changing Reality of Journalistic Practice in China." In *Power, Money and Media: Communication Patterns and Bureaucratic Control in Cultural China*, ed. Chin-Chuan Lee, 68–111. Evanston, Ill.: Northwestern University Press.

Pan, Zhongdang, and Ye Lu. 2003. "Localizing Professionalism: Discursive Practices in China's Media Reforms." In *Chinese Media, Global Contexts*, ed. Chin-Chuan Lee, 215–236. London: Routledge Curzon.

Pickowicz, Paul G. 1989. "Popular Cinema and Political Thought." In *Unofficial China: Popular Culture and Thought in the People's Republic*, ed. Perry Link, Richard Madsen, and Paul G. Pickowicz, 37–53. Boulder, Colo.: Westview.

Polumbaum, Judy. 1990. "The Tribulations of China's Journalists after a Decade of Reform." In *Voices of China: Interplay of Politics and Journalism*, ed. Chin-Chuan Lee, 33–68. New York: Guilford.

———. 1994. "Striving for Predictability: The Bureaucratization of Media Management in China." In *China's Media, Media's China*, ed. Chin-Chuan Lee, 113–128. Boulder, Colo.: Westview.

Radhakrishnan, R. 1996. *Diasporic Mediations: Between Home and Location*. Minneapolis: University of Minnesota Press.

Rosen, Stanley. 2000. "Seeking Appropriate Behavior under a Socialist Market Economy: An Analysis of Debates and Controversies Reported in the *Beijing Youth Daily*." In *Power, Money, and Media: Communication Patterns and Bureaucratic Control in Cultural China*, ed. Chin-Chuan Lee, 152–178. Evanston, Ill.: Northwestern University Press.

Ruan, Ming. 1990. "Press Freedom and Neoauthoritarianism: A Reflection on China's Democracy Movement." In *Voices of China: Interplay of Politics and Journalism*, ed. Chin-Chuan Lee, 123–131. New York: Guilford.

Schwarcz, Vera. 1986. *The Chinese Enlightenment: Intellectuals and the Legacy of the May Fourth Movement of 1919*. Berkeley: University of California Press.

Silverstone, Roger. 1994. *Television and Everyday Life*. London: Routledge.

Tai, Yingban. 2003. *Tebie shiqi de tebie zhuchiren [Special Anchor in Special Times]*. http://www.personbox.com/Data/Ent/20070807/422.html (accessed 31 March 2008).

Tuchman, Gaye. 1978. *Making News: A Study in the Construction of Reality*. New York: Free Press.

Walder, Andrew. 1986. *Communist Neo-Traditionalism: Work and Authority in Chinese Industry*. Berkeley: University of California Press.

Wang, Guangwu. 1991. *The Chineseness of China: Selected Essays*. Hong Kong: Oxford University Press.

Wang, Jin. 1999. "Dazhong wenhua xue de guihua [Plan for the Study of Mass Culture]." *Dushu*, no. 10:36–43.

Yu, Haiqing. 2006. "From Active Audience to Media Citizenship: The Case of Post-Mao China." *Social Semiotics* 16, no. 2:303–326.

———. 2007. "Talking, Linking, Clicking: The Politics of AIDS and SARS in Urban China." *Positions: East Asia Cultures Critique*, 35–63.

Yu, Xu. 1994. "Professionalization without Guarantees: Changes of the Chinese Press in Post-1989 Years." *International Communication Gazette* 53, nos. 1–2:23–41.

Zelizer, Barbie. 1993. "Journalists as Interpretive Communities." *Critical Studies in Mass Communication* 10, no. 3:219–237.

Zhang, Jie. 2003. Seminar on Wang Zhi. CCTV, September. http://www.cctv.com/anchor/compere/0087/20030922/3.shtml (accessed 25 May 2004).

Zhao, Yuezhi. 1997. "Toward a Propaganda/Commercial Model of Journalism in China? The Case of the Beijing Youth News." *International Communication Gazette* 58, no. 3:143–157.

———. 1998. *Media, Market, and Democracy in China: Between the Party Line and the Bottom Line*. Urbana: University of Illinois Press.

Zhou, Yuezhi. 2000. "Watchdogs on Party Leashes? Contexts and Implications of Investigative Journalism in Post-Deng China." *Journalism Studies* 1, no. 4:577–597.

Building a Chinese "Middle Class": Consumer Education and Identity Construction in Television Land

This essay studies the development of television formats catering to the emerging urban middle class by examining the influential consumer guide and lifestyle programs of major television stations in China. It also analyzes factors contributing to the popularity of this genre and new trends affecting its prospects in the Chinese television industry. I argue that although television consumerism in China plays an important role in the manifestation of social identities by mediating the imagination and participation of selected audience groups, as it does elsewhere, the Chinese context and history are also specific. In many other countries, television is associated with the development of the mass market. In China, however, early consumer programs were not so concerned with market development, but instead offered advice to viewers, whom they addressed as ordinary citizens with limited budgets. On the other hand, although almost all Chinese citizens have access to television, more recent consumer programming has become increasingly specialized and upscale, addressing and shaping the growing middle-class market with programs on everything from the latest technological gadgets and foreign travel to art investment. These programs embrace icons of global consumer culture and highlight their symbolic meanings, while acknowledging the middle class's striving for empowerment and self-expression within the sphere of consumption. Meanwhile, the client focus and interactive features of the programs indicate a significant shift in the relationship between television and the audience in contemporary China.

New consumption patterns in China bring new possibilities for individuals to shape their own images and identities, offering them new social spaces in addition to their domestic realms or workplace positions (Yan 2000). Chinese consumers have rapidly expanded their exposure to international cultural products through electronic entertainment media, air transportation, mass tourism, and a surge of global commodity imports. After decades of isolation and tight ideological control under the rule of Mao, Chinese audiences were exposed to a dazzling media world of affluence and leisure, and of seemingly limitless consumption options. A wide variety of television advertisements, infomercials, shopping programs, and Hollywood-style entertainment programs, both imported and locally produced, bombard Chinese audiences with messages and ideas about consumption. Many of these programs openly proclaim their goal of making viewers into knowledgeable and sophisticated consumers, informing them about the latest trends in the market, and teaching them the skills needed to meet the demands of a modern lifestyle.

Currently in China more than thirty provincial and large municipal TV stations offer service programs on lifestyle and consumer information, encompassing many aspects of the daily lives of the public, from traditional domains of food, clothes, shelter, and transportation to leisure activities like tourism and exercise. Beijing TV (BTV), Hunan TV, and Dalian TV all founded their own Life Channels after China Central Television (CCTV) took the initiative in 1996. This essay examines such consumer guide and lifestyle programs in the context of the nation's transformation from a subsistence economy to a consumer society, and analyzes their content and format as they relate to the production process. It also explores how these programs might influence concepts of value, aesthetic styles, and class identities.

Mediated Imaginations and the Middle Class

The rise of a Chinese middle class in the years of structural reform has been remarkable in the eyes of China observers in the West, as a *New York Times* report indicates:

China's middle class savors its new wealth. . . . Like a phoenix rising from the ashes of Communism, the last few years have seen the stunning growth of a flourishing Chinese middle class. . . . [T]he rapid accumulation of material things has left its psychological mark as well, infusing this group with a kind of independence and carefree optimism that has not existed in China for decades. (Rosenthal 1998)

Although scholars have not reached any consensus on the criteria that define the Chinese "middle class," the rising economic power of this social group and its political and cultural significance have drawn increasing attention. They suggest that in today's China, decades of economic reform have eroded the institutional bases of a cadre-dominated social hierarchy established in the Mao era and brought in new patterns of social stratification (Bian et al. 2005). Apparently, economic success in the more privatized market is becoming an important determiner of status, which was earlier primarily based on political standards.

The classic Marxist definition of class, which focuses on one's relationship to the means of production in a capitalist society, seems not so helpful in comprehending the class divisions in contemporary China, which is shifting from a state-controlled planned economy to a market-oriented system. Max Weber's theory sheds more light on the understanding of a society's "intermediate strata," or what he referred to as the "middle classes," which are often not directly linked to the process of industrial production. Weber points out that there is a difference between "class" and "status." According to him, a "class" is a category of people with common economic opportunities and common "life chances," while "status" describes intermingling and intermarrying social groups who share a common "lifestyle" (Weber 1953: 69). In other words, class is defined both by relations of production and by the ability to consume goods and services. The middle class relates to economic or productive processes not primarily as sellers of labor or owners of capital but as consumers in the marketplace. Through mediated economic privileges in the forms of education, honor, and lifestyle, the middle class exercises and maintains its social position in a constantly evolving dynamic.

While social classes are being formed during China's globalization process, self-identified "middle-class" or "petty-bourgeois" groups have emerged, particularly among the urban professional population (Wang 2005). Many in these groups distinguish themselves from the masses by identifying with international consumer trends and youth culture. A survey published by the Chinese Academy of Social Sciences in 2004 reports that China's middle class accounted for 19 percent of the total population by 2003. It defined "middle class" as families with assets valued from RMB 150,000 to RMB 300,000 (US$18,072 to US$36,144) (Xin 2004). This is a diverse body of people comprising private entrepreneurs, managerial staff working in domestic and foreign firms, technical professionals, and other "white-collar" workers. More and more international investors have been attracted to China by the purchasing power of this group and its growing interest in cars, housing, tourism, education, and entertainment.

According to a recent report issued by a Washington-based think tank, China has become the world's leading consumer:

> In China's consumer economy, sales of almost everything from electronic goods to automobiles are soaring. Nowhere is the explosive growth more visible than in the electronics sector. . . . Among the leading consumer products, China trails the United States only in automobiles. (Brown 2005)

The Chinese public's engagement with modernity demonstrates many characteristics specific to the Chinese context, shaped by the communist legacy and the Confucian past. Contrary to the common Western perception of television as "the lowest of media" (Seiter 1999: 131), associated with a lack of education and with idleness and unemployment, television is a symbol of modernity in China. The images and symbols that flow in through television usher in a new cultural order that challenges long-standing habits and ideologies. Compared with the print media, which is censored more meticulously, television is more representative of an open global culture.

A study of television and consumer culture in contemporary China would illuminate the role of consumption in the overall system of communication. According to Baudrillard, "consumption is a system which assures the regulations of signs and the integration of the group: it is simultaneously a morality (a system of ideological values) and a system of communication, a structure of exchange" (1988: 46). Consumer goods are components of structures of meaning through which people develop and maintain social identities, with their own symbolic values as well as use values. The commercial nature of media products provides a systematic way for images of the "modern lifestyle" to circulate among television viewers, creating texts as "mirrors of reality" (Carter and Steiner 2004: 20). Through television, the symbolic values of various consumer items, especially those available only to a few, become regenerated, highlighted, and magnified. In *Television, Audiences, and Cultural Studies*, David Morley also points out the dual layers of meaning in the relationship between television and consumerism, as viewers are consumers both of the medium and of the goods that television displays:

> If television has to be understood as "doubly articulated," in so far as its messages are themselves consumed (with meanings that are both predefined in design and marketing and negotiable—of which, more later), it also enables consumption. Through its combined messages it brings news of further consumption possibilities; and in some cases, through its interactive capacities, decisions to consume can now often be communicated, goods ordered, etc. (1992: 214–215)

As Appadurai (1996) points out in discussing the role of the desire for objects in the imaginative processes of identity, this desire enables viewers to partially identify with a global consumer culture through their aspirations and "taste," even though not all of them have the ability to materialize these aspirations. They fantasize about new lifestyles, appreciating, enjoying, and learning to adopt new status symbols, and these fantasies contribute to the construction of their subjectivities as citizens in an "advanced," global, capitalist world.

Television not only brings viewers images through which they can associate meanings with mundane consumption activities, but also allows them to display and communicate their consumer knowledge and competence through interactive activities. Mediated imagination and symbolic participation are part of a cultural process through which an emerging middle class creates itself as a social entity. According to Mark Liechty, middle-class culture can be seen as a mixture of practice, production, and performance. "Class culture is always a work-in-progress, a perpetual social construction that is as fundamentally bound to the 'concrete' of economic resources as it is to the cultural practices of people who jointly negotiate their social identities" (2002: 4). People can use media to rehearse their self-expression and to imagine those who share their communal identity through forms of entertainment and recreation. "Consumption is a significant part of the circulation of shared and conflicting meanings we call culture. We communicate through what we consume. Consumption is perhaps the most visible way in which we stage and perform the drama of self-formation" (Storey 2003: 78). Television stations across China have recently begun to solicit audience participation or feedback in the form of calls to telephone hotlines, cell phone text messages, and posts to internet discussion groups, and this development suggests that television is emerging as a public space for the middle class to rehearse and exhibit its new communal identity.

In the following sections, I will delineate how television in China plays a distinct role in the rise of consumer culture in society through its creation and circulation of images of a "modern" lifestyle and the possibilities of symbolic involvement by audience members. I will also discuss how this role may signify a new relationship between television and the public, with the media serving the audience as clients or "players."

Redefining "Serving the People"

In 1979, three years after Mao's death, China Central Television (CCTV) debuted its earliest lifestyle/service program, *At Your Service*. At a time when television was still a novelty to the majority of Chinese, the program met the desire of the public to retreat to a private sphere and build up a cozy domestic life after the social and political chaos of the Cultural Revolution. Viewers were encouraged to enjoy freedom and leisure through creative activities at home. The program offered viewers tips on mundane matters such as cooking, family health, house decoration, sewing, and knitting. The program's slogan was "Serving You Wholeheartedly" and it emphasized the public service function of television. Family life was the show's main focus, and in its early years it paid little attention to the consumer market and product trends. Throughout the 1980s the program maintained a steady audience. It had a down-to-earth style and easygoing pace, and featured mature women hosts respected by viewers for their friendliness, caring, and warm-hearted attitude. While the producers regarded married women as their target audience, some men were also regular followers of the show. According to critics, this was partly because a large number of Chinese men were participating in household chores, and partly because they were attracted to the hosts' combination of "traditional femininity" and "sense of understanding of intellectual women" (CCTV 2005c).

In the mid-1990s, amid the tide of consumer revolution in China and the rapid emergence of new television formats, the matter-of-fact style and content of *At Your Service* appeared outdated. The program faced declining ratings and harsh competition from more trendy service programs on national and local channels. In 1994 the station leadership decided to suspend broadcasting of *At Your Service*.

In 1996 CCTV-2 launched a regular magazine program, *Life*, focusing on new consumption trends and lifestyle in urban China. According to Yang Weiguang, chief of the television station at that time, the program was intended to "adapt to the changes in the economy and people's lives in the era of transitioning from socialist planned economy to socialist market economy." Its policy was to get "close to people and their lives, guiding scientific consumption and raising the quality of life" (Liu 1999: 110). Compared with *At Your Service*, *Life* provides more market-related information, providing information on interesting new consumer trends to an audience with higher-than-average income. The show is brisker and its content more colorful, and energetic and fashionable young college graduates are employed as hosts. It is also more accommodating when sponsors want the hosts to demonstrate their new products on the show.

Over the years, as more and more programs pursuing hot trends in the consumer market appeared on screen, some viewers felt nostalgic for the homely tone and down-to-earth style of *At Your Service*. Recognizing the good-old-times appeal of the program to the mid-income audience, CCTV reintroduced *At Your Service* to the public in 2000 after a makeover, with new content to suit the changing needs of urban viewers and to accommodate the concerns of advertisers. For example, one segment of the show features a month-long home cooking competition, broadcast mostly around holidays and with a seasonal focus, and another segment recommends tourist itineraries several weeks before every long holiday. The program also has an information series for parents of high school students preparing for the national college entrance exam. The hosts provide information on colleges and universities and advise families on filing applications, the nutritional needs of students, what to do if a student fails the exam, and so on. *At Your Service* also offers a legal help segment with a studio hotline through which legal experts and lawyers discuss selected cases and respond to audience questions.

After another format change in 2003, the program ventured into a wider range of topics, from exposés of poor-quality merchandise and pet care to the process of applying for a home mortgage. Topics covered in 2005 in the program's regular section on household management included the scientific way of drinking coffee, the easiest way to peel garlic, and tips for selecting a washing machine. Topics specifically aimed at women viewers included "What to do with expired lipsticks," "Carry the weight-loss effort through to the end," and "Preparing for your child's enrollment in preschool."

Currently *At Your Service* is a regular fifty-minute program on CCTV-2, the station's economic information channel, and is broadcast every weekday in the early evening and rebroadcast at midnight. The program is positioned to serve audiences in the age group of 30–45, with a post–high school education, who are interested in topics such as nutrition, health and safety, child care, seasonal change, and household matters. Although *At Your Service* still faces pressure to enliven its style and brighten its look, in the last few years the program has managed to maintain a position among the top ten service programs nationally. With no ambition to appeal to the high-end section of the audience, it finds loyal followers among the average urban residents who prefer to avoid flashy programs resembling infomercials. According to its host, the program is like "a big bowl of tea," soothing and homely, always a good choice even when viewers could have gone for "the flavor of coffee or the freshness of fruit juice" (CCTV 2005c)

Targeting Special Audience Groups

As the media continue to commercialize, television stations in China rely more and more on advertising instead of government funds for revenue. At present China's traditional broadcast TV channels count on advertising for 90 percent of their revenue (Landreth 2005). Market research measures such as audience surveys have been widely utilized by stations to assess the financial success of specific programs. Obviously it is not just the size of the audience that matters. More important is its value to sponsors and advertisers. Therefore, an increasing number of television programs have been created in recent years to cater to the taste of the so-called "three-high" population: viewers with high incomes, high educations, and high social positions. Because consumer guide programs strongly appeal to advertisers and sponsors and are relatively simple to produce, both national and provincial television stations have invested heavily in them. They provide an excellent platform for the creation of commercially successful programs aiming at a selected audience that has a special need for consumption-related information. Some programs come to stand out in this genre for their fresh content, unique style, or particular expertise.

High-Tech Observer

Beijing TV premiered a program in September 1999 called *High-Tech Business Observer*, targeting the growing number of consumers in Beijing knowledgeable about new technological trends and gadgets. The program was an immediate success and was soon renamed *High-Tech Observer*. Unlike other television production teams, its staff is mostly graduates of universities in Beijing who majored in scientific or engineering fields. The program has two segments—*In-Depth Reports* covers topics such as industrial development, new products, employment trends, educational technologies, IT peripheral industries, and portraits of white-collar lives; *Pioneers of Our Time* specializes in interviews with movers and shakers in the high-tech industries, including business executives at international companies.

As part of its effort to provide up-to-date industry information, *High-Tech Observer* has reporter teams stationed in Taiwan, the U.S., and South Korea. The hosts frequently visit important global high-tech exhibitions, such as the Asia Telecommunication Exhibition held in Singapore in 2005. The program is broadcast on BTV-3, the station's science channel, four times a week, in the morning, at noon, in the evening, and at midnight. According to data from Nielsen Media Research, the show is the highest-rated of all science and technology programs in the Beijing area.

The 2005 Beijing Telecommunication Exposition opened the day after Nokia announced that it had manufactured 200 million cell phones in China. In the episode of 31 October 2005, *High-Tech Observer* hosts toured the exposition and described selected new products, such as Nokia's business cell phone 6708, specifically designed for the Chinese market. A host pointed to the phone's large touch screen, which can read Chinese characters written on it. The host then demonstrated a useful gadget for business people, made by a Chinese company:

> You can use its 4-million-pixel CCD scanner to scan any business card you receive, and all the information will automatically get into your address book through its identification software. Also, you can choose to have a fingerprint

identifier attached to this cell phone; that way, if you lose it, other people simply cannot use it. This feature can also be used to protect your documents.

The program usually features dialogues between a young male and a female host, who try to lighten the tone and soften the dryness of technological terms. In many cases the female host asks simple questions and expresses amazement and surprise, whereas the male host explains the details of the state-of-the-art item. For instance, an episode aired on 9 October 2005 included this exchange:

> Male host: This is a pair of walkie-talkies with a GPS system. You can see not only your own position, but also the position of your friend if a group of people visit Disneyland. . . . It can also record the route traveled. . . .
> Female host: Oh, this is amazing! This way parents and children will be able to go to separate attractions. But isn't GPS for cars?
> Male host: Actually, the handheld ones are more useful.

High-Tech Observer does not limit itself to informing viewers about new products in the high-tech market. One episode in October 2005 reported that banks in Beijing were using more and more self-help facilities in place of cashiers. This not only shortens the lines but also offers 24-hour banking convenience to the customers. The hosts introduce the use of a deposit machine, a payment machine, and a device specifically for printing out receipts. Also featured in the episode is a machine that dispenses foreign currency. Other examples of topics covered by *High-Tech Observer* in 2005 include "Is your computer protected? (Electromagnetic radiation prevention)," "Who can you sell your old cell phone to?" "New Year digital gifts," and "A cell phone photo studio."

Investing in Works of Art

In order to attract audience groups with high incomes and high educations, CCTV has begun providing information on collecting, taking advantage of its authoritative status as the national station and its expert resources. CCTV-2's regular program *Investing in Works of Art* introduces its audience to the collection and appreciation of artworks, both ancient and contemporary, and provides information on developments in the business of art collection. While many may tune in out of curiosity, the program speaks to the growing interest among the new rich in decorating their mansions with art or investing in Chinese and foreign artworks. Topics range from art valuation, art auction sites, and price fluctuation in the market to tips on recognizing counterfeits. In an episode broadcast in summer 2005, viewers got to watch a twentieth-century painting by Lin Fengmian being sold for RMB 2,530,000 at an auction in Beijing. Then the host discussed with experts from well-respected institutions the artist's life, creative style, and market success.

As many viewers are still novices in the art business, producers of the program make a point of showcasing the risks as well as the impressive profits involved in this business. For example, the 8 August 2005 episode started with these words:

> In the porcelain artwork market, if you bought an item eight years ago, it would not be surprising if its value has increased fifty times. But if the item depreciated five times you would feel really bad. Here we have a case like this. Ms. Bai from Beijing is very frustrated, because recently she asked someone to evaluate a porcelain jar she bought eight years ago for 60,000 yuan. Do you know how much it is worth now? 10,000 yuan. We can understand how Ms. Bai feels. So why did this happen?

Investing in Works of Art invites volunteers to participate in its weekend segment called *Identifying Treasures*. Selected participants display their own treasured items on screen and share stories about them while audiences compete to guess the value of each, after which experts appraise them and offer comments. In various surveys, *Identifying Treasures* has been consistently ranked among the top four CCTV-2 programs, and its ratings have climbed since its debut in October 2003 (CCTV 2005a). Although the majority of items that appear on the show are artworks from various Chinese dynasties, Western artworks are also featured from time to time. For example, the episode of 9 August 2005 demonstrated a nineteenth-century Italian violin, which a team of experts valued at US$250,000 after discussing its quality and the latest trends in the international market.

While the producers claim that this program encourages viewers to appreciate the gems of national culture, its focus and target audience are clearly different from those of CCTV's traditional programs dealing with Chinese culture and civilization, which focus mainly on patriotic and historical education.

Consumer Participation in Sitcom and Reality Shows

The recent development of satellite television and paid channels in China has led to a proliferation of new program formats offering opportunities for audience participation, including game shows, talk shows, and various kinds of reality shows. Many of these shows target the urban middle class specifically, addressing aspects of their effort to establish and maintain a modern lifestyle and balance the demands of home and career. These programs provide a space for the growing middle class to play a role in public media outlets, share their views on social issues or consumer matters, and express their creativity without endangering themselves politically.

In the meantime, competition among the different channels and programs within CCTV is also increasing, forcing production personnel to renovate old formats. According to a 2003 decree by the station, all shows more than one year old are subject to a system of warnings and elimination (China News Net 2003). Station authorities issue warnings every quarter to programs whose ratings are problematic, and three or more warnings in a year will lead to elimination. Elimination of the show also means that it will not be allowed another rerun; the department responsible for it may not add a new show to the channel for a year; and its producer will not be allowed to produce a new show for two years. Although CCTV-2's *Life* and *At Your Service* still enjoy steady shares of the market, partly as a result of the strength of the national station and their own head start in the service program field, competition among programs in this genre has become rigorous. Producers use various tactics to enhance the appeal of their programs, often borrowing ideas from successful shows in foreign countries or in Hong Kong or Taiwan (Keane 2002). Lifestyle and service programs that package useful information and practical knowledge with entertainment have become very popular.

One of the producers' new tactics is to turn a consumer guide show into a sitcom. One example is Beijing TV's *Happy Life, Simple Tips*, which debuted in early 2004. In this program, practical knowledge and consumer information are deftly packaged into the story of a three-generation Beijing family. The fictional family consists of a happily married young couple, their smart little boy, and two loving grandparents. The family is portrayed as energetic and efficient, keeping in touch with new trends in the consumer market while economical in daily matters, capable of finding satisfaction in handling everyday chores in creative ways and helping each other out. BTV staff claim, "They love life enthusiastically and make their ordinary life colorful and full of fun by using all kinds of small strategies. They spend as little money as possible to achieve as much as possible. The family tradition of the Chinese nation is well integrated in the program" (Beijing TV 2005). In July 2005, the show covered such topics as protecting the little boy from mosquito bites while he is studying in the evening, measuring body temperature with a watch, making a nutritious and simple meal with only tomatoes and noodles, and cleaning the kitchen cutting board. *Happy Life, Simple Tips* also features life skills competitions, through which viewers can join the show as extras and win various consumer items as prizes.

To inject entertainment elements into consumer education programs, CCTV-2 created a shopping competition show named *Supermarket Winner*, bringing participants from all walks of life and various nationalities to shop on camera. The show offers participants a free shopping trip on which they guess the prices of thousands of items, working together to win an opportunity to fight for their dream items. The winning team is awarded a surprise prize. One episode in 2004 featured Chinese athletes who had just returned from the Olympic games, including a gold medalist in men's pommel horse, a bronze medalist in women's gymnastics, a gold medalist in women's freestyle wrestling, and a silver medalist in women's track cycling. Another episode had three families compete to demonstrate shopping skills and cooperation. In a section designed to test whether parents' understandings match their children's wishes, a group of parents had to choose, within a certain time, items they thought their children would want. Later each child named his or her own favorite item from the list. One episode featured Western students in Beijing who shopped in a Chinese supermarket and also entertained viewers by singing Chinese folk songs or performing martial arts.

In response to the rapidly expanding automobile industry and the rising number of adults getting their driver's licenses for the first time, CCTV created in 2004 a reality show called *Happy Heroes*, whose theme was cars and driving. The show was first aired during the 1 May holiday with a subtitle *Driving Boot Camp*, followed by more episodes subtitled *Car Training Camp* during the 1 October holiday. After both holiday seasons received impressive ratings, seven more episodes of *Car Training Camp* were aired in evening prime time during the 2005 Chinese Spring Festival season. While the May episodes showcased participants' impressive driving skills and the October ones highlighted the relationship of people, nature, and automobiles, the Spring Festival episodes placed more focus on romance and family in a cosmopolitan setting. The ten participants in the show—five men and five women—were selected from thousands of online applicants after many rounds of elimination. An important criterion was a youthful look, so that they would bring a sense of energy and vitality to the show. The young men and women went through difficult tests of their driving and survival skills in tropical settings, which challenged their physical abilities and stamina as well as their intelligence and imagination. The two winners were able to bring their family members to the camp in the end. Exotic settings and visual effects were also used to enhance the atmosphere of adventure.

While television producers strive to appeal to the middle-class dream of automobile and home ownership, they also have created Chinese versions of home remodeling shows. Debuted in April 2005, *Space Exchange* is CCTV's only reality-based decorating/remodeling show, the first of its kind in China, inspired by the popularity of this kind of reality show in more than a dozen other countries. In every sixty-minute episode, while one family is away, members of another renovate, redecorate, and reinvent one of their rooms or even their whole apartment in forty-eight hours, with the help of a professional designer and a budget of RMB 8000. Each space will showcase the latest in flooring, furnishings, cabinetry, and appliances, although producers claim they practice "environment-friendly" remodeling.

By late 2005 episodes of *Space Exchange* had been shot in five cities: Beijing, Shenzhen, Shanghai, Shengyang, and Chongqing. According to the station, every episode of *Space Exchange* attracts 10 million faithful viewers. When the program advertised for participating families in *Chongqing Business Daily* in 2005, it required that they own their living space; that the rooms be of decent size; and that family members be able to express themselves well, which meant they had to speak Mandarin instead of a local dialect. Most viewers are between 24 and 45 years old, with more than three years of college education and a monthly income of more than RMB 2,600. In other words, viewers typically are either homeowners or aspiring homeowners, or they are professionals with jobs related to home improvement—for instance, designers and building material retailers. One of the rationales for CCTV-2's creation of *Space Exchange* is that the show has the potential to bring in new advertisers in the area of home furnishing and remodeling. Since China is the world's largest market for building material, presumably there should be no shortage of businesses interested in a home improvement show, and therefore no shortage of potential buyers of advertising time (CCTV 2005b).

Reality television usually involves formalized or ritualized formats enriched by the relatively spontaneous performance of participants (Lunt 2004). As public exposure of emotions on camera is still rare in China, participants in *Space Exchange* sometimes make the program quite dramatic by their reactions to the changes in their homes after forty-eight hours. In one episode a homeowner is stunned by a black gauze screen that the designer used as a sectioning device. Black is usually associated with mourning in traditional Chinese culture. The homeowner indicates that he would have never imagined or agreed to the use of this color in the living room, but he is impressed with the well-coordinated effect and accepts it. In another episode an Australian-Chinese woman designer is assigned the task of remodeling the bedroom of two little girls. The designer insists on using pink even though the color is rare in Chinese households; everyone in the group considered it a bold selection. Upon seeing the dreamlike pink bedroom, the two girls burst into tears of surprise and excitement.

The programs rely on homeowners' participation to boost ratings, and at the same time offer them a sense of empowerment by involving them as players in the landscape of consumerism. In this sense the audience/consumer is seen not as a passive follower of ever-changing market trends but as an active inventor of a personal lifestyle, making individual choices and demonstrating individual aesthetic values and tastes. Although the range of options available is rather limited, this is a huge leap from the top-town pattern in which media provides mass education and entertainment to the public.

The online discussion forum hosted by CCTV-2 indicates that the messages *Space Exchange* sends out to viewers have caused some controversies. While the program claims that the remodeling on the program is based on a principle of frugality, one discussant questions, "Why does a house remodeled two months ago need remodeling again? Is it frugal to use a hammer to smash a piece of glass of about 100 by 60 or 70 cm to get broken pieces to decorate a flowerpot?"

Emerging Trends

Consumer guide and lifestyle programs have attracted many sponsors and advertising agencies, because they allow information about brand names and commodity features to be delivered to a select group of viewers who are more likely to buy the relevant products than the general public. According to Alex Abplanalp (2004), CEO of Zenith Media Asia, the cost of advertising on Chinese television has been driven prohibitively high, especially after the State Administration of Radio, Film, and Television ordered in late 2003 that no more than 15 percent of total airtime between 7 PM and 9 PM could be occupied by commercials. The price of a thirty-second slot soared by 40 percent in 2004 (Chen and Penhirin 2004). As stakes get higher, media agencies and advertisers are searching for more efficient means to break through the clutter of messages to convey brand messages to Chinese consumers. For example, Beijing TV's weekly lifestyle program *Jojo Good Living*, which debuted in 2002 and later became available nationwide on cable television's Tourism Channel, has been very successful in promoting Western household items. According to the host, Zhou Zhu, who is acclaimed in U.S. media as "China's Martha Stewart," the show has "tie-ins with McCormick spices, with . . . Fissler pots and pans . . . Fanini cabinets, a German floor-maker, with Starbucks, and even with Toto toilets" (French 2004). Generally speaking, provincial and local television stations are more willing than CCTV to allow hosts to act like spokespersons for a commercial brand.

With an increasing amount of consumer information available to the Chinese public in recent years, television viewers are growing more selective and practical about the types of merchandise and service they pay attention to. For example, fashion is not as significant a status symbol as it was in the early years of economic reform. In the 1980s, a program called *Fashion Galaxy* by Guangzhou TV introduced European and U.S. fashion trends to its audience, addressing the desire of Chinese urban residents at that time to draw attention to their consumption power and individuality through their attire. For several years the show dominated Guangzhou's television market with huge numbers of fans, mostly young people. However, nowadays it has become very difficult for a fashion program to sustain success of this kind, whereas television programs providing information on big-ticket items in the local market, such as cars, digital cameras, and household appliances, have flourished in all major Chinese cities.

Automobile-related consumer information programs are currently carried by more than twenty television stations in China, covering topics from car functions and maintenance to car races and self-guided tours across the country. Most of the programs emerged in the last five years to capitalize on the growing importance of cars as status symbols. The public reaction to Guangzhou TV's program *Automobile Magazine* illustrates how necessary a program in this category is if a station wants to find a niche in the television marketplace. Two segments of this show, *Driving Experiences* and *Car Fever*, which provide information on the features and models of different cars, faced declining viewership a few years after its debut. However, a segment called *Car Owners' Club*, which focuses on car maintenance and repair, has become more popular because of its relevance to the swelling numbers of first-generation, first-time car owners in the southern coastal area.

As the fantastic merchandise and exotic lifestyle on television constantly create new desires, viewers have to negotiate a path between the media image frenzy and the materiality of daily existence. Although Chinese viewers, like many middle-class Western families, must juggle multiple tasks in their daily lives, simply copying Western lifestyle programs would not lead to high ratings. Chinese audiences' relations to global media culture are mediated by local conditions, such as the legacies of Confucian moral codes and a living standard far below that of developed nations. For instance, the model urban family in BTV's *Happy Life, Simple Tips* consists of three generations living harmoniously together in one apartment, which illustrates the power of tradition in a rapidly changing society. While the smart grandson is the center of attention, "the little emperor," the grandparents are portrayed as wise and kind, and are respected by everybody. The family members are also amiable to neighbors and strangers on the street, as well as cleverly using their brains on matters of money and labor-saving inventions. These images indicate an interplay of cultural and commercial forces in the construction and maintenance of family values, as well as the complexity of the process of social transformation.

Conclusion

The client-focused and participatory nature of the lifestyle programs that promote consumer awareness and individual choices indicates a significant change in the relationship between television and the audience in contemporary China. Consumer guide and lifestyle programs bring their viewers a land of fantasy and create a myth that they can achieve the lives they dream of through personal consumption. The programs also provide them a chance to radically expand their frames of cultural reference and empower themselves symbolically. By bolstering the sense of privilege of selected viewers, which is associated with their "taste" or consumption power, television distinguishes between those deserving its special service and the rest of the population.

The trend toward audience participation in Chinese consumer guide and lifestyle programs indicates the audience's growing role as customers or players in their relationship with the media. Communication scholars in Europe have suggested that new technologies and the pursuit of audience size have profoundly transformed the way television serves the public. According to Trine Syvertsen, the relationship between television and the viewing public can be seen through four ideal type perceptions—television may serve the public as citizens, audiences, customers, and players. In the new media environment of competition, convergence, and digitalization, the relationship between broadcasters and their publics has undergone significant changes. In the early days of television, the public was served more as citizens. New communication technologies have opened up a wide range of possibilities for serving the public as customers or players. "Opportunities are created for viewers to engage with television and each other in a more playful fashion, acting out other aspects of their character than the previous three ideal types allowed for" (Syvertsen 2004: 363). This is also true of the television industry in contemporary China, with its growing client focus and interactivity. When new automobile owners demonstrate their adventuring spirit and their excitement driving across the desert, when homeowners exhibit on screen their creativity and imagination in decorating their or each other's rooms, the participants and viewers are engaged with the media as "players," though at different levels.

Lifestyle programs enable viewers to construct new individual identities, and at the same time they acknowledge the viewers' efforts to achieve empowerment and self-expression in the sphere of consumption. The programs provide a space where individuals can relate to the changing world outside and reassert a measure of choice and control over their lives. Cultural practices in the form of symbolic participation in television, while limited to certain socio-economic groups, open up new room for the Chinese middle class to envision a group identity in the emerging public sphere. This resonates with their growing interest in participation in other media forms, such as talk radio (Xu 1998) or online forums. Although it is still debatable to what extent this kind of awareness and activities will translate to political power, it is nonetheless a crucial step toward the growth of a robust civil society.

References

Abplanalp, Alex. 2004. "Yet More Changes in China's TV Market—But at What Cost?" *Brand Republic*, 7 May. http://www.brandrepublic.com/login/News/210345/ (accessed 28 February 2008).

Appadurai, Arjun. 1996. *Modernity at Large: Cultural Dimensions of Globalization.* Minneapolis: University of Minnesota Press.

Baudrillard, Jean. 1988. "Consumer Society." In *Jean Baudrillard: Selected Writings,* ed. Mark Poster, trans. Jacques Mourrain, 29–56. Oxford: Polity.

Beijing TV. 2005. *Kuaile shenghuo yidian tong* [*Happy Life, Simple Tips*]. www.btv.org/gb/node/sszy2-dx.htm (accessed 18 November 2005).

Bian, Yanjie, Ronald Breiger, Deborah Davis, and Joseph Galaskiewicz. 2005. "Occupation, Class, and Social Networks in Urban China." *Social Forces* 83, no. 4:1443–1468.

Brown, Lester. 2005. *China Becoming World's Leading Consumer.* February 21. http://www.earth-policy.org (accessed 12 August 2005).

Carter, Cynthia, and Linda Steiner. 2004. "Mapping the Contested Terrain of Media and Gender Research." In *Critical Readings: Media and Gender,* ed. Cynthia Carter and Linda Steiner, 11–35. Maidenhead, UK: Open University Press.

CCTV (China Central Television). 2005a. *Jian bao* [*Identifying Treasures*]. http://www.cctv.com.cn/program/jb/index.shtml (accessed 16 December 2005).

———. 2005b. *Jiaohuan kongjian* [*Space Exchange*]. http://202.108.249.206/program/jhkj/01/index.shtml (accessed 19 December 2005).

———. 2005c. *Wei ning fu wu* [*At Your Service*]. http://www.cctv.com/lm/494/6.html (accessed 13 December 2005).

Chen, Yougang, and Jacques Penhirin. 2004. "Marketing to China's Consumers." *McKinsey Quarterly,* special issue, 62–73.

China News Net. 2003. *Yangshi liangchu hong huang pai* [*CCTV Issues Red Cards and Yellow Cards*]. http://www.chinanews.com.cn/n/2003-06-27/26/318440.html (accessed 11 August 2005).

French, Howard W. 2004. "China's Martha Stewart, with Reasons to Smile." *New York Times,* 10 April, A4.

Keane, Michael. 2002. "As a Hundred Television Formats Bloom, a Thousand Television Stations Contend." *Journal of Contemporary China* 11, no. 30:5–16.

Landreth, Jonathan. 2005. "China: Changing Channels." *Hollywood Reporter,* 30 August. http://www.hollywoodreporter.com/hr/search/article_display.jsp?vnu_content_id=1001050615 (accessed 28 February 2008).

Liechty, Mark. 2002. *Suitably Modern: Making Middle-Class Culture in a New Consumer Society.* Princeton, N.J.: Princeton University Press.

Liu, Lianxi, ed. 1999. *Dianshi Zhongguo shenghuo: Shenghuo de baodao* [*China Television Life: Reports of Our Lives*]. Beijing: China Economy Press.

Lunt, Peter. 2004. "Liveness in Reality Television and Factual Broadcasting." *Communication Review* 7, no. 4:329–336.

Morley, David. 1992. *Television, Audiences, and Cultural Studies.* London: Routledge.

Rofel, Lisa. 1994. "*Yearnings:* Televisual Love and Melodramatic Politics in Contemporary China." *American Ethnologist* 21, no. 4:700–722.

Rosenthal, Elisabeth. 1998. "China's Middle Class Savors Its New Wealth." *New York Times,* 19 June, col. 2, p. 1.

Seiter, Ellen. 1999. *Television and New Media Audiences.* Oxford: Clarendon.

Storey, John. 2003. *Inventing Popular Culture: From Folklore to Globalization.* Oxford: Blackwell.

Syvertsen, Trine. 2004. "Citizens, Audiences, Customers, and Players: A Conceptual

Discussion of the Relationship between Broadcasters and Their Publics." *European Journal of Cultural Studies* 7, no. 3:363–381.

Wang, Jing. 2005. "Bourgeois Bohemians in China? Neo-tribes and the Urban Imaginary." *China Quarterly*, no. 183:532–548.

Weber, Max. 1953. "Class, Status, and Party." In *Class, Status, and Power*, ed. Reinhard Bendix and Seymour Martin Lipset, 63–74. Glencoe, Ill.: Free Press.

Xin, Zhigang. 2004. "Dissecting China's 'Middle Class.'" *China Daily.* 27 October.

Xu, Hua. 1998. "Talk Radio in Urban China: Implications for the Public Sphere." In *Communication and Culture: China and the World Entering the 21st Century*, ed. D. Ray Heisey and Wenxiang Gong, 329–345. Amsterdam: Rodopi B.V.

Yan, Yunxiang. 2000. "Of Hamburger and Social Space: Consuming McDonald's in Beijing." In *The Consumer Revolution in Urban China*, ed. Deborah S. Davis, 201–225. Berkeley: University of California Press.

Chinese Television Audience Research

TONGDAO ZHANG

This essay provides a brief overview of the evolution and current state of Chinese television audience research. As an active participant in the field, I have helped to conduct some of the more recent major quantitative and qualitative research projects on Chinese television viewing, and I begin the chapter by introducing those projects. Together with other large-scale national surveys, they have revealed much about Chinese television audiences' overall viewing patterns. To explain why my own recent work and that of my colleagues in academia has focused on the social circumstances and consequences of television viewing in China, the rest of this essay will locate recent work in the short history of both academic and commercial Chinese television audience research. Over the past twenty years, Chinese television audience research has developed from scratch and made tremendous achievements. However, much of it has been dictated by the agendas of funding bodies and limited by the frequent lack of training and experience among researchers. It is even more disturbing that commercial interests overwhelm the standpoints of many academic studies. Furthermore, because television has been hailed as a symbol of modern civilization, little attention has been paid to the negative impact of certain television programs on society at large and on children in particular. Such shortcomings mean there is still much to be done in Chinese television audience research.

My Own Involvement in Audience Research

I have organized several television audience research projects since 2000, including "A Study of Young Television Viewers in Six Major Cities," "The Study of College Student TV Viewership in Beijing," "Television Entertainment in the Eyes of Beijing Young Women," and "The Viewing Habits and Patterns of Beijing Residents" (see Zhang 2002). These research projects focused on the psychology and viewing patterns of specific demographic groups such as youth, students, and young women, as well as general populations such as Beijing residents. They aimed to discover the social function of television in the viewers' daily lives and to further explore television's social impact.

These studies confirm the conventional wisdom that watching television is part of Chinese people's daily routine, and that people watch television in many locations, such as the home, military camps, schools, trains, buses, public squares, and even the temporary tents that house migrant workers. My studies find that different viewing locations have different effects on the television viewing atmosphere. This special relationship between television viewers and viewing environments forms a "viewing field." Different human relationships create two distinct types of viewing fields: the stable and the fluid. Viewing fields in which relationships are durable, such as homes, offices, dormitories, and military camps, tend to be stable, while viewing fields in which human interactions are temporary, such as trains and public squares, tend to be fluid. Stable viewing fields could be further divided into heterogeneous and homogenous fields. Homogenous viewing fields are those in which viewers are one another's equals. In such viewing fields, like colleges and military camps, viewers are similar or identical in age, hobbies, income, intelligence, and social status. Therefore, they share similar tastes in television viewing. Heterogeneous viewing fields, such as the family, are those in which viewers are different in age, interests, income, intelligence, social position, and so on. Therefore, their relationships are more hierarchical, which affects what and how television programs are viewed.

Viewing fields determine the range, extent, and nature of viewing activities.[1] For example, in a college dormitory that normally houses between four and six students per room, television viewing is mainly a collective activity. Forty-four point one percent of students choose to watch television with all their roommates; 27.8 percent choose to watch with only two or three of their roommates; and 7.4 percent prefer getting friends to come over and watching together. These results indicate that 80 percent of college students watch television in small groups. Students are on an equal footing and share similar hobbies, which bring them together, and they watch television mainly for entertainment. The relationships among them are also relatively simple.

Chinese Family Television Viewing Patterns

As I report in "The Viewing Habits and Patterns of Beijing Residents," "Family is the basic unit of Beijing residents' television viewing. 96.1 percent of the 1160 surveyed individuals are part of families of at least two members. 77.2 percent watch television with their families, composed of more than two individuals" (Zhang 2002, 350). The viewing environment of a family is relatively relaxed, and television is viewed mainly for entertainment and information. However, 23.2 percent of those surveyed indicated that they watch television to promote a better family relationship. Elderly people seem particularly eager to participate in family viewing for this purpose. This suggests that television viewing at times becomes a ritual that brings the family together and deepens relationships among its members. Television provides them with topics of conversation. More than a third (36.6 percent) of the viewers surveyed said that they prefer watching a favorite program with their families, and 27.3 percent discuss the program with the family. More than a quarter (29.3 percent) do not mind watching a program that is not to their own liking, so long as they are watching it with the family. This suggests that television can not only provide entertainment but also enhance family bonding and improve domestic relationships. Television may also cause disturbances. A fifth of the people surveyed (20.2 percent) expressed the negative impact of television viewing; 11.2 percent had disagreed with family members about choosing channels, and 9 percent became distanced from their families as a result of heavy television viewing. Nevertheless, more than half of those surveyed believe that television does not hurt their family relations, and 27.2 percent believe that television provides topics for discussion among family members and improves their relationships. Women especially tend to think this way. Although more than half of the 1160 surveyed individuals indicated that television doesn't influence their family life, television clearly plays a significant role in domestic life.

Generally speaking, the most popular programs for family viewing are entertainment programs, followed by education programs. Cultural programs are relatively neglected.

Because family is the core environment for television viewing, family viewing patterns imply a social phenomenon with unique Chinese characteristics, which is the dominance of children. In most families with children, the children decide what is watched. The remote control is a miraculous invention. It is much more than a simple accessory to the television—it is a symbol of the modern age of television culture, and a signifier of power over television viewing. The person with the remote has the power to choose what program to watch. According to our research, 32.8 percent of those surveyed indicate that children are in command of the remote control and therefore at the center of television viewing in the family. Children are in control of the remote in 43.3 percent of families composed of seniors, adults, and children; in 42.8 percent of families composed of only adults and children; and in 52.9 percent of families composed of only seniors and children.

In other words, children have power over the remote in approximately half of families with children. Husbands (17.3 percent) and fathers (11.9 percent) also have an important position in the power structure of family viewing. While the Chinese male is the secondary center of family viewing, wives (11.7 percent) and mothers (7.7 percent) are at the bottom of the structure. The domination by children is an extension of the trend toward single-child families, a uniquely Chinese social phenomenon. This completely overturns the hierarchical power structure of traditional family ideology. "Television Entertainment in the Eyes of Beijing Young Women," a study conducted in November 2000 that targeted women aged between 13 and 39 who were more independent and had a stronger feminist consciousness than most of their peers, indicates that only 40.6 percent of married women control the remote. The majority actively or passively give up this power, which suggests that women are still playing subordinate roles in the family, struggling under pressures from both men and children (Zhang 2002: 350–351).

Research indicates that 22.9 percent of those surveyed switched channels after finishing a program, 30.5 percent switched channels during the commercials, and 31.1 percent were habitual channel surfers. Since more than one-third of all family television viewing is controlled by children, viewing patterns exhibit the characteristics of children—impatience and difficulty with watching one program for a long period of time. This characteristic is contagious, infecting older people. In the end, impatience is spread out among the entire audience.

Patterns of possession of the remote control indicate that the power structure of family viewing among Beijing residents is dominated by children and supported by males. TV viewing psychology is oriented toward physiological stimulus; watching television to some extent becomes nothing more than operating the remote control; and the meaning of television goes beyond the existence of the television itself.

Overall Characteristics of Chinese Television Viewing

The history of the Chinese television industry and the basic nature of Chinese television viewing can be learned from the four national audience research surveys conducted by China Central Television (CCTV) in cooperation with many provincial and local television stations. As indicated by chart 9, the number of Chinese owning a television and the number of households containing one have steadily increased since 1987. There were a total of 116 million televisions in use in China in 1987, averaging 10.7 per hundred people. Television penetration of households was 73.0 percent, and there were 590 million television viewers aged 5 or older. By 1992, the number of televisions in use in China had grown to 207 million, averaging 19.5 per hundred people. Television penetration was 81.3 percent, with 806 million television viewers. The number of televisions in use in China continued to grow, reaching 317 million in 1997, an average of 26 per hundred people. Television penetration was 86.2 percent, with 1,094 million television viewers aged 5 or older. By 2002, there were a total of 448 million televisions in use in China, averaging 107 per 100 households. Television penetration was 93.9 percent, with 1.15 billion television viewers aged 5 or older.

China is now the country with both the greatest number of televisions and the greatest number of people watching television in the world. According to the CVSC-Sofres Media (CSM) *Chinese Television Rating Yearbook 2005*, the television population has reached 1.188 billion, and television penetration is 95.6 percent. Televisions are owned by 98.1 percent of Chinese households, and 32.6 percent own more than one.

From 1987 to 2002, Chinese people spent more and more time in front of the television. In 2002, the average time spent watching television was 174 minutes per person per day, compared to 131 minutes in 1997 and 118 minutes in 1992. However, the numbers have declined since then; the average time spent watching television was 168 minutes in 2004, six minutes less than in 2002.

The viewing habits of Chinese television audiences are strongly affected by the calendar. Viewing time often peaks on weekends, as well as on holidays such as Labor Day, National Day, New Year, and Chinese New Year. The average TV viewing time per day on weekends is sixty minutes higher than on weekdays.

For Chinese audiences, the top ten television genres are weather forecasts, domestic news, television drama, international news, movies, large-scale live shows, variety entertainment shows, news forums, programs on the law, and music programs. Most people dislike commercials. Their reasons for watching changed very little from 1987 to 2002. "Entertainment," "knowledge of policies of the party and the government," "learning current news and politics," and "general education" have consistently ranked as the top four. Television is the major entertainment medium for Chinese audiences. Virtually all (99 percent) of those surveyed report watching television "sometimes," "often," or "almost every day," which suggests the significant role that television plays in Chinese mass culture. The television set is a one-time investment and viewing is free, which fits well with the consumption pattern and power of ordinary Chinese

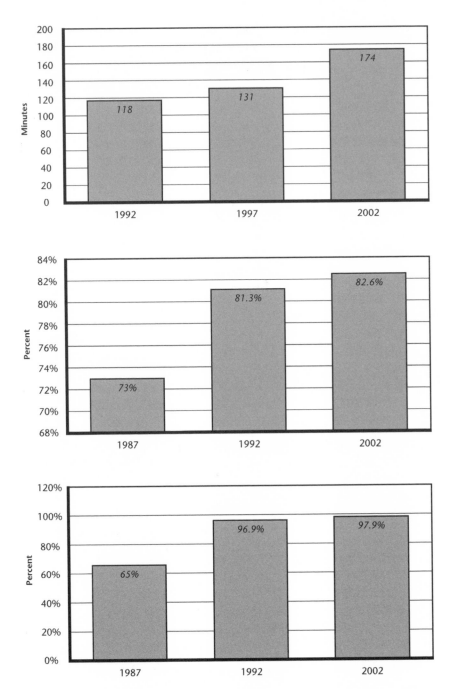

Chart 9. [first part] Average viewing time per person, per day, in minutes. [second part] TV penetration in China. [third part] TV penetration in urban China.

people. The majority of Chinese television viewers are in the lower economic classes with relatively little education. Of rural television households, 63.1 percent have a monthly income below US$150; 69.7 percent of the urban television households have a monthly income between US$150 and US$450. Both students and the poorly educated unemployed are important audiences. Four-fifths (80 percent) of urban viewers have graduated from middle school, while only 15.4 percent of rural viewers have done so.

Chinese audiences speak highly of the overall value of Chinese television but are not satisfied with the quality of many of the programs, including the news programs. They expect to hear more stories about everyday people, as well as more exposés and critiques of social injustice.

The History of Audience Research Studies in China

The history of Chinese television started in the late 1950s. However, the term "audience research" did not exist in the lexicon of the Chinese television industry until the 1980s. Even then, the term signified only a lack. The Chinese television industry was structured by a strictly political hierarchal system from the national to the local level. CCTV was the only channel that could broadcast nationwide. In such a system, which was free from competition, Chinese television was always centered on the broadcasters, and audiences were neglected. Audience research received only lip service and did not go beyond answering viewers' letters.

In 1982, the Institute of Journalism at the Chinese Academy of Social Science initiated an audience research project together with several media companies and institutions, including the newspapers *The People's Daily, The Workers' Daily,* and *China Youth Daily,* as well as the Beijing Broadcasting Institute. This was a general research project on three media: radio, television, and newspapers. The Beijing Statistics Bureau selected a survey sample from among the Beijing population aged 12 or above. In an effort to meet professional standards, the sampling process used computers for the first time and strictly followed random sampling strategies to cover multiple demographic sub-groups. The research took the form of walk-in surveys, and sampled a total of 2,430 individuals in 295 institutions. It also verified 10 percent of the samples. The response rate was 99.7 percent; 2,423 valid surveys were collected. This was the first audience research study using scientific methods in Chinese broadcasting history.

In 1983, the Chinese government instituted a policy of "four-level management of television." This meant that four levels of administration—national, provincial, city, and county—could manage television enterprises. The result was a rapid multiplication of television stations, as well as an increase in television broadcasting penetration. More importantly, because the number of television stations increased but government funding was cut, audiences were given more choice, television-viewing demands were diversified, and market competition emerged in the television industry. To attract viewers, for whom they were now competing, the broadcasters had to attend to their desires and needs. Therefore, the television rating system, which had been operating in Western countries for a long time already, finally came into the Chinese television picture. Increasing competition promoted the rapid development of audience research.

In 1986, CCTV began its audience research, establishing the first television ratings analysis system in Beijing, with a sample of five hundred households. This was the beginning of corporate analysis of television audiences in China, and it was forty years behind that in Western counties. In 1987, CCTV, along with twenty-seven provincial and local stations, conducted a nationwide survey of television viewers. Since then, such efforts have been carried out four times, once every five years. Between 1989 and 1999, provincial television stations joined the satellite broadcasting system, which dramatically changed the Chinese television industry. The old geographic boundaries were broken down, and every provincial satellite channel was available nationally. A television ratings battle quickly spread across the entire country—the ratings determined the cost of commercial slots, which by then had become almost the only source of revenue for Chinese television. The success of the Hunan Satellite Television Channel made it a significant challenge to CCTV's entertainment programming. In 1993, the Chinese government had already raised the issue of television industrialization—television would no longer be purely a "propaganda machine," but would also be a profitable enterprise. Meanwhile, overseas capital and domestic corporate capital began to flow into the Chinese television markets. Foreign advertisers who bought commercial time on Chinese television demanded ratings data, which forced the industry to adopt international ratings systems.

In 1997, CVSC-Sofres Media (CSM) was set up by CCTV's China Viewing Survey Center (CVSC) and the French company TN Sofres Inc. CSM provides television ratings and analysis and develops related software and service systems. CSM has the largest audience measurement network in China and dominates the Chinese television rating industry. The American market research leader, Nielsen Media Research, also entered the Chinese market in 1996, and ranks second. Although corporate research serving the television industry is flourishing, academia has been relatively resistant to audience research. Numerous academic studies have been conducted by various institutions, including the Institute of Journalism at the Chinese Academy of Social Science, the School of Communications at the People's University of China, the Beijing Broadcasting Institute, the School of Communication at Fudan University, and the School of Arts and Communication at Beijing Normal

University. These studies focused on the relationships between television and modernity, children, youth, and college students, and that between television viewing patterns and psychology. Since empirical studies are usually time-consuming and highly dependent on funding, they are often beyond the reach of purely academic scholars. On the other hand, corporate research normally lacks theoretical insight. Therefore, despite gradually increasing interest in academia, original studies are still very limited.

Corporate Research on Chinese Television Viewing

Corporate research on the television viewing market has been the driving force in Chinese television viewing research. Since the first study in 1982, Chinese audience research has gone through two phases: a period of independent studies followed by a period of collaborative research with overseas agencies. The watershed was 1997, when CSM was founded and Nielsen entered the Chinese market.

The period of Chinese independent television audience research began with the founding of the country's first provincial audience feedback network, which was established by Zhejiang Television in 1985. It peaked with CCTV's establishment of its ratings network in the Beijing area in 1986 and the launching of its five-yearly surveys in 1987. In 1992, CCTV launched a national TV ratings system, and in 1995 it created the China Viewing Survey Center (CVSC), the first of its kind in China.

Collaborative research with overseas agencies began with the foundation of CSM. The CVSC is the largest marketing analysis company in China and owns the largest media research system. It has more than ten years of experience in television ratings research, and is very familiar with the Chinese market. TN Sofres has substantial software for TV ratings analysis and decades of experience in European television audience research. After several years of operation, CSM has become the largest professional television ratings service in China, and dominates the field. By 2002, it had established a national audience measurement network using people meters, fourteen provincial ones using diaries and one using meters, and seventy city ones using diaries and twelve using meters. The total sample size is 26,000 households. This huge system tracks 24-hour viewing data for almost seven hundred major stations across the country. Taking 80 percent of the market share, CSM dominates the Chinese television ratings industry.

Nielsen Media Research entered the Chinese market in 1993 but did not begin doing its own ratings research until 1996. Currently Nielsen Media Research has established ratings networks in seventy cities, monitoring 1,200 television channels. The company is competing for the Chinese TV ratings market with its slogan of "neutrality and transparency."

Profit-driven commercial viewing research lacks much in-depth analysis of the background, psychology, and cultural orientation of viewers. Furthermore, the negative influence of television viewing is rarely touched upon.

Academic Research on Chinese Television Viewing

Empirical study is the key methodology for audience research. Chinese academia has borrowed from the United States many social scientific methodologies in mass communication, such as "agenda setting," "usage and gratification," and "the silent spiral." These have become popular theoretical approaches among Chinese scholars.

The 1982 audience research study was the first one co-organized by Chinese academics and entertainment enterprises. The most meaningful discovery of that research was that only 24 percent of the 1,966 people surveyed believed that news broadcasts were credible. Common responses included "many reports are not factual" (44.3 percent); "some reports lack opposing opinions, which tends to give a biased picture" (43.7 percent); and "only reporting good news but not bad" (29.2 percent). These data showed the Chinese media, for the first time, that Chinese people were longing for credibility in news journalism.

If Chinese audience research in the 1980s concentrated on reporting and ratings, the audience studies of the 1990s were more academically grounded. Academics were not satisfied by commercially driven television ratings, but were more interested in exploring the underlying relations between television culture and human life, as well as the viewers' psychological patterns and viewing habits. The most fruitful fields included the relationship between media and modernity, demographic patterns of television viewing, viewer psychology, and patterns of viewing.

In 1991, Chen Chongshan, a researcher at the Institute of Journalism at the Chinese Academy of Social Science, led a research project, "Broadcasting and Modernity," that focused on the relationship between journalism broadcasting and the modernization of viewers. This study surveyed 1,366 samples in Zhejiang Province and defined modern thought as consciousness of independence, efficiency, and creativity. The research indicated that media significantly increase modern consciousness and that better-educated people are more receptive to programs that address the issue of modernity.

Bu Wei, also of the Chinese Academy of Social Science, conducted a longitudinal study of mass media and children. In her book *Mass Media's Impact on Children* she suggests a "conditional theory" of mass media: "The impact of broadcasting on children is conditional. The media impact on individuals results from interactions among social differences, media usage patterns, and children's physiological differences" (2002: 20). She cited research data from 1992 and 1996 showing that children aged between 9 and 15 in major cities increasingly preferred programs designed for adults, while the percentage of children who liked children's programming was decreasing. "Among four different kinds of programs—children's drama; action dramas such as martial arts, crime, gangster, and war genres; documentary; and adult drama and entertainment programs—the percentage of children preferring children's drama decreased from 70 percent to 48 percent, whereas the percentage of children preferring adult drama and entertainment programs increased from 31.5 percent to 49 percent. There was no change for documentary programs" (2002: 50–51). This study indicated that Chinese television programs were catering more and more to adults. "This tendency in television programming is reflected in the replacement of children's demands with adults' demands. Either children's experience is 'expanded' into adults' experience, or it is 'reduced' into a kind of childish mentality that is completely divorced from adult imagination. This situates children in a uneasy position" (2002: 51). Therefore, she points out, "the children's media are based on their responsibility to fulfill the requirements of children's mental development. The key point is to put children first in the children's media that adults create for them. Adult knowledge, opinions, and experience are also helpful, but their value relies on their ability to help children to form their own ideas instead of assigning this knowledge, these opinions, and this experience to children. Our study believes that the development of the media for children should follow the principle of putting children first" (2002: 60).

Professor Yu Guoming at the People's University of China has been promoting empirical methodologies in academic studies. He has directed many studies of media and viewing. One of them, "Beijing Television Market Analysis and Lifestyle Guide Programs," was a marketing research study specifically conducted for Beijing TV's Life Channel. After analyzing Beijing viewers' viewing habits and the audience of the program, the study pointed out defects in the business model of lifestyle guide programs:

> The so-called weak position of lifestyle guide programs in the media market is in fact the weak position of its business model. It should be noted that, in a niche market (a market that does not target the general audience), one is doomed to fail if one follows a business model for the mass market. Within the niche market, you either occupy a dominant position and maximize market share—under the condition that you have enough resources (talents, content, network) to guarantee dominance—or you adopt a multiple-interactive value production model to create interactive value association across the screen and combine the program content with services such as competitions,

exhibitions, marketing, and informatics. Event organizing is programming and vice versa. This can double or multiply value within a limited market. (Yu 2005: 138–139)

Competition in the Chinese television market has intensified rapidly as television channels have multiplied and more and more foreign programs and investments have poured in. Viewers have also become more and more diverse. Therefore, corporate research on television viewing will be more internationalized, and more academic attention will also be paid to audience research. Academic research on TV viewing will absorb diverse methodologies and at the same time broaden its scope to cover the viewing interests of the rural population and other marginalized social groups often ignored by both broadcasters and scholars.

Notes

1. For detailed research results, see "The Study of College Student TV Viewership in Beijing" and "The Viewing Habits and Patterns of Beijing Residents" (Zhang 2002, 153–255, 320–354).

References

All references were published in Chinese.

Bu, Wei. 2002. *Mass Media's Impact on Children*. Beijing: Xinhua.

Chinese Broadcasting and Television Publishing House. 1988. *Chinese Audience Survey 1987*. Beijing: Chinese Broadcasting and Television Publishing House.

———. 1993. *Chinese Audience Survey 1992*. Beijing: Chinese Broadcasting and Television Publishing House.

———. 1998. *Chinese Audience Survey 1997*. Beijing: Chinese Broadcasting and Television Publishing House.

———. 2003. *Chinese Audience Survey 2002*. Beijing: Chinese Broadcasting and Television Publishing House.

CVSC-Sofres Media. 2006. *Chinese Television Rating Yearbook 2005*. Beijing: CVSC-Sofres Media.

Yu, Guoming. 2005. *Change the Media*. Beijing: Huaxia.

Zhang, Tongdao. 2002. *TV Audiences*. Anhui, China: Anhui Education.

4

Going Global

Hong Kong Television and the Making of New Diasporic Imaginaries

AMY LEE

Hong Kong Television and Transpacific Linkages

The globalization of cultural products such as television programs across multiple reception contexts has raised many questions about the role of context and contextual analysis in our interpretation of televisual meanings. In delineating the "discursive concept and object of an East Asian Popular Culture," Chua argues for the necessity of bringing to bear both the culture of production and the culture of consumption to understand how "programs criss-cross the cultural boundaries in the region to reach non-home-audiences" (2004: 212). This essay explores the ways in which production contexts interanimate with reception contexts to discursively construct a transnational diasporic imaginary. As more and more scholars working on Asian television are pointing out, the transnationalization and multiplication of production and consumption contexts for Asian television programs within Asia play a crucial role in demarcating the boundaries of inter-Asian relations and in constituting an Asian imaginary

(Chua 2004; Iwabuchi 2004; Leung 2004). Yet the proliferation of production sites outside Asia and the distribution of Asian television shows via diasporic routes have widened the scope of the social formations and relations under consideration. A diasporic audience position, in this sense, not only represents an audience's relationship with its homeland but also provides a framework for thinking about cross-ethnic and cross-racial relations transnationally. What kind of transnational imaginary do diasporic television programs help to construct? How does Asia envision its position in the world through television? How are inter-Asian, cross-racial, and diasporic relations narrated within diasporic television's economy of signs, and how are they forged through the practices of global circulation? What are the implications of a diasporic reception context and audience position for the interpretation of televisual meanings?

In particular, I am interested in the ways in which the circulation of Hong Kong television dramas to Chinatowns has mediated inter-Asian and cross-racial relations in a transpacific and diasporic framework. These dramas are primarily produced by Hong Kong's Television Broadcasts Limited (TVB), which boasts of owning the world's largest library of Chinese television programs and capturing more than 30 million viewers worldwide, making it the premier exporter of Hong Kong media (To and Lau 1995: 108; TVB 2006).[1] In fact, Hong Kong could be considered a primary conduit of Chinese diasporic culture worldwide. According to Cindy Wong (1999: 97), cultivating diasporic audiences' "feeling[s] of connectedness with a homeland is a key to the international marketing strategy of TVB." The transnational circulation of Hong Kong television dramas and films, due to their cultural intimacy with immigrant communities (exemplified by Chinatowns), plays a large role in forming an immigrant mass culture in the U.S. and elsewhere (To and Lau 1995: 111; Wong 1999: 97). Though little known to the larger national imaginaries outside immigrant communities, immigrant mass culture (e.g., Chinatown culture) is a key participant in the formation of a global diasporic culture, which problematizes the notion of Chinatown as an isolated ghetto and as simply a byproduct of local racism.

The concept of diaspora offers a way for immigrants to make affiliations outside the confines of the nation-state, which allow them to rethink "home and nation-state across multiple identity formations and numerous locations 'out here' and 'over there'" (Eng 2001: 219). Media form many of these affiliations by connecting viewers in disparate locations. The cultural logic of media plays a large role in consolidating and mediating transnational Chinese publics. As the one medium that "interpenetrates public and domestic spheres," television can "serve as a facilitator for the public sphere" and open up a space for critical democratic discourse (Yang 1999: 27). Chinese immigrants most certainly partake in these transnational publics, but they are also a part of other local and national publics. Hong Kong television in the diaspora mediates not only Chinese diasporic publics but also in tangential ways these other publics, thus illuminating the complex ways that television as a social formation works and reworks new power relations in a changing world.

The discourse of a Chinese or Hong Kong diaspora mediated by a homeland has now been replaced with evolving notions of diaspora that take into consideration the different ways in which Chinese subjects all over the world experience the discrepant modernities underwriting contemporary globalism (Chu 2004; Lu 2000; Lo 2001). More specifically, these new theorizations of diaspora understand identity formation as a process that is intricately intertwined with economic processes. I am interested in the roles that race and gender play, as they intersect with economic concerns, in constructing the contrapuntal modernities that constitute the Hong Kong diaspora and the global system in which it operates.

Postcoloniality and 1997, the year marking the end of British colonial rule in Hong Kong, are perhaps the key focal points in studies of Hong Kong. The postcolonial experience of Hong Kong is intricately intertwined with the city's experience of modernity and globalism. Unlike other postcolonial states, which are often preoccupied with the processes of decolonization and national independence, Hong Kong could never become an independent state under the transfer of its rule to China. Instead, Hong Kong's postcolonialism is centered on resituating itself in relation to China, the Asian region, and the world in its new predicament as a special administrative region of China. Given the fervor of its capitalist development under British colonialism, which has defined much of what Hong Kong stands for, it is not surprising that Hong Kong's current identity crisis is circumscribed by its imbrication in the global economy, marked as it is by the rise of China as a global economic power, in what has been labeled the "Asian century." In short, today's Hong Kong and the contradictions of its gender, class, and race politics are positioned within the cusp of the postcolonial and the global. If, as Chow (1992: 158) argues, "it is in postcoloniality that the modernity of Chinese cities . . . is most clearly defined," then postcoloniality has set Hong Kong up as a possible "paradigm of Chinese urban life in the future." At the same time, Hong Kong migrants are, according to Ong (1999), paradigmatic transnational subjects (i.e., "parachute" or "astronaut" families). Hong Kong culture, therefore, is a central site for the articulation of the experiences of Chinese modernity, inter-Asian relations, globalism, and postcoloniality.

This essay follows a cultural studies approach that takes into account the discursive work of television as well as the ways in which the cultural contexts of production and consumption are themselves discursively constructed and understood. I am interested in the cultural work of these televisual representations when they circulate across borders. Since the work of representation—its narrative strategies and thematic concerns—often brings to light a society's unconscious and sensibilities, how do these shows appeal to a wider diasporic or global unconscious? Such a study requires, as Lee (1993: 173) aptly sums up, "'form sensitive' analyses that can specify which particular cultural forms located in what institutions have acted as mediators between different public fields both within and between societies." What are the formal elements of these television dramas that allow them to circulate across immigrant spaces, and what transnational social relations do they put in place?

Travel Narratives: Globalism and Identity Crisis

In the past, most Hong Kong television programs took place in the domestic spaces of Hong Kong, such as the home, the local restaurant, and the workplace, and were concerned with "making home." Recently, however, a growing number of television programs have been produced by TVB in which a good part of the action takes place in sites such as the airport, the cruise ship, and locations in Africa and Southeast Asia. These travel narratives are thematically concerned with transnational formations of identity and questions of travel and intercultural communication. They also point to new formations of labor and capital under conditions of neo-colonialism. From family empires to the growth of middle-class professions (e.g., medicine) to tourism, the change in emphasis on Hong Kong television serials parallels the development of the Hong Kong economy over the last quarter century. Gone are the days of manufacturing and building up corporations, the foundation of Hong Kong's economy, as seen on many of Hong Kong's family melodramas. Hong Kong television's focus has shifted away from the rags-to-riches myth of corporate-family melodramas (or epics) to the cosmopolitan lifestyles of young professionals. TVB's recent shows *Triumph in the Skies* (*Chongshang yunxiao*), *Ups and Downs in a Sea of Love* (*Shiwandun qingyuan*), and *Fantasy Hotel* (*Kaixing bingguan*), for example, feature airplane pilots and flight attendants, tour guides, and workers in Hong Kong's burgeoning service, travel, and tourism industries, respectively. Many programs also focus on the trials and tribulations of Hong Kong's growing middle and professional class—hence the accumulation of shows on the lives of doctors, lawyers, bankers, and teachers.[2] If the family melodrama anticipates the crisis of 1997, the travel narrative responds to its aftermath, namely by securing Hong Kong's position in the region and the world as a capitalist power, cultural center, and site of knowledge and ideological production.[3] It is also important to note that travel narratives do not represent a complete break from earlier television dramas. Travel narratives, like other Hong Kong television dramas, are melodramatic in nature, seeped in emotional intimacies and excesses, and follow many of the same generic conventions (e.g., crime serials and romantic narratives).

The two shows that I will focus on in this essay, *Split Second* (*Zhengfen duo-miao*) and *The Last Breakthrough* (*Tianya xiayi*), introduce not so much a new class of workers as a new role for traditional careers, such as medicine and detective work. That role is to centralize Hong Kong's influence in the world. In *Split Second*, the Hong Kong police force collaborates with police in Thailand to crack down on the transnational operations of a Chinese-Thai triad run by an ethnic Chinese godfather who is living in exile in Thailand after fleeing Hong Kong, where he is wanted for murder. The local Hong Kong police have become the regional police. In *The Last Breakthrough*, medical volunteers at Life Force, an organization similar to Doctors without Borders, go on missions to Kenya and Guanxi in China to educate Africans and ethnic minorities in China on proper healthcare and nutrition. Though they try to respect the beliefs and practices of the African tribes and Chinese ethnic minorities they work with, they nonetheless see these beliefs and practices as a hindrance to proper healthcare, thus promoting the righteousness of their own liberal humanist beliefs and practices. They have long discussions and debates about work and personal ethics, and in the process universalize their own principles and ethics to all of humankind.

These recent serials are highly intertextual, a characteristic that both helps them travel well and implicates their viewers in an increasingly complex web of global relationships. *Split Second*, for instance, borrows from popular Hong Kong films such as *PTU* and the three *Infernal Affairs* films and from popular American television shows such as *24*.[4] The narrative forms of *Split Second*, *24*, and *PTU* are adopted from popular crime and detective genres. Like *24* and *PTU*, *Split Second* is obsessed with the passage of time. The narrative of *Split Second* takes place over one month (whereas *24* takes place over one day). The show is divided into thirty episodes, each documenting the events of a single day. The narrative segment of each episode unfolds linearly; our attention is periodically drawn to the time as it is printed on the screen. The narrative suspense is raised by a question constantly repeated in the show: "What will the world look like in thirty days?" The police narrative, which relies on instituting control and social order, seems a particularly well suited response to the tyranny of time and anxieties about not having enough time in a world increasingly saturated by time-space compression (Harvey 1989).[5] A world taken over by the overwhelming demands of global capitalism needs an international police force that can not only guarantee social order in an increasingly chaotic world but also withstand the domination of time. The film attempts to arrest time into an eternal present. For example, when his friends and colleagues advise him to get some sleep, Huang Sir, a police officer working around the clock hoping to find enough evidence to defeat the triad's operations, tells them he has no time. He wants everything that needs to happen to happen *now*. Ironically, this arresting of time works to create an atmosphere of doom, in which nothing appears to be happening. This produces the effect of a diminishing past (i.e., historical amnesia) and future (i.e., there is no foreseeable future).

In *Split Second*, the past functions as a puzzle that needs resolution but resists it. A man named Wong Sir is slated to become the new Hong Kong police chief, to be officially inaugurated in exactly thirty days. But the triad wants him dead and plans to expand by incorporating all the other triads. The police work against time to stop its operation. Later, a secret is revealed. The leader of the triad—an overseas Chinese man by the name of Zheng Kwan currently living in Thailand—is suspected to be Li Man Ho, a wanted suspect who fled from Hong Kong back in the '60s. If the police can verify his identity, they can arrest him on the old charges and thus shut down the triad's operation. While Kwan wants revenge against Wong Sir for driving him out of Hong Kong, he also exposes Wong Sir as a corrupt cop who took bribes from Kwan only to betray him in the end. Indeed, police corruption was rampant in Hong Kong in the '60s, a theme that is often taken up by Hong Kong televisual serials, and with which audiences in Chinatowns can identify. In Chinatowns, the police were likewise often accused of either colluding with the powerful elite, many of whom had associations with organized crime, or of turning a blind eye on their operations (Kwong 1996: 126).

This revelation throws a wrench into Huang Sir's efforts to prevent the triad's expansion, by raising doubts about the true identity of Wong Sir. All along, Huang Sir is a self-righteous and moralistic officer who believes his job as a police officer is to seek justice unconditionally by going after all criminals, without hesitation or doubt. In scenes where others raise doubts about the efficacy of their operation or where he is told to take his job less seriously so that he can rest properly, he retorts, "I am a cop." In this way, he idealizes the role of police officers as the ultimate purveyors of justice. To the extent that a coherent modern social order depends on the successful subjectification of bodies, policing and the legal system that serves as its foundation play important roles in modernity; they are among the major mechanisms through which people are interpellated into the social order as self-controlled, rational, liberal subjects. It is no wonder, therefore, that police officers and others who work on the side of the law (lawyers, judges, etc.) have become the paradigmatic figures of modern liberal subjectification in Hong Kong television serials. They work, often self-righteously, to forge equivalence between ethics and legality, thus conceiving justice as only possible within the terms of the law. The statement "I am a cop" functions as an alibi, as the last vestige of certainty, for the modern liberal subject threatened by the contradictions of globalism.

But when Huang is thrown into a state of confusion about what is right and who is criminal, he begins to question his ambitions, and as a result his sense of identity. Dong, a Hong Kong Chinese undercover cop whose job is to find evidence against the triad, also questions his identity. He repeatedly asks, "Am I a cop?" For him, the line between being a cop and being a triad member is continually blurred. His question, unlike Huang's, points to the impossibility of being a knowable subject. No longer able to "know" his identity, Dong fails to become a liberal subject aware of his consciousness, intentions, and agency, thus putting in question the ways in which we can come to know and impart justice. Sam, an undercover officer in Thailand, admits, "The longer I work for him [Kwan], the less I know him." Personal relationships between triad members and police officers continually trouble the boundaries that exist between their purported social roles, thus raising questions about the commensurability of legality and ethics that Huang Sir insists on.

Split Second is a new type of Hong Kong television serial that no longer replays the clichéd trope of good vs. evil, and as such, it radically challenges our notions of justice. Toward the end of the serial, the operation falls apart and Huang Sir ends up on friendly terms with Kwan. Vacillating between their identities as cops and crooks, these hybrid characters mirror the promiscuous relationship between the state (as represented by the police) and capital (as represented by the triad). As the world of the serial degenerates into a dystopia and both systems are brought to the point of crisis, the show clears a space for, but ultimately postpones the possibility of, extralegal justice. Hong Kong may have achieved postcoloniality, but as the serial dramatizes, the city still lives with the consequences of hands-off colonial policies that had allowed corrupt practices to go unchecked. Similarly, in Chinatown, racist policies spawned an insular society that was left to its own devices, making collaborations possible between the business and political elite and organized crime.

The officers' identity crises resonate with Hong Kong's fractured sense of identity, both of which are symptoms of the city's globalizing, post-1997 predicament. Split Second portrays a Chinese mafia seeking to become the most powerful triad in Hong Kong history by taking over all the other Hong Kong triads and merging them, along with its own domestic and transnational affiliations and operations, into a corporation. To keep up, the Hong Kong government likewise has to delocalize its police operations and expand them transnationally. The impossibility of achieving transnational justice corresponds to the officers' crises of subjectivity. That is, Hong Kong's inability to achieve a footing in the region and a global identity for itself parallels the officers' inability to become subjects and citizens in a global order they can no longer understand. In a way, Hong Kong's identity crisis is an indicator of the end of Hong Kong exceptionalism (i.e., its exceptional nature as an economic miracle and one of the freest economies in the world). Hong Kong and Thailand (where the other half of the serial was filmed) become similar sites in the sense that neither is able to maintain social order. Unable to maintain social order, Hong Kong won't be able to maintain its exceptional economy either. Instead, it is the underground economy, in the form of the mafia, that strives for exceptionalism in the new world order. As the site of transnational-ization, the mafia acts as a foil to corporate globalism. Relying on ethnic kinship and diasporic ties for its survival and growth, the mafia thrives in places like Hong Kong and Chinatown where familial and ethnic relations are especially strong in the absence of state support.

At the same time, Hong Kong TV travel narratives direct our attention to the global system in which Hong Kong is imbricated by acknowledging Hong Kong modernity's dependency on the developing world, such as Thailand, rural China, and Kenya. Viewers from Chinatown, also a "Third World" site of Hong Kong modernity, may begin to feel a kinship with these locations and to take into account the perspectives of other non-Chinese groups, thus forming a basis for interethnic solidarities.[6] In the Chinatown context, this means letting go of any sense of ethnic parochialism to acknowledge kinship with other racialized groups. An identity crisis becomes an opportunity to align with other groups.[7] Furthermore, like Hong Kong, which no longer represents the model moder-nity, the overseas Hong Kongers and Chinatown can no longer bathe in Hong Kong's glory as paradigmatic figures of the myths of the model modernity and the model minority. In this sense, inter-Asian and interracial relations provide a point of departure for different possibilities of modernity that do not rely solely on diasporic relations, corporatism, or the state.

Form, History, and Spatiality

Unable to solve the mysteries of history, hence leading to the failure of subject formation, *Split Second* resorts to spatiality and form to map the global systems responsible for these rupturing effects. *Split Second*'s hybrid form, which relies on quotations of other popular television shows and films, is exemplary of the post-modernist tradition. According to Simon Malpas (2001: 8), postmodernism can be characterized by a suspicion of metanarratives, otherwise known as "grand narrative[s] of progress." Postmodernism signals the death of grand narratives by calling literary forms and genres into question, thus marking a different relation-ship to conceptions of historical change, knowledge, and truth.[8] *Split Second* and other television shows like it mark the death of the Hong Kong grand narrative of progress and modernity. It generates a desire for historical explanation which the narrative never fulfills, leaving us with a chaotic world of uncertainty, disorder, and unpredictability. This lack of explanation indicates not only that the historical content has changed but also that the meaning and uses of history as an interpre-tive mode for understanding the past need to be put up for questioning. The prior-ity of space over time in *Split Second* is a clear sign that historical changes in Hong

Kong are tied to a larger global system. Understanding the spatial relationships forged in the serial may help us chart this global system, which is rendered indecipherable by teleological narratives of history. Furthermore, popular culture, with its emphasis on the everyday, is perhaps always ahead of other cultural forms in attempting to register change and hence most able to help us understand contemporary changes brought on by late capital.

In *The Last Breakthrough*, the show about medical volunteers, there is no sense of any kind of historical relationship or shared experiences between Kenya and Hong Kong, even though both are Commonwealth nations, or between Africa and Asia more generally. Television offers a way to clean the slate, so to speak, and forge a new historical relationship between Kenya and Hong Kong based on humanitarian aid. Television grounds Hong Kong's and Kenya's postcolonial histories in relation to the changes brought on by globalization rather than in the frameworks of nationalism and imperialism. The playful intermingling of various televisual genres across cultures in these shows defies common invectives against television's ahistoricism (as demonstrated by its banality, repetition, and clichéd content) and forms instead a repository of history that is defined by popular practices.

The popularity of Hong Kong television amongst the overseas Chinese ensures a diasporic intimacy with Hong Kong popular culture and current events. While historical claims and myths of origins may wane as a collective imaginary is formed, the global circulation of Hong Kong popular (and consumer) culture upholds affective links between audiences and Hong Kong Chinese identities. The history of popular culture, therefore, becomes the shared history of the members of the Chinese diaspora. Travel narratives like *Split Second* and *The Last Breakthrough* are both intertextual and intercontextual, borrowing from international (i.e., American) televisual forms and filming in disparate locations. This not only helps these serials travel well; it also helps to establish diasporic ties where they no longer or do not yet exist. In a Chinatown context, the ways we relate to these serials are determined as much by the ways in which we relate to popular culture and popular genres as by the serials' actual content.

Class, Race, and Gender

By setting Hong Kong against Africa, Southeast Asia, and China, *Split Second* and *The Last Breakthrough* map the uneven development that marks the current international division of labor. Hong Kong is the global finance center that dispenses tourists and aid workers to the rest of the world. A "modern," cosmopolitan Hong Kong is set in contrast to the "backward" world of Africa, China, and Southeast Asia, where disease and crime run rampant. These "other" places become sites of romanticism and idealism, ways to find a meaningful future. Africa in *The Last Breakthrough*, for example, is a site of courage and life. The Hong Kong doctors who work there find their own problems trivial in comparison to the problems that the Africans face. They also tap into the courage of survival they find in Africa as inspiration to live their own lives to the fullest. They adopt the ideals they learn from Africa as the operating principles of a community-based clinic called Long Sing that they run in Hong Kong. By traveling to other places, these Hong Kong people are able to find the identity and futurity they need in order to live within a crisis-ridden Hong Kong, where imaginations of identity and the future are continually put up to question. Travel, in this sense, is a way not to leave Hong Kong but to imagine a global community of which Hong Kong is the center. For Chinatown viewers, Hong Kong's path to becoming a global center becomes the site of futurity, a new kind of diasporic vision, that, unlike conventional diasporas, does not nostalgically advocate a return to a lost past.[9] This vision is made possible partly by the contemporaneity of Hong Kong television's travel narratives, in both their content and their mode of circulation (i.e., simultaneous broadcasting). Furthermore, the ways in which "home" becomes a transnationalized concept rather than a site-specific location (i.e., Hong Kong), facilitated by a common language, cultural practices, politics, and ideology, work to broaden the scope of Hong Kong culture's influence on other locations by mediating a sense of Hong Kong as a transnationalized local of which Chinatown is a part.

In a world networked according to the needs of the new global economy, *The Last Breakthrough* and *Split Second* try to put in place a new kind of internationalism that prioritizes humanism and moralism over profit. *Split Second* provides a critique of the global economy through its portrayal of the international Chinese mafia, which typifies the processes of transnational corporatization and late capitalism. Kwan and his son, Hao, aim to incorporate all the Chinese triads (which are broken into factions) into one body that they, as chief executives, will run as a corporation, one not unlike the family-run corporations widely depicted on Hong Kong TV melodramas. All of these triads have become transnational in nature, with branches in other parts of the region, such as Thailand, run by wealthy *huaqiaos* (overseas Chinese). These triads are both offsprings and generators of transnational capital. The program also shows the ways in which the Chinese diaspora is responsible for the uneven development and violence in the region and within the diaspora itself, such as the fact that co-ethnic employers are some of the worst exploiters of labor. The transnational triad that strives for exceptionalism in the global economy is an indication of globalism gone awry. A transnational police force tries to reestablish moral order in the face of the violence that threatens to undo it. Where transnational corporatization supersedes policing by state regimes, the transnational police emerge as a new regulatory body that attempts to do what the state cannot do alone. This new regulatory body represents the collaboration of police forces from multiple locations, whose purpose is to put a stop to transnational corporatism, or monopoly capitalism by another name, in the form of the transnational Chinese triad. The fraternal sentiments that unite the police, however, recall too much of the familial and diasporic binds that support transnational corporate capital, making it impossible at times for the state and its representatives to distinguish between these two structures.

While the transnational police provide an implicit critique of the transnational mafia and the global capital it represents, *Split Second* equally problematizes the values of the police and the state that it represents. When Hao is urged by his best friend, who is a police officer, to abandon his triad operations, he retorts, "Why must everything be black and white? Why can't there be grey in the world?" *Split Second* seems to imply that although values must be found that are not associated with capital, we cannot find them in existing moral regimes. When the police operation and the triad's vision both fail to materialize results, the serial clears a space for us to envision alternative values and morals that might finally enact the justice that capitalism (as represented by the triad) and state structures (as represented by the police) could not. By revealing the violence embedded in diasporic affiliations (e.g., the transnational Chinese mafia and co-ethnic exploitation), the serial also troubles the subversive potential of diasporic unity as a counter-hegemonic force to capitalist exploitation and racism.

While *Split Second* gestures toward the impossibilities of liberal subjectivity, *The Last Breakthrough* portrays international healthcare workers as the new humanist, liberal, cosmopolitan subjects. They are the agents of a new internationalism based on spreading Western science and its version of universal healthcare. These doctors go to underdeveloped and traditional societies in Kenya and Guanxi (China) to teach them the principles of nutrition and of disease prevention and management. A fundamental part of their job is to change the way people think—their ideologies and their principles. They are liberal subjects who try not to be arrogant or judgmental about the beliefs of other cultures. Their lectures and discussions with volunteers serve as primers for understanding cross-cultural differences. In this way, they try to be open-minded humanistic subjects, and their sympathy and compassion for others turn out to be the frame of mind suitable for dealing with transnational differences and inequalities.

The entire philosophy of the Long Sing clinic is to establish a trusting and intimate relationship with patients and to listen to their wishes. The serial establishes a distinction from the beginning between the compassionate doctor, whose healing powers go well beyond his scientific skills, and the arrogant doctor, who relies on advanced technology and the superiority of Western ethics. Curing the ailments of individual patients is often beyond the ability of technology and science, thus implying that medicine cannot be entirely grounded in science. One of the doctors, for example, is criticized by another for using unscientific and "irrational" means to cure his patients (e.g., he talks to his patients during operations; he knows how to draw out his patients' feelings of strength), yet he is able to perform "miracles." Long Sing is contrasted to the private hospital that funds it, which is more interested in making a profit and balancing the budget. All in all, Long Sing represents a new kind of medicine, one that relies on emotions and sympathy. By viewing this new medicine as superior, the serial implicitly critiques the so-called advances made by technological and economic development. Unlike the political internationalisms of an earlier period (i.e., Marxist and Maoist movements of the 1960s) or the economic internationalisms of global capital, *The Last Breakthrough* proposes a new internationalism based on sentimentalism and nostalgia, facilitated by the needs of medicine and public health. Through its international circulation, this serial uses affect to mobilize identification with Hong Kong and across cultures.

The doctors' liberal open-mindedness is equally based on a certain kind of paternalism. They romanticize Africa as the site of life, courage, and lost love. One of the doctors has a girlfriend who is a devoted member of Life Force. Unfortunately, she dies in an accident. Going to Africa is a way for her boyfriend to remember her and be with her in spirit. Moreover, the shots of the sweeping and breathtaking African landscape buttress the nostalgia and sentimentalism that run through the entire serial. The bird's-eye views of the land we are given place us in a position of power, allowing us to take ownership of the land. Righteous outbursts against the "incivility" of African practices pepper the serial throughout. Although these doctors try not to be overly idealistic or to assume that they can become heroes and change society single-handedly, their belief that their values are better proves that their humanism and openness are parochial in nature. Eurocentric ideals are carried through the non-European body, an indication perhaps that Hong Kong (as the paradigmatic "modern" Asian city) is emulating and even co-opting Western forms of modernity. An international human rights movement (in the sense that the serial is advocating for improvements in international healthcare) is still inevitably racialized.[10]

The serial begins with one of the new doctors, who encounters Africans for the first time. When two Kenyans chase after him to return a pen he dropped, he thinks they are trying to threaten him. He cannot stomach the food he eats. He doesn't know how to take blood from African patients because he cannot find their veins. Gradually, however, he overcomes his prejudices and ignorance. By learning to deal with racial differences, albeit in paternalistic ways, these traveling doctors reestablish Hong Kong's exceptionalism as a global and cosmopolitan culture that is immune to racial prejudice (although not in the sense of an exceptional modernity or economy). They replace, in this sense, the exceptionalism and paternalism of the Western liberal subject.[11] The fact that these cosmopolitan characters are often Western-educated or returnees from the West leads us to ask an interesting question: Can their cosmopolitanism be considered a form of Chinese American, Chinese British, or Chinese Australian identity? Is the Chinese American, just to take one example, as a subject able to straddle multiple hybrid identities, exemplary of the transnational, cosmopolitan subject of Hong Kong?

These narratives of travel also explore the possibilities of new sites of intimacies under globalism. In *The Last Breakthrough* and *Split Second*, travel opens a path for romance, but unlike earlier romance serials these shows explore interracial relationships. In *Split Second*, Rita, a Thai police officer, falls in love with Dong, a Hong Kong Chinese undercover cop. In *The Last Breakthrough*, Susan, a Hong Kong Chinese volunteer who speaks American English, marries Don, one of the Kenyan medical workers. Though Susan has problems with the patriarchal nature of Don's culture, love conquers in the end and they resolve their differences. In this sense, romantic heterosexual love offers a way for us to connect cross-culturally in a globalizing world.

Split Second offers another, more interesting take on intimacy. The distinctions between the cops and the robbers in the series gradually erode as each side gets involved with the other in intimate ways. Sam, for instance, is an undercover cop who, having worked with the godfather of the triad for more than ten years, sees him equally as a father figure and as the criminal he is supposed to arrest. The serial directs our attention to the intimacies between men of different backgrounds, interests, and personalities and to how these intimacies are used to subvert their roles as cops or robbers in terms that can help us build deep and politicizing cross-racial and cross-cultural relationships.

Split Second and *The Last Breakthrough* call for a new Hong Kong identity, based not in heroism or insular forms of fraternity (as is the case in Hong Kong family melodramas) but in intimacy, flexibility, and humility. In *Split Second*, the undercover officers are told they can become good officers if they don't strive to become a hero or a "brother." The doctors in *The Last Breakthrough* are told they shouldn't be too idealistic or try to change society single-handedly. Instead, they need to become more flexible by letting go of moral orthodoxies. However, the officers in *Split Second* all lose their sense of themselves as their world devolves into chaos. In the end, they all find a new purpose in life and, faced with despair and death, want to give up their careers and wealth in exchange for new futures with the women they love. Unfortunately, it's too late. Sam, the Thai undercover officer, and Dong, the Hong Kong Chinese one, are both shot and struggle, as they die, to reach the women they love. As Fung, another police officer, is being chased by Thai officers, he hallucinates that he sees his girlfriend waiting for him. Huang Sir calls Vicky, a colleague who's in love with him, to tell her that he's done with his business in Thailand and would like her to pick him up at the airport the next day. But he is riddled with brain cancer, and as he closes his eyes to take a nap, we are left wondering if he'll ever wake up. Whereas the characters in *The Last Breakthrough* were able to achieve subjectivity by emulating Western liberalism, for the men in *Split Second* liberal subjectivity is neither achievable nor sustainable in the face of transnational corporatism and the crisis of the state. They can point to, but realize only belatedly, the intimacies and moral flexibility that might have made a difference in their quest for subjectivity.

Split Second registers Hong Kong's identity crisis as it is embodied by primarily male middle-class subjects. In fact, these subjects seem to point to the impossibility of becoming proper liberal autonomous subjects in a capitalist and global world order. Instead, they gesture toward the women in the shows as solutions to their identity crises. While the men have trouble finding a role in the new global economy, the women seem untroubled by the uncertainties of the new world order. No longer relegated to the domestic sphere, women can adapt to the uncertainties of globalism, and this ability makes them the most suitable subjects for the future upkeep of Hong Kong's place in the global sphere. From being domestic housekeepers, women promise to become global housekeepers.

Always seen as an ethnic ghetto existing on the fringes of American society, a place that failed to become a small Hong Kong and is instead a passive receptacle of Hong Kong media, Chinatown, it seems, will always be the "other" of these televisual discourses (Kwong 1996). Its proletarian and working-class profile, policing by state institutions, and marginalization from U.S. national culture prevent Chinatown from identifying with the rising Hong Kong middle class, the romance and privileges of travel, and Hong Kong's role as regional police and moral missionary depicted in these serials. Yet, in a paradoxical way, these programs also provide a way for Chinese diasporic viewers to form identities vis-à-vis the "others" within the televisual texts—the Kenyans, ethnic minorities, and Southeast Asians. This dual process of interpellating and "othering" Chinatown publics works on the one hand to consolidate a wider Hong Kong diasporic imaginary and on the other to reveal the uneven power relations implicit in diasporic and racial or cross-cultural relationships.

The television serials discussed in this essay are important contributions to racial discourses in the U.S. Instead of focusing on white–Asian relations, these shows ask that we consider inter-Asian and interminority dynamics vis-à-vis Hong Kong, which in turn help us reflect upon Asian American and minority identities in the U.S. An analysis of these texts within a Chinatown context helps us to, as Lowe (2001: 273) suggests, "supplement an Asian American notion of racial formation within one nation-state with an understanding of the multiple contexts of colonialism and its various extensions within the uneven development of neocolonial capitalism." In other words, racial identity in any given Chinatown is bounded by racial relations not only within the country where it is found but also within the larger Chinese diaspora as it intersects with East Asian, Southeast Asian, and African contexts. How, in other words, do we understand the Afro-Asian relations depicted on *The Last Breakthrough* with respect, for example, to Asian American and African American relations in the U.S.? How do representations of Afro-Asian relations compare with those of inter-Asian relations? What kind of racial hierarchies do they set up?

Conclusion

In the American context, the circulation of Hong Kong TV travel narratives in Chinatowns has produced a cross-border geography of shared cultural imaginaries and disjunctive modernities, which in turn have mediated formations of Chinese immigrant identities that have little to do with the narratives of "claiming America" and becoming "American" that have dominated an earlier period of Asian American politics. These televisual encounters produce a transnational imaginary centered on similar experiences of modernity and shared cultural practices while simultaneously exposing the racial, class, and gender contradictions and differences that modernity requires. They highlight Hong Kong and Chinatown's mutual dependency: Chinatown's investment in fantasies of a future like Hong Kong's; Hong Kong's imbrication in a globalism that relies on developing and informal economies like Chinatown's. The travel narrative provides an opportunity for Chinatown and Hong Kong to situate themselves within a larger global network and, by doing so, to rethink their relationship to modernity as mediated through each other and other sites of modernity. While Hong Kong television shows have always been thematically concerned with the experiences of modernity, the rise of the travel narrative since 1997 has elucidated the particular anxieties and consciousness of a historical moment in which modernity coincides with global, postcolonial, and postmodern forms. Travel emerges as a key force in articulating and coping with the predicament of global modernity.

Hong Kong television provides fantasies of travel as mechanisms for coping with the feelings of isolation and carcerality that structure the experiences of Chinatown's modernity within the fabric of imperialism and globalism. Travel narratives valorize travel by focusing on the love and romance of self-discovery that faraway and exotic places (e.g., Rome, Hawaii) stir up. They provide a means for Hong Kong and diasporic viewers to travel to these places by way of the televisual medium. These shows essentially aid the circulation of both commodities (e.g., technology, popular culture) and persons (e.g., through travel), two circulations that are key to a globalizing economy. Yet travel takes on a different register when we consider Hong Kong television as a traveling medium that traverses multiple boundaries. James Clifford considers travel in the form of watching television as a kind of travel-in-dwelling. Clifford also stresses his use of travel as a "term of cultural comparison" and as a "translation term" (1997: 110). Hong Kong television provides a site of encounter between Hong Kong and global Chinatowns that elucidates the transnational diasporic networks that connect them. By examining how reception contexts that are not reflected on the television screen can nonetheless be figured in televisual narratives, this essay provides a framework for thinking about Hong Kong television as a location that activates translation and comparison between different diasporic spaces, sites and experiences of urban modernity, and colonial models.[12] At the same time, viewers and critics must also bring to bear their own knowledge of these different contexts in order to draw out the nuances of the text.

Notes

1. TVB's programs have all been recently subtitled in Chinese, as the company aims to move beyond its Cantonese markets to capture a wider Chinese audience in Taiwan, China, and Chinese diasporas all over the world.

2. See, for example, *Healing Hands I, II, III (Miaoshou renxin I, II, III)* (aired 1998, 2000–2001, 2005) and *Files of Justice I–V (Yihao huangting I–IV)* (aired 1992–1995, 1997).

3. The growth of these travel narratives also coincided with TVB's development of satellite broadcasting, which helps these shows spread faster and more widely. The obsession with time and space in these narratives is perhaps a timely response to advances in telecommunications and technology.

4. In *Split Second*, some police officers are actually undercover agents for the triad. This gimmick was used in the *Infernal Affairs* trilogy (Hong Kong: Miramax, 2002, 2003, dir. Andrew Lau and Alan Mak), in which an undercover triad member works as a police officer. The serial also makes numerous references to Buddhism (e.g., the triad members are fervent believers), again resonating with the Buddhist expressions capping the end of each movie. One of the officers in *Split Second* loses his gun, which partly mirrors the plot line of *PTU* (Hong Kong: Palm Pictures, 2003, dir. Johnnie To). The popular American television show *24* runs over twenty-four episodes, each episode recounting the events of one hour of a day. Its narrative suspense derives from the necessity of stopping a criminal operation within the twenty-four hours. The 2007 season of the show, for example, features an anti-terrorist operation that must succeed against the limits of time if the United States is to be saved from terrorist attacks. Similarly, *PTU's* narrative takes place over the course of one night and tells the story of a police officer's race against time to recover his missing gun before dawn, when he will have to file a police report, and before it can be used to commit a crime.

5. For example, Huang Sir in *Split Second* works on his case for days without sleeping. He feels a sense of urgency because he has a life-threatening brain tumor. He chooses to battle against time instead of his illness.

6. Restructuring in and differential state support for media industries have made it often cheaper and more appealing to film overseas, and many Hong Kong television

serials now do so. Therefore, Hong Kong's kinship with Thailand may be partly due to new intricate linkages between the two countries' economies.

7. Similarly, the residents of major U.S. Chinatown, who are largely Hong Kong Cantonese, must also reckon with the growing number of co-ethnic compatriots emigrating from mainland China, just as the people in Hong Kong must. Parallels can be drawn between Hong Kong's identity crisis as a postcolonial society and the racialized identity crisis of Chinese Americans.

8. This breakdown in form can be characterized by fragmentation, schizophrenia, pastiche, the priority of space over time, intertextuality (which erases the boundaries between high and low culture), the death of the unitary subject, and an emphasis on the image (or simulacrum, i.e., a photographic negative of the world). I have gleaned most of these postmodernist features from Fredric Jameson (1984: 65), who describes schizophrenic writing as a breakdown in the signifying chain and pastiche as a "neutral form of mimicry."

9. Even though *Split Second*, unlike *The Last Breakthrough*, ends on a dystopic note, the serial does gesture toward "home" as a redemptive site (each of the dying male characters tries to imagine a different life, in which he can return to a heterosexual home).

10. For more on Afro-Asian relations in popular media, see Marchetti 2001; Joseph 1999.

11. Some of the new Hong Kong serials have also begun to use more English, the lingua franca of the new global economy. See, for example, *Yummy Yummy*, which is partly filmed in Singapore and features several Singaporean actors. In *The Last Breakthrough*, Kenyan and Hong Kong translators communicate with each other in English.

12. Yet it is also important to bear in mind, as Clifford (1997: 110) warns, that these types of translations are used "for comparison in a strategic and contingent way. . . . [I]t offers a good reminder that all translation terms used in global comparisons . . . get us some distance and fall apart."

References

Anderson, Kay J. 1991. *Vancouver's Chinatown: Racial Discourse in Canada, 1875–1980.* Montreal: McGill-Queen's University Press.

Chow, Rey. 1992. "Between Colonizers: Hong Kong's Postcolonial Self-Writing in the 1990s." *Diaspora* 2, no. 2:151–170.

Chu, Yiu-Wai. 2004. "Introduction: The Politics of Home, Memory, and Diaspora." In *Between Home and World: A Reader in Hong Kong Cinema*, ed. Esther Cheung and Yiu-Wai Chu, 112–126. Hong Kong: Oxford University Press.

Chua Beng Huat. 2004. "Conceptualizing an East Asian Popular Culture." *Inter-Asia Cultural Studies* 5, no. 2:200–221.

Clifford, James. 1997. *Routes: Travel and Translation in the Late Twentieth Century.* Cambridge, Mass.: Harvard University Press.

Eng, David L. 2001. *Racial Castration: Managing Masculinity in Asian America.* Durham, N.C.: Duke University Press.

Fong, Timothy. 1994. *The First Suburban Chinatown: The Remaking of Monterey Park, California.* Philadelphia, Penn.: Temple University Press.

Harvey, David. 1989. *The Condition of Postmodernity: An Enquiry into the Origins of Cultural Change.* Oxford: Blackwell.

Iwabuchi, Koichi, ed. 2004. *Feeling Asian Modernities: Transnational Consumption of Japanese TV Dramas.* Hong Kong: Hong Kong University Press.

Jameson, Fredric. 1984. "Postmodernism, or the Cultural Logic of Late Capitalism." *New Left Review* 146:53–92.

Joseph, May. 1999. *Nomadic Identities: The Performance of Citizenship.* Minneapolis: University of Minneapolis Press.

Kwong, Peter. 1996. *The New Chinatown.* New York: Hill and Wang.

Laguerre, Michel S. 2000. *The Global Ethnopolis: Chinatown, Japantown, and Manilatown in American Society.* New York: St. Martin's.

Lee, Benjamin. 1993. "Going Public." *Public Culture* 5:165–178.

Leung, Lisa Yuk-Ming. 2004. "Ganbaru and Its Transcultural Audience: Imaginary and Reality of Japanese TV Dramas in Hong Kong." In *Feeling Asian Modernities: Transnational Consumption of Japanese TV Dramas,* ed. Koichi Iwabuchi, 89–106. Hong Kong: Hong Kong University Press.

Lin, Jan. 1998. *Reconstructing Chinatown: Ethnic Enclave, Global Change.* Minneapolis: University of Minnesota Press.

Lo, Kwai-cheung. 2001. "Transnationalization of the Local in Hong Kong Cinema of the 1990s." In *At Full Speed: Hong Kong Cinema in a Borderless World,* ed. Esther C. M. Yau, 261–275. Minneapolis: University of Minnesota Press.

Lowe, Lisa. 2001. "Epistemological Shifts: National Ontology and the New Asian Immigrant." In *Orientations: Mapping Studies in the Asian Diaspora,* ed. Kandice Chuh and Karen Shimakawa, 267–275. Durham, N.C.: Duke University Press.

Lu, Sheldon. 2000. "Filming Diaspora and Identity: Hong Kong and 1997." In *The Cinema of Hong Kong: History, Arts, Identity,* ed. Poshek Fu and David Desser, 273–288. Cambridge: Cambridge University Press.

Malpas, Simon. 2001. Introduction to *Postmodern Debates,* ed. Simon Malpas. New York: Palgrave.

Marchetti, Gina. 2001. "Jackie Chan and the Black Connection." In *Keyframes: Popular Cinema and Cultural Studies,* ed. Matthew Tinkcom and Amy Villarejo, 137–158. London: Routledge.

Okihiro, Gary Y. 2001. *The Columbia Guide to Asian American History.* New York: Columbia University Press.

Ong, Aihwa. 1999. *Flexible Citizenship: The Cultural Logics of Transnationality.* Durham, N.C.: Duke University Press.

Palumbo-Liu, David. 1999. *Asian/American: Historical Crossings of a Racial Frontier.* Stanford, Calif.: Stanford University Press.

To, Yiu-ming, and Tuen-yu Lau. 1995. "Global Export of Hong Kong Television: Television Broadcasts Limited." *Asian Journal of Communication* 5, no. 2:108–121.

TVB (Television Broadcasts Limited). 2006. "Corporate Information." Hong Kong: Television Broadcasts Limited. http://www.tvb.com/affairs/faq/tvbgroup/tvb_e.html (accessed 15 May 2006).

Wong, Cindy H.-Y. 1999. "Cities, Cultures, and Cassettes: Hong Kong Cinema and Transnational Audiences." *Post Script* 19, no. 1:87–106.

Yang, Mayfair Mei-Hui. 1999. Introduction to *Spaces of Their Own: Women's Public Sphere in Transnational China,* ed. Mayfair Mei-Hui Yang, 1–34. Minneapolis: University of Minnesota Press.

Zhou, Min. 1992. *Chinatown: The Socioeconomic Potential of an Urban Enclave.* Philadelphia, Penn.: Temple University Press.

Globalizing Television: Chinese Satellite Television outside Greater China

CINDY HING-YUK WONG

Within contemporary global communication, television has been character-ized by a localized/nationalized public sphere, oftentimes hierarchical. Broad-cast television caters to geographically and culturally defined audiences, whether via "local" news in an American corporate sense or in cultural citizen-ship shaped by national broadcasting networks, both public and private, world-wide (see, e.g., Bullert 1997; Hong 1998; Streeter 1996; Hartley 1999; Mankekar 1999; Kumar 2006). Even when "content" (e.g., programs) "moves" from one national context to another—Latin American soap operas across the Western hemisphere or U.S. hits like *Dallas* onto international screens—criticism has engaged the delocalization of the global within national distribution and audi-ence interpretation (Ang 1985; Sinclair 2000). Moreover, governments have constantly intervened in, operated, or regulated broadcast television as a part of the construction of nation-states as imagined communities and thus have sought to limit incursions from abroad, whether broadcast across borders or "sold" for transnational use (Anderson 1991; Hong 1998; Streeter 1996; Kumar 2006).

Satellite television, however, embodies technologies that ignore national borders and even population geography through broad and diffuse dissemination. Its viewers may be widespread, connected through voluntary (paid) choices that differentiate them from their neighbors. At the same time, satellite television offers global immediacy. Rather than repackaged programming (which it may incorporate), satellite television promises live connections through transnational shared visions: Arabic-language reports on the war in Iraq from correspondents uncensored by Allied forces, or live coverage of "local" crises or celebrations for distant viewers. Governments can construct political, economic, or technical barriers to undesirable programming. The material structures of production and paid distribution also delineate selected audiences. Yet other techniques overcome limitations and share satellite transmission beyond commercial limits (e.g., videotaping soap operas). In the end, the culture of satellite television as a "global/local" medium is incompletely filtered through negotiations of sovereignty and desire.

In China, as other essays in this volume show, television has long been controlled by and reinforced the nation-state, with minor spillage across the Hong Kong and Macau borders into already-suspect Guangdong. In recent years, Rupert Murdoch's international STAR TV and the Chinese Phoenix Television also have entered Chinese airspace from Hong Kong. Murdoch once prophesied that satellite television would end authoritarian regimes; Chinese authorities, in turn, cracked down on STAR's satellite broadcasts. Murdoch's stormy negotiations with China produced the hybrid Xing Kong (Starry Sky) channel, which broadcasts Mandarin/Putonghua repackaging of Western programs via cable in the south and via satellite elsewhere to luxury hotels and expatriate homes. Meanwhile, these media have raised international controversy over whether Western conglomerates have kowtowed to Beijing authorities for access to the Chinese market (J. Chan 2003; Curtin 2005; Barboza 2006; Thompson 2006).[1] Chinese producers have also created alliances with foreign networks in Guangzhou TV and NBC Asia (Kwong 1998). And wealthier Chinese who own pirate satellite dishes easily receive world news, Filipino evangelization, and pornography.

Apart from debates about globalizing media within China, another creative televisual universe has emerged through satellite television transmission abroad of content in Chinese languages. Here, diverse linguistic, political, economic, and cultural forms of production look outward from China and "Greater Chinese" points of dissemination beyond the nation-state to a larger imagined diasporic Chinese "audience" worldwide. Globalized, yet diverse, satellite television in Chinese languages projects China (or a Wittgensteinian set of Chinese family resemblances) to diasporic but equally diverse Chinese speakers.

Satellite television entails commercial expansion as well as more political and cultural attempts to foster a new Greater China, but broadcasts are repackaged within different Chinese contexts, including the U.S. Global Chinese thus receive "non-Hollywood" media content that originated mainly from "home," but these Chinese recreate these media through spectatorship in new contexts.

This essay concentrates on Chinese-language satellite television in the United States (with glances toward other overseas Chinese and other ethnic immigrant American audiences). I first situate satellite production within a range of choices open to culturally diverse American Chinese. I then look more closely at content through the Hong Kong–based TVB/Jadeworld package. Hong Kong, initially a British colonial creation within South China coastal society, retains certain freedoms of ownership, expression, and creativity that situate it outside China and its national media. It has long been a gateway linking mainland China to overseas Chinese through trade, transportation, and global networks (Cartier 2001; McDonogh and Wong 2005). Hence it represents a vanguard for both Chinese praxis and global communication. Hong Kong media, especially television, also raise interesting questions about the local language (Cantonese) and its cultural implications for Greater China. In discussing context, I will compare TVB/Jadeworld both to state broadcasts by CCTV and to the hybrid Hong Kong–based Phoenix satellite station, especially with regard to news. Finally, I also seek to understand a global or pan-Chinese audience, drawing on textual data as well as limited ethnographic experience with these media among family and friends.

Chinese-language(s) satellite TV represents only one of the many communicative tools mainland and overseas Chinese have used to construct a global community. In the nineteenth century, communication was often interpersonal and fragmented, mediated by *jinshanzhuang* (Golden Mountain Chinese firms), especially in Hong Kong, that transmitted remittances and other communications between Chinese in North and South America and Australia and families left behind (Hsu 2000). Overseas Chinese soon produced their own media in new worlds, primarily newspapers mixing local news, reports from Guangdong, shipping and business news, and advertisements. The reopening of Chinese immigration to the U.S. since the 1960s has sustained several score Chinese newspapers available in global and local editions in Chinatowns and on the web. American-based newspapers and radio, like books, magazines, and videotapes from Greater China (Wong 1999), have facilitated communications amongst Chinese in different parts of the world and have reproduced aspects of Chinese culture in geographically dispersed places, as have more interpersonal channels like telephones, faxes, and most recently, the internet.

Phoenix's chairman, Liu Chang-le, has claimed that "Phoenix uses its own platform to spread Chinese culture and unites the Chinese communities around the world, with Mainland China, Taiwan and Hong Kong as its main target. With the help of experienced staff, Phoenix can surely maintain its position in the highly competitive global Chinese language television market and deliver the best programming to the Chinese people worldwide" (Liu Chang-le 2004). Through commercial interests, immigrants' desire to connect to the homeland, and attempts by the mainland Chinese government (and other entities) to build relationships with overseas Chinese, a diverse, multi-faceted mosaic has been created that reminds us that globalization in media does not simply drop "from the sky" (Curtin 2005) or even "from the West." By examining the global reach of Chinese-language satellite television, then, this essay strives to understand how diverse senses of "Chineseness" are mediated and how this multiply transmitted China becomes a modern, cosmopolitan project beyond national boundaries.

Producing and Distributing Global Chineseness

Chinese satellite content providers who reach U.S. markets are based in China, Hong Kong, Taiwan, and the U.S. Transmission requires gaining access to satellites owned by companies or national or international authorities, such as the Chinese government and Eurosat. Those who subscribe to satellite television are primarily served by companies that have their own wide distribution systems and satellite dishes, including major American companies like DirecTV and Echostar (Dish Network). Another kind of satellite dish, known as "the little ear," requires direct contact with producers, such as small Buddhist networks, and reaches a much smaller audience. In its early years, Hong Kong–based Television Broadcasts Limited (TVB) was only available through the little ear; in 2003, its subsidiary, TVB Satellite Inc., negotiated a new package, called Jadeworld, for American distribution through DirecTV. KyLin TV (discussed below) is the first U.S.-based retransmission package to become available through the internet instead of a dish.

There are an estimated 2 million Chinese-speaking households in the U.S., although it is not clear how many subscribe to cable or satellite television services. Jadeworld, for example, claims 50,000 subscribers. Obviously, this market is dwarfed by that of China itself, with 340 million or more TV households and perhaps 25 million digital TV households, but the sheer level of U.S. competition suggests high interest among satellite television providers and their sponsors and advertisers.[2] Programs are produced in Mandarin, Cantonese (Hong Kong/Guangdong), Min (spoken in Fujian), Taiwanese, and Japanese; some bear subtitles in Chinese (and occasionally English for Hong Kong films). Political, cultural, and stylistic differences in programming, as well as in differences in language, depend on place of origin (and its ties to local audiences). Yet many packages for American subscribers combine mainland, Taiwanese, and Hong Kong channels and languages.

The most important satellite broadcaster of mainland China is the nationally run CCTV (Chinese Central Television), the official channel of the People's Republic. CCTV represents a dynamic nationwide network of stations with many channels in Mandarin. Both CCTV-4 (Mandarin) and CCTV-9 (English) have an international orientation. Through them, CCTV reaches all over the world, boasting an international viewership of 10 million for CCTV-4 and 40 million for CCTV-9. DirecTV offers both as part of its basic satellite package. Yet CCTV also responds to international markets. In 2004, two channels changed format to court new audiences: CCTV-3 (general) and CCTV-5 (sports) became CCTV-youth and CCTV-music, respectively. Some provincial and metropolitan stations, such as Guangzhou TV and Jiangsu TV, also transmit abroad. While CCTV has announced plans for other foreign-language channels, including French and Spanish, these have not yet emerged (Christy Liu 2004).

To attract U.S. subscribers, CCTV and Echostar launched the Great Wall Platform in October 2004. This package offers sixteen channels, ATV from Hong Kong and fifteen mainland channels: Beijing TV, four CCTV channels, China Movie Channel, DRAGN, FUJTV (from Fujian), GUAND (from Guangdong), HUNAN, JIATV (from Jiangsu), PACTV, Phoenix Info, Phoenix, and SHANX (from Shanxi). Shortly after its launch, the Chinese International TV Corporation made the package available throughout Vietnam, Thailand, South Korea, Myanmar, Hong Kong, Macau, and Taiwan. This wide availability suggests that producers believe in a core Chineseness that will appeal to widely separated and extremely heterogeneous Chinese populations. CCTV has expanded in cooperation with Hong Kong's Tom Group, offering new programming borrowing Western models (*TV Court*) or inverting them, as in the male beauty pageant of *Women in Control*. These innovations have been picked up by Murdoch's Starry Sky Channel (Borton 2004a). China's most popular recent program, *Super Girl*, originated on Hunan Satellite TV. Despite such variety and international outreach, CCTV has often been identified with stultifying political broadcasts and anodyne features on China's beauty or other patriotic themes reifying its role as a national television broadcast network (J. Chan 2003).

Taiwan also boasts a long history of competing commercial and cable networks that provide a foundation for satellite distribution. ETTV Eastern Television, a division of the huge Eastern Multimedia conglomerate, signed a deal in 2003 with Echostar for a distinctive "Taiwan" package offering ET-News, ET-Drama, ET-Global, the Yoyo children's channel, and JET-TV, a Japanese-language channel with Chinese subtitles. The package is unique in its appeal to a (Mandarin-speaking) children's market, while JET bridges Taiwan's colonial past with the formidable presence of Japanese modernity throughout East Asia (Heaney 2003). Smaller producers in Taiwan offer three Buddhist channels to American markets: Buddhist Light TV, Tzu-Chi TV (affiliated with Da-Ai TV), and Hwazan Satellite TV. These broadcast in both Mandarin and Taiwanese; their content contrasts with the secularization of television in the mainland and Hong Kong.

Despite its small size and anomalous status as part of "One Country, Two Systems," Hong Kong represents a major site for Chinese television production, as it does for film production. Hong Kong was the first British colony to get television; under colonial rule it had the government station and two private commercial stations, Asia Television Limited (ATV) and Television Broadcasts Limited (TVB), both of which have aggressively courted global markets. ATV was founded in 1957 as a cable channel named Rediffusion. It changed to free-to-air broadcasting as ATV in 1982. Since then, it has been owned by Hong Kong and Australian investors; Phoenix has invested heavily in it since 2002, expanding its reach in satellite bundling. TVB originated in 1967 as a private firm controlled by transnational media mogul Sir Run Run Shaw. This conglomerate owns 45,000 hours of archived programming and produces 6,000 hours of programming annually for local Hong Kong viewers and international distribution. Its international subsidiary, TVB International (TVBI), established in 1976, distributes TVB-produced programming, from serial dramas and sitcoms to documentaries, news, musical specials, variety and talk shows, and travelogues, through videotape and DVD, cable, and satellite. It also handles advertising and licensing TVB programs and stations abroad, reaching audiences in Taiwan, Southeast Asia, Australia, Europe, and North and South America.

Since 1984, TVB has owned and operated North American cable TV stations, first in Los Angeles and then in San Francisco, which distribute its Chinese-language Jade Channel cable service. Even before 1997, TVB saw its local income stagnating; a small territory of 6.6 million people could hardly sustain more growth. In December 1994, TVB (USA) Inc. began delivering the 24-hour Jade Channel via satellite directly to Chinese-speaking audiences nationwide; according to its website, "the combined reach of the Jade Cable and Jade Satellite services measured nearly 50,000 American Chinese households—an estimated 200,000 affluent, influential viewers!" Like the Hong Kong film industry, TVB can only be viable with a global market (Curtin 2004)

Since 2003, TVB has been available through DirectTV, which boasts a major American satellite system and widely standardized equipment. For $36.99 monthly, subscribing American households receive five Jadeworld Channels—Jade East, Jade West, Jade Super, Movie Channel, and CCTV4 (DirectTV channel numbers 450–454). Jade East and West are Cantonese-language stations relaying TVB programming geared to East and West Coast time zones. Jade Super is TVB's Taiwan (Mandarin) satellite station. Some have accused Jade Super of being a mainland mouthpiece because of its criticisms of Taiwanese president Chen Shui-Bian, who has advocated the independence of Taiwan.

But this criticism may also represent Hong Kong's ambivalent political status. The Movie Channel utilizes TVB's vast movie library, including Cantonese- and Mandarin-language films, while establishing nostalgic connections to those who grew up in the golden age of Hong Kong cinema. Finally, CCTV4 is the free Mandarin-language international channel. Subscribers receive monthly program listings for all channels. (While not part of the package, CCTV-9, the English channel, comes free of charge to DirectTV subscribers.)

This package thus offers channels that originate in three different Chinas: Hong Kong, Taiwan, and the mainland. Even though the Taiwan channel is a Hong Kong–owned station, this TVB package evokes an audience beyond immigrants from Hong Kong or other Cantonese-dominated areas (including past immigrants). In fact, most dramatic programs are broadcast in both Cantonese and Mandarin, emphasizing the bilingualism of overseas Chinese. Still, American audiences, eight thousand miles away from these divergent Chinas, can see China from different perspectives and through languages not heard in the same way in official channels.

As noted, Hong Kong also hosts Murdoch's STAR TV, a global supplier of Western content in Asia (Kumar 2006), and Phoenix TV, where Murdoch joins Liu Chang-le, who had a career in the People's Liberation Army in China before leaving for the U.S., and other mainland investors. Despite this web of interests, Phoenix may raise "dangerous issues" and seem to challenge CCTV: "Phoenix's three-year-old InfoNews Channel offers new ways to report the news, familiar in the West but new in China. . . . Viewers find innovative news shows modeled after Western media such as CNN. The channel also provides live, exclusive (for China) reporting on Taiwan—a first since the government banned virtually all news from the island that it considers a renegade province" (Borton 2004b).

Phoenix launched its programs in the U.S. in 2001 as the Phoenix North American Chinese Channel (PNACC), distributed initially through DirecTV and subsequently through Echostar. In the U.S., however, Phoenix has faced continuing suspicion because of its close associations with the Chinese government, especially because these are frequently reported in *Epoch Times*, a free periodical distributed by followers of the religious sect Falun Gong, which is highly critical of the Beijing regime (and has been banned in China). A report in *Epoch Times* quoted Wu Guoguang, of the University of Victoria, as asking,

> "Why doesn't it [the Phoenix TV] have a Cantonese channel or Cantonese programs, given that it is stationed in [Cantonese-speaking] Hong Kong?" . . . Wu's answer, in short, is that the majority of the people in China have lost both their confidence and interest in China's state media. "Overseas" media—media from outside China—are believed to be credible. Therefore, the Chinese government now has to use "overseas media" to spread its political propaganda. (Zhou 2005, annotations in original)

Other commentators, including Joseph Chan (2003), have emphasized Phoenix's close links to mainland power structures, which belie stylistic differences in form and programming. However, if Phoenix is friendly to the PRC government, it is also a commercial venture whose owners understand that propaganda does not always generate revenue. Phoenix, for example, was the first news network in China to broadcast news of the death of Zhao Ziyang, a highly sensitive subject.[3]

Some complaints about mainland Chinese control of Chinese American media may reflect the competing interests of *Epoch Times* and New Tang Dynasty Television (NTDTV), which has produced its own Mandarin and Cantonese satellite programming for China, the U.S., and the world since 2002. Based in New York City, NTDTV, in turn, continually faces accusations of affiliation with Falun Gong, whose activities are anathema to the mainland government. The company has also had difficulty broadcasting, since governments and private owners of satellites may feel pressure from Chinese authorities not to transmit it (BBC Monitoring 2005b).

In New York, a few hours of New Tang Dynasty TV appear on the public access channel, although it can be seen only on pay cable. New York is one of the few places in North America (along with Los Angeles, San Francisco, and Vancouver) where cable and broadcast Chinese media complement satellite transmissions. New York City also offers Sinovision, a New York–based Mandarin station that broadcasts news and entertainment programming via cable and over the air. The Nightly News hour covers not only American, international, and Chinese news, but also city news. Hence Sinovision, like Channel M (Multivision Television) in Vancouver, is closer to a traditional local TV station whose producers and audience come from the same space, actively building a New York–based Chinese American citizenship.

Satellite packages and providers also face new competitors on the internet. Late in 2005, KyLin TV began to offer limited service through Internet Protocol Television (IPTV), offering CCTV-4, CCTV-9, and SunTV, a Phoenix spinoff based in Hong Kong. SunTV, broadcast in Mandarin, specializes in Chinese history, art, and culture for a global audience. It also carries programs on Chinese America produced by Duowei TV, a U.S. content provider owned by Chinese Media Net, Inc. KyLin's main strength is its massive library of movies and videos on demand. Founded by Charles Wang of Computer Associates and Charles Dolan of Cablevision, KyLin has turned to traditional Chinese American media outlets for marketing, teaming with World Journal Bookstore in Canada and the U.S. to advertise its somewhat cheaper service (US$15/month) in Chinatowns across North America. More aggressive promotional efforts were made in March 2006 in Washington, D.C., and Philadelphia Chinatowns (PR Newswire 2005).

Chinese televisual satellite media in the U.S. thus suggest an array of choices about who and what Chinese may be. Within China, television production ranges from anthems of the People's Liberation Army to pop stars, and the producers may be government channels, increasingly privatized Chinese companies, and those who cross into Chinese "airspace." Outside of mainland China, television production in Taiwan, Hong Kong, and the United States offers different cultural perspectives, sometimes in complex packages. To explore the implications of this satellite China further, I turn to a more detailed albeit personal reading of TVBI/Jadeworld.

Content, Context, and Experience

The weekday line-up of the 24-hour programming of Jade West includes 8.5 hours of serial dramas, 6 hours of magazine programming, 4.5 hours of news, 2 hours of children's cartoons, 1.5 hours of music, and 1.5 hours of other programs (financial advice, documentaries on contemporary Hong Kong issues, travel). About a third of these programs are repeated during the day. Weekend programming adds an extra hour of children's programming on Saturdays and some programs from Radio Television Hong Kong (RTHK). Except for American news, all programs come from Hong Kong.

This localization of production, in turn, raises questions about how satellite programs bridge the gap between production and reception. I begin my analysis with news programming, since these shows are transmitted live with compelling immediacy. As primary services, news programs also represent a global battleground on which the ideological agendas of Phoenix TV, CCTV, and NDTV can be compared. The content of each show allows us to suggest preferred readings of Chineseness within each global package and its alteration as transnational localism.

Jade East and West transmit live news from both Hong Kong and the U.S. Hong Kong news is broadcast directly, so that the 8 AM Hong Kong news appears live at 7 PM EST on the previous day. U.S. news, produced on the West Coast, follows at 9:30 PM EST. Both are repeated later that night. Having casually watched these programs for years, I analyzed them more intensely for this paper. I took the half-hour midnight Hong Kong news show broadcast on January 24, 2006, five days before the Chinese New Year (repeated at 1 AM EST), as a typical example of Jade News. Here I list the stories that night in the order they were reported, categorizing each as local, Chinese, or international:

- Sum Shui Po, a food stall on Ap Lui Street, sold long-expired food (LOCAL)
- 200,000 kg of "pirated pork" was found in lorries entering the New Territories (LOCAL/CHINESE)
- Chinese New Year tourism has Hong Kong hotel occupancy rates at 90%; most visitors are from China; border crossings are busy (LOCAL/CHINESE)

- Macau has arrested mainland pickpockets (LOCAL/CHINESE)
- There has been an explosion in a Shanxi mine (no pictures) (CHINESE)
- A seventh person has died in mainland China (Sichuan) from avian flu (CHINESE)
- Japan suggests North Korea had an avian flu death (INTERNATIONAL)
- Natural gas problems appear in Russia and Ukraine (INTERNATIONAL)
- An Australian oil tanker has had an accident near the Great Barrier Reef (INTERNATIONAL)
- Iraq TV says American soldiers killed one of its photographers (INTERNATIONAL)
- The 2004 arsonist at Admiralty Subway Station is given life imprisonment (LOCAL)
- Doctors advised pediatricians about harmful medicines and decried patient expectations (LOCAL)
- A ban on cigarettes is instituted in all public places in Hong Kong, even mahjong parlors (LOCAL)
- House sales fell in the U.S. in the second quarter of 2005 (INTERNATIONAL)
- The American crude oil reserve dropped, and a Hong Kong financial official spoke about rising interest rates (LOCAL)
- China Bank will be listed on the Hong Kong Stock Exchange (LOCAL/CHINESE)
- Chinese insurance companies issue a warning on earnings (CHINESE)
- A report is given on global stock indexes and exchange rates (INTERNATIONAL)
- A report is given on a malfunction on Kowloon East Rail, with interviews (LOCAL)
- The Hong Kong Dept. of Justice will not sue a judge over an ethics violation (LOCAL)
- RTHK (Radio Television Hong Kong), facing an impending government review, says it wants to be free from government interference and should not become CCTV (LOCAL)
- A vendor sold frozen lamb as fresh (LOCAL)
- Report is given on the Palestinian vote and on U.S. and Israeli concerns about Hamas (INTERNATIONAL)
- Iran blames England for an explosion (INTERNATIONAL)
- The whale in the Thames died (INTERNATIONAL)
- Suggestions are made for Valentine's Day gifts, including chocolate and a diamond in the shape of Africa, because Africa produces both diamonds and cocoa (INTERNATIONAL)

- Sports news—soccer, the German World Cup, the Australian Open semi-finals (with the first Chinese player to earn a Grand Slam title) (CHINA/INTERNATIONAL)
- Weather (LOCAL/INTERNATIONAL)

This brief broadcast includes twenty-five stories. Hong Kong local news dominates with eleven items, several with China border connections; two others have Hong Kong "hooks." Two stories deal only with China; four more deal with China but underscore links to Hong Kong. Six stories deal with international news. There are five financial stories (some with Hong Kong links) and brief segments on sports and weather: the sports story highlights a Chinese connection at the Australian Open.

Presentations are quite conventional, with the anchor announcing the main story, a turn to visual materials, and a reporter at the scene continuing, with occasional interviews with everyday people at the scene or with officials or experts. TVB, however, lacks field reporters for global stories and relies on wire feeds.

The news on TVB takes an extremely local—that is, Hong Kong—perspective on what topics are relevant, as well as what places. Typical local stories encompass food issues, crime, and transportation problems in concrete spaces recognizable to Hong Kongers—street markets at Shum Shiu Po and the subway station at Admiralty. Hence, the news and visuals evoke memory of place and deepen any emigrant connections to Hong Kong. Business and financial news, including the stock market, banking, interest rates, oil prices, and tourism, also show this Hong Kong focus.

At a more abstract level, this news is local in how it criticizes the local government. The story on the impending review of RTHK exemplifies a Hong Kong, rather than PRC, perspective: the piece carries the onscreen statement of a dissident Democratic Party legislator who had harshly criticized the pro-China executive branch. His claim that he does not want to see RTHK turned into CCTV places Donald Tsang, the chief executive of Hong Kong, in opposition to Beijing. Freedom of the press has been an extraordinarily volatile issue in Hong Kong since 1997; this report continues that debate. Rather than shocking the local audience, it immerses them—and American Hong Kong audiences—in active, mediated citizenship.

Finally, the news becomes localized through Hong Kong's vantage on global participation. Since 1997, Chinese news itself has become more common; the staid *South China Morning Post* now includes pages of "national" (Chinese) coverage. In this newscast, China stories are less evident than China linkages—not always favorable—in border issues, pirate pork, and avian flu. These underscore continuing personal and commercial links between Hong Kong and China that shape "national"/global coverage. (By comparison, mainstream U.S. news at this time was preoccupied with flu outbreaks closer to "the West," in Turkey.) These stories also refract Hong Kong attitudes toward mainland China, involving dependence on Chinese tourism, fear of crime from mainlanders, and economic cooperation as contradictory visions of China.

As the news reaches the U.S., it can challenge the United States' enclosed televisual world, too. Of the twenty-five stories broadcast, few appeared on major U.S. news at all—the Palestinian vote, the Ukraine gas crisis, the Thames whale, or avian flu. A Valentine's Day chocolate feature is hardly novel, but the inclusion of Africa would be unusual in U.S. media. And the story of an Iraqi TV journalist killed by Americans was omitted by U.S. media in the days I reviewed these materials, highlighting the different gatekeeping filters in U.S. and Chinese national televisual media. Here, perspectives and choices in satellite news might construct a more complicated Chinese American subject than would mainstream American news media.

TVB, finally, represents Hong Kong abroad insofar as it is an alternative to other Chinese mainland-oriented news. While freedom of the press and of expression are debated in Hong Kong (as in the U.S.), TVB's criticism of governments and coverage of stories uncomfortable to China clearly distinguishes it from other satellite news broadcasts.

A broadcast of Phoenix Mandarin News Express on 3 March 2006, for example, illustrated the station's higher production values as well as its ideological slant. The lead story was the People's Congress meeting in Beijing, followed by official PRC views on Taiwan and President Chen Shui-Bian's plans to scrap the Mainland Affairs Council and the National Unification Guidelines (moves that suggest Taiwanese independence). The American State Department's reaction to Chen followed, stressing American commitment to recognizing only one China. Phoenix also showed the Taiwanese opposition party (KMT) reacting to Chen's move and footage of mass demonstrations in the streets of Taipei against Chen. Phoenix had reporters in Beijing, Washington, D.C., and Taipei presenting the stories, converging on the Chen case into a powerful statement of global opinion. It also has field reporters in Moscow and India, who covered the Hamas visit to Moscow and the Bush visit to India.

Another long story covered drills by the People's Liberation Army, a deeply patriotic display of military hardware and soldiers in training. Another story on avian flu featured a health official reassuring everyone that the country was well prepared for the epidemic and that the disease had become a global phenomenon (rather than a Chinese responsibility). With regard to Hong Kong, Donald Tsang's visit to Beijing led the broadcast, followed by the proposed merger of the Broadcasting Department with the Department of Telecommunication. The lack of questions about the merger contrasted sharply with TVB's critical coverage. All in all, this broadcast was clearly friendlier to the mainland. As Liu has stated, "I think Phoenix can play a role in promoting the construction of China's democratic system . . . but it must be orderly and gradual" (Pan 2005). Phoenix offers American viewers an orderly China as a global project.

The CCTV-4 news program, *Chinese News*, reports on China, Hong Kong, Macau, Taiwan, and the world from a somewhat different mainland/global Chinese perspective. The broadcast of 28 January 2006, for example, just before the Chinese New Year, showed how different parts of China celebrated the New Year and claimed that some U.S. states have made it a holiday. It highlighted yellow and red lights on the Empire State Building and red lanterns in London. It also reported that Donald Tsang had visited Hong Kong's flower market, discussed how the Hong Kong economy had picked up, and showed New Year's traffic in Taiwan.

Besides this New Year's news, more substantive reports discussed Hamas's victory in Palestine, with interviews with Hamas leaders. No Israeli or Western diplomats appeared in the report, as they did in Western coverage. CCTV's Taiwan coverage also emphasized criticism of Chan and persecution of the KMT. Obviously these news stories are carefully selected. The Palestinian story was important, but the news was clearly more sympathetic to Hamas perspectives than comparable American reports were. The Taiwan news, in particular, emphasized the failures of Chan's ruling government and its heavy-handed tactics.

This brief comparison of the three news programs suggests the ideological slants of each. TVB remains very local (Hong Kong) and relatively open. Phoenix seems more pan-Chinese and international but sympathetic to the mainland. CCTV supports a traditional party line. Very different Chinas are being projected through this programming, to audiences that may compare and select.

Still, TVB news may have less regard for an audience beyond Hong Kong or "Hong Kongers" in selecting stories and perspectives. Compared to that in Hong Kong, the American audience of TVB is very small, and thus generates limited revenue. While transmitting Hong Kong news programs is cheap, it makes no economic sense to cater to this small American audience. On the other hand, both Phoenix and CCTV news cover China on a more global level. Since neither program is made for any specific local audience, neither carries stories on restaurant hygiene or local weather. TVB simply transplants its local news to audiences beyond Hong Kong, but Phoenix and CCTV have imagined—and clearly targeted—a broadly placed, Chinese-speaking audience potentially receptive to broad albeit specific visions of Greater China.

Besides providing Hong Kong news to American homes, TVB also produces a thirty-minute American news program in California. The 26 January 2006 broadcast of Jade East Cantonese covered the following national (U.S.) stories in Cantonese:

214 · Globalizing Television

- Rumsfeld's comments on troop levels
- Bush's comments on NSA spying
- Congressional hearings on Samuel Alito
- Sales of questionable second-hand cars after Katrina
- Health issues among 9/11 rescue workers in New York
- A suspected arson in Maryland
- A Maryland child involved in a gun accident, whose father was charged
- Window on Society, a ten-minute magazine on infertility that interviewed two doctors, one of them Chinese (Mandarin-speaking)
- The weather (presented with a U.S. map, using Fahrenheit)
- American financial news: crude oil was cheaper, oil stocks were lower, residential sales had fallen
- Stock indexes, stock prices, and exchange rates

This American news from TVB is obviously less extensive and comprehensive than national or local general-audience news shows produced in the U.S., but it combines elements of both—major national stories, vaguely concrete local stories, weather, and finance. Like USA Today or Metro, this show is a supplementary news source; someone who wants to be informed about local or national events would need additional sources, whether Chinese or English. As in Chinese American newspapers, stories on immigration or U.S. relations with China inevitably lead. Neither CCTV nor Phoenix offers this localization overseas.

While news represents the most compelling and ideologically tinged transmission of China to the U.S., TVB also provides popular continuing programs—especially serials and soap operas that convey everyday life as well as everyday speech (Tsai 2000). This presentation of the contemporary everyday intersects with nostalgic older movies from TVB's archives of film and television. Here, TVB embodies Hong Kong identity and culture through transnational media. Many of the TVB magazine programs also are extremely local, including stories about how to invest while in college and how to invest in jade, and cooking shows that use local ingredients. Another TVB program, E-buzz, is an entertainment and gossip show that interviews Hong Kong actors and would be fairly incomprehensible to people unfamiliar with the Hong Kong entertainment scene (again, a major theme in Chinese American print media).

TVB and other stations also link concrete Chinese worlds to the diasporic audience through special events—pageants, fundraisers, and especially their Chinese New Year line-ups, which are a focus for competition among all Chinese satellite networks. TVB carries the annual Tung Wah Hospital charitable show as an exclusive, showcasing a Hong Kong elite associated with the century-old institution. It also has created the Miss China International Pageant, which has been won by Chinese women from Hong Kong, Thailand, Malaysia,

Canada, and South Africa. For New Year's 2006, TVB offered Hong Kong popular song contests, a star-studded variety New Year's Eve show, New Year's soccer, New Year's movies like *Himalaya Stars,* live coverage of the recently created Hong Kong New Year's Day Parade (with Disney's Mickey and Minnie Mouse), New Year's fireworks over the harbor, and finally the Miss Chinese International Pageant. By March, ads for the Miss Hong Kong competition were ubiquitous, with the 2005 winner urging overseas Chinese to compete. These events provide a buffet of immediate local images, celebrities, and outreach, drawing an overseas audience into a Hong Kong world.

Finally, TVB is a profit-making corporation; revenues come from advertising and subscriptions, including "infotainment" slots. Hence, ads provide further insights into globalization and localization. On Jadeworld, primarily Chinese American vendors sell air fresheners, ginseng, health supplements to fight diabetes, poultry, and beauty products. Most of these products are extremely culturally specific, and many vendors are actually located in California: regional, then, to a primary market but accessible to other subscribers by telephone, fax, or internet. This reflects the materiality of satellite subscriber distribution as well as loci of production in California and New York. In terms of the localization of reception, southern California, especially the San Gabriel Valley, still represents the largest market, followed by northern California, the New York City area, and the Sun Belt. However, because ads are transmitted by satellite, these packages cover any part of the country that has a sales agent (or an internet connection to one). Like earlier Golden Mountain firms, these enterprises make Chinese goods or services available within an American national market and community, bridging transnational communities through goods and everyday needs.

Goods and services also contribute to a project of Chineseness through different forms of inclusion. Beyond bringing Hong Kong, or China as seen from Hong Kong, into American living rooms, these ads normalize a community of American Chinese as targeted viewers. The specialized goods they offer highlight differences between Chinese, who might need Lee Kum Kee sauces or Japanese herbal supplements, and other Americans, who are presumed not to. The absence of ads for general Americana—Pepsi, McDonald's, or Toyota—raises questions about how American producers read these media (a theme apparent in Chinese-language radio). By comparison, advertising on CCTV-4 is more global, with higher production values and spots for Western Union, Beijing Beer, large corporations based in China, and global conglomerates such as GM, which showcases Buicks made in China for the Chinese market.

The diverse content of satellite broadcasts, however, still defines only part of the experience of global Chineseness, which is also re-created by reception and readership. Unfortunately, at this point, I can suggest negotiated readings of these materials only on a limited, personal basis. Every morning, in my house in suburban Philadelphia, the family wakes up to the blaring of TVB's news anthem emanating from my father's room. On a typical day, the anchor talks about Chief Executive Donald Tsang or how the Hang Seng Index (the official Hong Kong stock index) is doing, while other reports deal with local policy or neighborhood features. My father, who speaks limited English, considers this news program a daily necessity, but watches many other shows as well. He also goes to Chinatown nearly every day to purchase his Chinese newspapers, generally Hong Kong–based journals like *Ming pao* that cover similar political and economic issues. He then discusses the news over tea or by telephone with Cantonese-speaking friends in greater Philadelphia and around the world. In 2005, he also gave me daily digests of news on the Taiwanese election, Hong Kong demonstrations, and news on the WTO—news that he knew I would not hear on "American" television.

I, on the other hand, watch these programs infrequently, partly because of my non-Cantonese-speaking spouse and my children, for whom Cantonese is an acquired second language. For us, Chinese TV is not a major form of relaxation. However, during the Iraq War in 2003, I used these channels to obtain another perspective on the war beyond that of local American media. I also use them to check on important events, like Hong Kong elections, Chinese affairs, or protests. My children, however, rarely look at Chinese television. Children's programming is limited, and CCTV's programs in Mandarin are not comprehensible to Cantonese speakers.

To put my experiences in a somewhat wider context, I also spoke with parents and teachers at Philadelphia's Chinese Academy. Of seventeen families, ten received Chinese satellite television in their homes. Since this is a Cantonese school, all except two had the TVB Jade package; one had Phoenix, and one had KyLin TV. Most identified the news as the most important program; some, however, were fans of different TV dramas. Households whose members do not speak much Chinese or where the parents are both English-dominant American-born Chinese do not have satellite. On the other hand, Chinese-dominant households all do. Other research suggests that in multi-generational households where the middle generation speaks English, Chinese TV serves their monolingual Chinese parents, acting as a babysitter for the elderly in an increasingly suburban American world (Wallack and Ning 2005). It deals with generational as well as immigrant displacement by offering reconnection to Hong Kong as a linguistic and social place.

I also asked about young people's viewing of Chinese-language television. While several parents had hoped, when they acquired these channels, that their children would watch them, they all agreed that this did not often happen, although older teenagers might get caught up in occasional dramas. This was confirmed in inquiries by my own non-watching daughter within her peer group at her Chinese school. Hence, the sense of re-placing or bridging China into a new world seems transient as well (as it does among Hispanic viewers [Navarro 2006]).

Such scattered data cannot explain the impact of Chinese satellite television in the U.S. Yet they remind us how such media, however strong they appear with an increased Chinese push abroad, intersect with larger issues of an imagined pan-Chinese community. Chinese mass media, whether newspapers or television, may rely on a fluency more common among immigrants and first-generation Chinese than among assimilated later generations of Chinese Americans. As with other ethnic media, we should not see a strong transnational market in the present as evidence that hybrid localism has a promising future. In the past two years, even Telemundo has explored bilingual broadcasting through "mun2" (i.e., *mundos* or worlds), in conjunction with NBC Universal. Comcast has launched the bilingual "Sí TV" as a Latino network in English. These broadcasters, based in the U.S., seem to have recognized an ever greater complexity in the large Latino audiences who watch transnational television (Navarro 2006). The worlds of Chinese satellite television may soon face similar challenges.

Conclusions

In his study of globalization and nationalism in Indian television, Shanti Kumar begins:

> We live in a dynamic world of electronic capitalism where traditional definitions of nationality, community, and identity are always in flux. We are only beginning to understand the significance of transnational networks such as CNN, MTV and STAR TV, which can bypass national governments and can connect with television viewers with the click of a remote-control button. We have scarcely recognized the growing influence of translocal media networks such as Eenadu TV, Sun TV and Zee TV, which can strategically use linguistic appeal to affiliate with the vernacular interests of domestic viewers and diasporic communities. . . . The location of culture is being constantly reconfigured on and off television through alternative imaginations of time, space, history, geography, identity and difference. (2006: 1)

This preliminary exploration of Chinese-language satellite television outside China must be read in dialogue both with the other essays in this volume, and their insights on the history, production, content, and readership of Chinese television, and with the changing contexts of global media and spectatorship. While moving outside a fixed national broadcast and ideological sphere, Chinese satellite television evokes many of the same mediated debates that face China itself. It asks, in a transnational sphere, what China means and who speaks for it. It also asks how China fits into a global framework, as nation-state and as producer and competitor. Finally, it asks about the future, not only of China and Chinese television, but of media and their global spectators.

At the same time, this inquiry poses questions about Chinese American identities. Historians and social scientists continue to elucidate the networks, places, and media through which Chinese have created identities "overseas." Certain features of this mediated world—its relation to politics, economics, and technology and its reliance on the extra-Chinese location of Hong Kong—raise questions for further study within this diaspora. Other features link Chinese immigrants to other immigrant Americans and their mediated histories in Spanish, Creole, Arabic, or Korean. Yet NTDTV's American production of satellite programming or KyLin's links with World Journal Bookstore remind us that Chinese Americans bring tradition and agency to global encounters as well. Together, these questions underscore the power and complexity of satellite television in a global world of imagined and emergent communities.

Notes

1. Recent reports have stated that Rupert Murdoch has been considering pulling out of Phoenix TV because of all the obstacles he faced in accessing the Chinese market (BBC Monitoring 2005b).

2. See various articles from *Digital Video Broadcasting* at http://www.dvb.org/about_dvb/dvb_worldwide/china/ (accessed 10 March 2008).

3. Zhao opposed the Tiananmen Square Massacre, and had been under house arrest for fifteen years before his death. The Chinese authorities cut off Phoenix's signal after news of Zhao's death was announced (Pan 2005).

References

Anderson, Benedict. 1991. *Imagined Communities: Reflections on the Origin and Spread of Nationalism.* London: Verso.

Ang, Ien. 1985. *Watching Dallas: Soap Opera and the Melodramatic Imagination.* London: Routledge.

Barboza, David. 2006. "Version of Google in China Won't Offer E-Mail or Blogs." *New York Times,* 25 January.

Barraclough, Steven. 2003. "Satellite Television in Asia: Winner and Losers." *Asian Affairs* 31, no. 3:263–272.

BBC Monitoring. 2005a. "China Launches Satellite TV Package in Asian Region." *World Media Monitor,* 1 February. http://news.monitor.bbc.co.uk (accessed 10 March 2008).

———. 2005b. "China/US/France: Media Watchdog Raps Eutelsat for Dropping US-Based Chinese TV." *World Media Monitor,* 15 March. http://news.monitor.bbc.co.uk (accessed 10 March 2008).

Borton, James. 2004a. "Face Off: China's Tom Group vs. Star TV." *Asia Times Online,*

18 November. http://www.atimes.com/atimes/China/FK18Ado1.html (accessed 10 March 2008).

———. 2004b. "Phoenix TV Spreads Its Wings in China." *Asia Times Online*, 9 December. http://www.atimes.com/atimes/China/FL09Ado1.html (accessed 10 March 2008).

Bullert, B. J. 1997. *Public Television: Politics and the Battle over Documentary Film*. New Brunswick, N.J.: Rutgers.

Cartier, Carolyn. 2001. *Globalizing South China*. Oxford: Blackwell.

Chan, Joseph Man. 2003. "Administrative Boundaries and Media Marketization." In *Chinese Media, Global Contexts*, ed. Lee Chin-Chuan, 159–176. London: Routledge Curzon.

Chan, Sucheng, ed. 2006. *Chinese American Transnationalism*. Philadelphia, Penn.: Temple University Press.

Cheng, Allen. 2001. "Phoenix Rising: A Former Propaganda Chief is Changing the Face of Chinese TV." *Asiaweek* 27, no. 9 (9 March). http://www.timeinc.net/asiaweek/magazine/nations/0,8782,100989,00.html (accessed 10 March 2008).

Curtin, Michael. 2002. "Hong Kong Meets Hollywood in the Extranational Arena of Cultural Industries." In *Sights of Contestation: Localism, Globalism, and Cultural Production in Asia and the Pacific*, ed. Kwok-Kan Tam, Wimal Dissanayake, and Terry Yip, 79–109. Hong Kong: Chinese University Press.

———. 2004. "Media Capitals: Cultural Geographies of Global TV." In *Television after TV: Essays on a Medium in Transition*, ed. Lynn Spigel and Jan Olsson, 270–302. Durham, N.C.: Duke University Press.

———. 2005. "Murdoch's Dilemma or 'What's the Price of TV in China?'" *Media, Culture, and Society* 27, no. 2:155–185.

Hartley, John. 1999. *Uses of Television*. Routledge: London.

Heaney, Bill. 2003. "Eastern Multimedia Sets Sights on US Satellite-TV Market." *Taipei Times*, 16 July, p. 10. http://www.taipeitimes.com/News/biz/archives/2003/07/16/2003059655 (accessed 10 March 2008).

Hong, Junhao. 1998. *The Internationalization of Television in China: The Evolution of Ideology, Society, and Media since the Reform*. Westport, Conn.: Praeger.

Hsu, Madeleine. 2000. *Dreaming of Gold, Dreaming of Home: Transnationalism and Migration between the United States and South China, 1882–1943*. Stanford, Calif.: Stanford University Press.

Hua, Vanessa. 2005. "Culture and Religion: Dissident Media Linked to Falun Gong." *San Francisco Chronicle*, 18 December.

Kumar, Shanti. 2006. *Gandhi Meets Primetime: Globalization and Nationalism in Indian Television*. Urbana: University of Illinois Press.

Kwong, K. F. 1998. "American Peacock on Chinese Soil—The Challenge Facing NBC Asia in Greater China." M.A. thesis project, Hong Kong Baptist University. http://home.netvigator.com/~kwongkf/4090proj.htm (accessed 1 December 2006).

Liu Chang-le. 2004. "Building a New Bridge." http://www.ifeng.com/phoenixtv/74594176003473408/20040902/362366_1.shtml (accessed 10 March 2008).

Liu, Christy. 2004. "CCTV Unveils Music, Youth Channels." *Media Asia*, 18 June, p. 12.

Mankekar, Purnima. 1999. *Screening Culture, Viewing Politics: An Ethnography of Television, Womanhood, and Nation in Postcolonial India*. Durham, N.C.: Duke University Press.

McDonogh, Gary, and Cindy Wong. 2005. *Global Hong Kong*. New York: Routledge.

Navarro, Mireya. 2006. "Changing U.S. Audience Poses Test for a Giant of Spanish TV." *New York Times*, 10 March, pp. A1, C4.

Pan, Philip P. 2005. "Making Waves, Carefully, on the Air in China: Head of Private TV Network Curries Party's Favor while Testing Limits." *Washington Post*, 19 September, section A.

PR Newswire. 2005. "KyLinTV to Visit Philadelphia, Washington, Chicago, and Boston." *Monitors Industry News*, 18 November. http://www.all-about-monitors.com/kylintv_to_visit_philadelphia_washington_chicago_and_edh.jspx (accessed 10 March 2008).

Sinclair, John. 2000. "Geolinguistic Region as Global Space: The Case of Latin America." In *The New Communications Landscape: Demystifying Media Globalization*, ed. Georgette Wang, Jan Servaes, and Anura Goonasekera, 19–32. London: Routledge.

Streeter, Thomas. 1996. *Selling the Air: A Critique of the Policy of Commercial Broadcasting in the United States*. Chicago: University of Chicago Press.

Thompson, Clive. 2006. "Google's China Problem (and China's Google Problem)." *New York Times Magazine*, 23 April.

Tsai, Yean. 2000. "Cultural Identity in an Era of Globalization: The Structure and Content of Taiwanese Soap Operas." In *The New Communications Landscape: Demystifying Media Globalization*, ed. Georgette Wang, Jan Servaes, and Anura Goonasekera, 174–187. London: Routledge.

Wallack, Todd, and Yu Ning. 2005. "Immigrants Turning to Foreign-Language Channels." *San Francisco Chronicle*, 20 April.

Wang, Georgette, Jan Servaes, and Anura Goonasekera, eds. 2000. *The New Communications Landscape: Demystifying Media Globalization*. London: Routledge.

Wong, Cindy. 1999. "Cities, Cultures and Cassettes: Hong Kong Cinema and Transnational Audiences." *Post Script* 19, no. 1:87–106.

Zhou, Meihua. 2005. "Is TV Network Implicated in Spying? The Sinister Role of Phoenix TV." *Epoch Times*, 10 November. http://english.epochtimes.com/news/5-11-10/34396.html (accessed 10 March 2008).

Relevant Websites

CCTV's English-language site: http://english.cctv.com/index.shtml
China Central TV: http://www.cctv-4.com/
The Chinese Channel: http://www.chinese-channel.co.uk/
Da-Ai TV: http://www.newdaai.tv/index.php
Fairchild TV: http://www.fairchildtv.com/
Guangdong TV: http://www.gdtv.com.cn/
Hwazan Satellite TV: http://www.hwazantv.com/
New Tang Dynasty TV: http://www.ntdtv.com
Phoenix TV: http://www.phoenixtv.com/
Skylink TV: http://www.skylinktv.us/
TVB: http://www.tvb.com/

Transnational Circulation of Chinese-Language Television Dramas

YING ZHU

A wave of dynasty drama serials began to dominate prime-time dramatic program-ming on television in the PRC in the late 1990s, and a viewing frenzy soon began among Chinese audiences around the world. Together with Taiwan's idol dramas and Hong Kong's martial arts sagas and contemporary social mobility dramas, the PRC's dynasty dramas had saturated a pan-Chinese media market by the early 2000s. Using transnational dramas from the three Chinese-language media pro-duction centers as a springboard, this essay explores two aspects of the global cir-culation of Chinese-language television dramas: the forces conducive to such dramas' transnational circulation and the cultural and economic ramifications of that circulation. It utilizes the theory of a "cultural-linguistic market" to sort out both the factors conducive to the formation of Chinese cultural-linguistic media and the products viable in that market. It further asks how the emergence of a Chinese cultural-linguistic market, together with other cultural-linguistic mar-kets, complicates the power dynamic of global cultural flow.

The Cultural-Linguistic Market and Chinese
Cultural-Linguistic Media Practic

Conventional geographic borders play a major role in a cultural-linguistic market, of course, but are not determinative, giving way to the virtual contours of shared language and culture. Cross-border, hopscotch commonalities are established by historical relationships of colonization and by the formation of diasporic ethnic enclaves deposited in the wake of global population flows. The assumption behind the descriptive frame is that these concatenations of shared language and culture describe real or potential international niche markets for media products.

The Chinese cultural-linguistic market is more or less synonymous with the notion of "Greater China." Formerly synonymous with "the pan-Chinese region," "Greater China" has lately shifted meaning to become an all-inclusive descriptor, incorporating the three Chinese homelands and the worldwide Chinese diaspora into a single community. "Greater China" in this sense is an "imagined community" or common cultural region united through the "time-space compression" of satellite broadcasting and the portability and reproducibility of video and other cultural products.

McAnany and Wilkinson (1996) emphasize that audiences within a given cultural-linguistic market must share the same or similar languages as well as intertwined histories and overlapping cultural characteristics. Yet language is a complex issue in the Chinese cultural-linguistic market (Chua 2004). Chinese people from different regions and origins do not necessarily speak the same language or dialect, even though they share a written language. This is why Chinese audiences are often found watching Chinese movies and television programs with Chinese subtitles. Even the written language comes in two versions, with "traditional" characters used in Taiwan and "simplified" characters used in China since the late 1950s to promote literacy. Most immigrants from Guangdong Province (Canton), Hong Kong, and parts of Southeast Asia speak Cantonese, which is not easily understood by Mandarin speakers. Mandarin, on the other hand, has been the official language of China and Taiwan for more than half a century. In fact, Cantonese-language film production was banned during the Republican era for the sake of national and linguistic unity. By now, most non-Cantonese Chinese are fluent in Mandarin even though they speak another dialect, such as Min, Hakka, or Shanghainese, at home (Zhou and Cai 2002: 421–423). Moreover, while Cantonese is still the dominant dialect in Chinatowns all over the world, Mandarin dominates among the more culturally sophisticated immigrants typical of recent arrivals from China and Taiwan.[1] Overseas Chinese schools are also predominantly Mandarin, reflecting parents' preference. Finally, Mandarin is promoted by the U.S. government as a strategic second-language choice, by elite U.S. and European businessmen in recognition of China's rising economic power, and by schools at every level, which offer instruction in Mandarin much more often than in any other dialect, making Mandarin the de facto official dialect of foreign learners as well.[2]

The current linguistic hierarchy is the reverse of that in Hong Kong and in Cantonese-speaking Chinatowns in the U.S. and Australia in the 1970s–1980s, when Mandarin speakers were ridiculed and occupied a low rung in media representations and in reality. The power dynamic has shifted as China has continued to increase in global political and economic power. Since the 1990s, the prospect of huge Mandarin markets has convinced Hong Kong producers to add Mandarin soundtracks to their media products and to venture into co-producing Mandarin dramas.[3]

China recently mandated that domestic variety show hosts use standard Mandarin only and stop affecting Hong Kong or Taiwanese slang and accents (Cody 2005). The affected tones were considered cool by the millions of Chinese youth who constitute the main audience for variety shows hosted by pop stars from Hong Kong and Taiwan, long the centers of teenage heartthrob production. Some hosts of mainland variety shows began affecting this pop lingo in an effort to associate themselves with the cool radiating from Hong Kong and Taiwan. Yet the use of Taiwanese and Hong Kong vernacular has gone out of fashion recently as the mainland's own pop stars increasingly craft their own cool. So instead of putting a new strain on mainland producers, the ban on Hong Kong and Taiwanese vernacular speech is actually a rare instance of accord between state regulators, media practitioners, and audiences.

Cantonese TV dramas and pop music have been on the wane since the early 1990s, and all popular dramas are now dubbed into Mandarin. DVDs follow the same pattern. In Australia, for instance, Mandarin and Cantonese are now on an equal footing in the non-broadcast Chinese media markets. The mainland Chinese and Hong Kong video industries formerly ran parallel in Australia, each with its own producers, distributors, rental outlets, and customers, with very little crossover. Subtitling has fostered more crossovers between the two markets. Meanwhile, pop music performers have switched to Mandarin in order to exploit the huge mainland market. This switch has enabled Taiwan and lately China to emerge as major recording locations for Mandarin dramas and pop music, helping to cultivate a newly Mandarin-dominated Chinese cultural-linguistic market. Mandarin films and television dramas from Taiwan and mainland China are rented and sold side by side at video stores in Chinatowns all over the world, in response to the demands of a cultural-linguistic market that is oblivious to the political rift between the two states.

Even as Mandarin continues to rise, local dialects do occasionally challenge its state-mandated dominance. A case in point is the debate over whether the imported cartoon *Tom & Jerry* should be dubbed into Shanghainese or not. The fur flew between advocates for the preservation of local dialects and those for the promotion of Mandarin over what dialect the mostly silent cat and mouse should deploy in their own antagonistic antics (Bodeen 2004).

Within the Mandarin-speaking market, tension also exists between China and Taiwan. With Taiwanese media products enjoying higher status for a variety of reasons, not least of which is Taiwan's more advanced economy, efforts have been made in China to return to using the complex ("traditional") Chinese characters used in Taiwan and elsewhere for subtitles. Some academics in China even suggest that Beijing should consider reintroducing complex characters alongside simplified characters, since the complex Chinese characters have been in use for thousands of years, making them part of the Chinese cultural treasury (see *South China Morning Post* 2004). Meanwhile, in an effort to unify Chinese characters for easy communication, the UN has officially adopted simplified characters as its own standard. Letters of protest have since been circulated alleging that this decision will have a devastating impact on Chinese language, culture, and history. Protesters charge that if the UN succeeds in its reckless effort, it will only be a matter of time before traditional written Chinese becomes the next Latin.[4] At the same time, Taiwan's effort to promote its own use of traditional characters is denounced in Beijing as "anti-Chinese."

Anxiety about what is China and what is not, and about the Chinese cultural and historical heritage, is not at all new, and for all the claims and counter-claims about who is the keeper of the Chinese flame, it provides a common theme. "Greater China" is not conceptualized just as a shared media market; the concept is thoroughly steeped in the ideology that the Chinese nation is a unified entity. Historical and ongoing mobilization efforts within China and the global Chinese diaspora by Nationalists and Communists alike have codified this conception of the Chinese as a single people with a unifying cultural and historical experience (Fitzgerald 1996). Yet Hong Kong, Taiwan, and China have developed as significantly different societies over the last century and a half, and television must negotiate the enormous social, economic, and political differences within Greater China in order to appeal to the collective market. Indeed, the successful exploitation of any cultural-linguistic market relies in varying degrees on programming that appeals to various sub-regions with diverse political and economic conditions and aspirations. TV in Greater China does this by taking advantage of the theme of Chinese unity, reaching across ideological divisions with two broadly drawn, uncontroversial variations on the shared characteristics of being Chinese: one points to the past, reveling in the kind of cultural nostalgia reflected in China's dynasty dramas, and one to the future, pining after the smart images of modernization depicted in contemporary urban dramas from Hong Kong and Taiwan. The successful genres of transborder Chinese television are thus paradoxically underpinned by simultaneous longings for Chinese tradition and modernity.

Genres for Transborder Television

Transnational TV dramas from the three Chinese production centers vary according to their different origins. The Hong Kong drama serial is the most established among the three regions. Most Hong Kong drama serials are either martial arts dramas or contemporary social mobility sagas focusing on the struggle of individuals who manage to rise to the top of the business world. The struggle-to-the-top serials are also keen on exploring conflicts within extended families, sometimes mixing in a general spirit of parody that injects humor into the melodramatic story. Meanwhile, the martial arts serial is a particularly enduring native genre of Hong Kong, with a solid Chinese fan base all over the world.[5]

In the past, most Hong Kong programs were set in domestic spaces—the home, the local restaurant, the workplace—and were concerned with "making a home." Recently, however, in a growing number of television programs produced by TVB, a good part of the action takes place in sites such as airports, cruise ships, and Africa or Southeast Asia. These travel narratives are thematically concerned with transnational identity formation and questions of travel and intercultural communication (see Lee, this volume). Gone are the days of building up corporations, the foundation of Hong Kong's economy, as seen in many of Hong Kong's family melodramas. Recent shows such as *Triumph in the Skies* (*Chongshang yunxiao*), *Ups and Downs in a Sea of Love* (*Shiwandun qingyuan*), and *Fantasy Hotel* (*Kaixing bingguan*) feature airplane pilots, flight attendants, tour guides, and other workers in Hong Kong's burgeoning service, travel, and tourism industries. Indeed, if the family melodrama anticipated the crisis of 1997 (the year of Hong Kong's reunification with China), the travel narrative responds to its aftermath, namely by securing Hong Kong's position in the region and the world as a capitalist power, cultural center, and leader in the global information economy.[6]

Popular serial dramas from Taiwan have traditionally been family melodramas known for their sentimentality and their lack of identifying historical referents. The youth-oriented idol drama brought a new look to Taiwanese TV drama, with its distinctively modern settings, narratives frequently based on Japanese manga series, and high school– to college-age characters. *Meteor Garden* (2001) is a mega-hit among young audiences in the pan-Chinese region and Southeast Asia generally, and has spawned two sequel series. Several similar serials from Taiwan have succeeded in the export markets—*It Started with a Kiss* (*Ezuoju zhiwen*, 2005), *Mars* (*Zhanshen*, 2004), *At the Dolphin Bay* (*Haitun wan lian ren*, 2003), and several others—but drama production in Taiwan currently faces overwhelming competition from imported dramas, particularly from Korea. The more popular, less expensive (relative to the cost of producing original domestic series), and often higher-quality imports have been pushing domestic drama series out of prime time and putting pressure on domestic production, so much so that Taiwan's Government Information Office has considered prohibiting foreign drama broadcasts in prime time. Many other measures to prop up, free up, and manage Taiwan's television industry for better performance (more and better domestic productions) under globalized conditions are currently under consideration in the midst of a major, ongoing structural and regulatory overhaul.[7]

The only genre from China that is able to compete in the transborder market with series from Hong Kong and Taiwan is dynasty drama. China's dynasty drama production teams have raised the genre to a high art, giving dynasty dramas a position in the Chinese market akin to the place of British television's singular period dramas in the English-language market. Moreover, within limits set by the state, mainland Chinese dynasty dramas have pursued provocative political and cultural themes relevant to contemporary Chinese society.

Allowing for a degree of oversimplification, then, the current configuration of the global Chinese-language television market looks something like this: history has become China's niche, while Hong Kong maintains its reign in the martial arts arena and Taiwan leads the pack in family melodramas and idol dramas. Historically, programming has moved in only one direction, from Hong Kong and Taiwan to China.[8] The most popular Hong Kong exports to China are martial arts serials adapted from works by the most popular martial arts novelist, Hong Kong's Jin Yong. The most popular Taiwanese exports are melodramas written and produced by Qiong Yao, the popular novelist specializing in Republican-era family melodrama. Yet in recent years both martial arts and family melodramas have given way in China to China's own dynasty dramas, particularly the Qing drama series of the late 1990s and early 2000s.

A cursory survey of Chinese-language websites that sell Chinese DVDs suggests that the overseas Chinese-language drama markets are likewise largely divided between contemporary idol dramas from Taiwan, martial arts dramas from Hong Kong, and dynasty dramas from China, with the dynasty dramas leading in numbers available for sale and rental.[9] One website even categorizes mainland TV series by dynasty, from the Qin (221–207 BC) to the Qing (AD 1644–1911). While some of the most popular serials, such as *Yongzheng Dynasty*, are available in both Mandarin and Cantonese, and with English and Chinese subtitles, all of the mainland serials are originally produced in Mandarin with Chinese subtitles (complex and traditional characters in most cases for Taiwan and the overseas market).

In fact, the generic and stylistic characteristics of the transborder genres produced in Hong Kong, Taiwan, and China began to blur in the late 1980s and 1990s amidst increasingly frequent cross-fertilization of production personnel and financing. For instance, China's costume dramas during this intensely transnational period produced a new sub-genre, the comedic dynasty drama, centered not so much on historical authenticity as on the legendary figures and tales of dynastic China. These dramas were mostly tongue-in-cheek and not at all concerned about historical accuracy and authenticity. Snubbed by elite critics in China, the dynasty comedies were popular in Hong Kong and Taiwan. Indeed, the dynasty comedies, with their humorous use of local slang, droll dialogue, and blithe caricatures of legendary figures, resembled Hong Kong's own pop comedies.

Historical dramas easily resonate with Chinese audiences everywhere, both overseas and at home, by tapping into the imagined glory of a bygone era and the active and residual nationalist sentiment associated with it. Contemporary dramas, on the other hand, need a little fine-tuning in order to appeal to audiences across all the social segments and regions of the Greater China cultural-linguistic market. China's prolonged modernization project, an encompassing existential concern running the gamut from technological and economic modernization to cultural and lifestyle transformations, frequently serves as a common denominator (Anagnost 1997). Modernization has become the unifying theme that transcends the political and ideological divisions between Hong Kong, China, Taiwan, and the rest of the Chinese-speaking populations.

Markets and Production Centers of
Chinese Cultural-Linguistic Media

McAnany and Wilkinson's discussion of cultural-linguistic markets also notes that within these markets there are significant co-production arrangements, frequent instances of cross-national and cross-regional media ownership, and fluid exchanges of personnel as well as cultural products. The three production centers of Chinese-language media are engaging in more and more exchanges of this sort as the Chinese cultural-linguistic market matures. Below I consider the three centers and the course of their development separately and as a cultural-linguistic triumvirate.

Media systems in Hong Kong, Taiwan, and China have followed their own distinctive paths. The free-market-based Hong Kong TV industry has four broadcast television channels operated by two networks (with two channels each), and four multi-channel cable television networks.[10] The leading television network is Television Broadcasts Limited (TVB), which owns the world's largest library of Chinese television programs and exports its programs all over the world (To and Lau 1995). The smaller Asia Television Limited (ATV) is Hong Kong's second television network.

While Hong Kong's media system has been almost exclusively private and commercial from the start (there is also a public radio and television operation, with public TV programs broadcast over the commercial networks), traditionally state-run systems in both China and Taiwan have been gradually deregulated and weaned from government funding since the 1980s, partly in a common effort to foment a more vigorous regional trade in Chinese-language programming.

As Sinclair and Harrison (2004) point out, deregulation in Taiwan was politically rather than economically motivated. The Taiwanese television industry was dominated by three commercial television networks, TTV, CTV, and CTS, which were commercial broadcasters owned by the provincial government, the ruling nationalist political party (the KMT), and the military, respectively (Thomas 2000: 104). These three arms of the state exercised political control over broadcast content. After the lifting of martial law in 1988, pressure grew to allow independence in broadcasting. In 1993, the government lifted the restrictions on new free-to-air stations that had been in place since 1971, allowing Formosa Television, backed by Taiwan's leading opposition party (the Democratic Progressive Party or DPP, itself legalized in 1991), to begin legal transmission, although preparations and licensing delayed actual broadcasting until June 1997 (Sinclair and Harrison 2004: 49). Formosa Television became the fourth over-the-air television station, providing an alternative viewpoint and liberalized entertainment to a ready audience. Further deregulation led to a proliferation of cable operators, and more changes are in the works, including divestment of government interest in Taiwan's three original television networks and the creation of a new public network.

Both Hong Kong and Taiwan began to export Chinese-language television programs to overseas Chinese markets in the 1970s. After initial program exchanges in the late 1970s with Hong Kong, Taiwan expanded its market to Chinese-language communities in Southeast Asia, the U.S., and Europe. Taiwan also founded the International Audiovisual Broadcasting Company in 1979 to facilitate television exports to Canada and the U.S. In 1991, Hong Kong and Taiwan began to deliver regular news broadcasts to Canada and the U.S. via satellite.

Hong Kong's TVB has positioned itself as the most resourceful international broadcaster in Chinese, serving international media markets from the Asia-Pacific region and Australia to North America and Europe. TVB formed a joint venture with a Canadian company to take over Canada's two Chinese-language cable networks, Chinavision Canada Corporation and Cathay Television Inc., which together cover the whole of Canada. Exclusive rights to broadcast TVB programs in Europe belong to a satellite channel, The Chinese Channel (TCC). TVB delivers 1,000 hours of programming to TCC each year, with a total target audience of 850,000 in Europe. Similarly, TVB contracts with two Australian stations to provide 1,000 hours per year (To and Lau 1995).

Through its international arm, TVBI, TVB exports most of its domestic production in various forms and in several languages, but principally to diasporic markets. TVB has its own video outlets in Southeast Asia, cable subsidiaries in the United States and Canada, and a satellite superstation aimed mainly at Taiwan, TVBS. TVB has also operated two regional satellite television channels aimed at Taiwan since 1993. Meanwhile, the Chinese Television Network (CTN) launched two satellite television channels in Chinese at the end of 1994, and another satellite broadcaster, Chinese Entertainment Television, was launched in March 1995. This marked the beginning of a new wave of ambitious expansion for Hong Kong's electronic media.

China's broadcast television system was originally built as a structurally integrated media system and was seen as an extension of the state, but regulatory changes beginning in 1983 led first to rapid expansion of China's television infrastructure and then to a gradual withdrawal of state financing in favor of a largely for-profit system operated according to commercial imperatives but still subject to close oversight, censorship, and regulation by the state (see Chan, this volume). Deregulation in China has also fostered the growth of officially sanctioned cable networks and the expansion of transborder satellite coverage. In August 1993, the CCTV-backed, Chicago-based American Eastern TV launched its twelve-hours-a-day Chinese programming service in the U.S., broadcasting programs from more than twenty provincial stations in China. CCTV now controls about 75 percent of the leading Chinese-language television stations in the United States and Canada (Donohue 1999).[11] Its most recent move was the February 2005 launch of a new satellite service under the auspices of the China International TV Corp. (CITVC), a subsidiary of CCTV (Goldkorn 2005). Dubbed "The Great Wall Satellite TV Platform," this initiative delivers a suite of Mandarin-language channels to Vietnam, Thailand, South Korea, Hong Kong, Macao, and Taiwan, as well as to U.S. cable networks and, soon, to Canada's leading cable network (*Korea Times* 2005). This is controversial in Canada, having met with some resistance from overseas Chinese there who regard the Great Wall channels as fronts for mainland propaganda (Wong 2007). The platform brings together seven of China's leading provincial television stations along with two Hong Kong–based channels, Phoenix Television and Asia Television (ATV), and the U.S. Huaxia Television station, all under the broad leadership of CCTV.

CCTV has relied almost entirely on revenue from commercials since the mid-1990s (Li 2002). Advertising became the major source of income for the whole industry by the mid-2000s. TV drama production is at the forefront of the transition from state subsidies to commercial finance. Prior to the mid-1990s, drama production units received an annual subsidy from the government, with CCTV's drama production department receiving the most funding. According to one report, the CCTV's Drama Unit received RMB 3 million to make one hundred episodes of television drama in 1993 (Cai 1993). The State Administration of Radio, Film, and Television (SARFT) estimated that in 1995 it allocated RMB 10,000 for every episode of television drama. By the 2000s drama series were financed primarily by advertising revenue, generally through a system of bartering advertising space. In practice, the production company receives program time from the broadcaster to fill with advertising. In many instances the production company functions as a de facto advertising agency, selling time and even producing commercial spots. TV drama has become a significant force in generating advertising revenue, accounting for 90 percent of all television ad revenue in 2002.

By the early 1990s, the three Chinese production centers were all selling programming to Greater China in a pan-Chinese media practice driven by commercial imperatives. Despite the differences in political and economic systems, the door had been opened to programming and systems of distribution that treated Greater China as a unified television market. The establishment of commercial cable and satellite networks, both local and multi-national, and the proliferation of videocassettes and video compact discs have facilitated the maturation of the market. Co-productions combining commercial expertise from Hong Kong and Taiwan with the ample production talent and resources available in China are common. Many of the co-productions also mix and match creative contributions from Hong Kong, Taiwan, and China. The veteran Hong Kong director Chan Ho-Sun's recent film *Perhaps Love* (2005) is a musical that features a transnational cast including Zhou Xun, from China, and Takeshi Kaneshiro, the half-Chinese, half-Japanese pop and film star from Taiwan. It is reported that even the most experienced movie fan cannot discern the movie's origins without looking at the credits (Jin 2005).

Some Theoretical Considerations

The debate concerning globalization and cultural identity hinges on two related issues: the economic reality of the burgeoning trade in cultural products at the transnational level, and value positions concerning the impact of imported culture on the integrity of local culture. From the 1970s until quite recently, the U.S. was singled out as the primary agent and beneficiary of a new imperialism, "cultural imperialism." Replacing the martial domination of colonialism with cultural domination, cultural imperialism was thought to be reshaping the values and structures of other societies in ways favorable to continued U.S. economic domination by means of a constant and overwhelming "one-way flow" of cultural goods and ideas from the U.S. to everywhere else. The preeminence of U.S. audiovisual products in international markets appeared to threaten the size and in some instances the viability of cultural industries in other nations. It was feared that hegemony, or domination at the level of unwitting conformity, would be the long-term outcome of this imbalance, compounding widespread concern about the erosion and homogenization of cultural values and identities in the receiving societies.

Many of the themes of global cultural domination by U.S. cultural industries were raised powerfully in the UNESCO (United Nations Educational, Scientific and Cultural Organization) debates of the 1970s, during which the Soviet Union, together with a number of third-world, Non-Aligned Movement countries raised questions about the danger of unwanted television programs and other media products emanating primarily from the U.S., and put forward their countering concept of a New World Information and Communication Order (NWICO), later outlined in the 1980 UNESCO report by the MacBride Commission titled *Many Voices, One World*. At the time, the U.S. was attempting to capitalize on emerging satellite communication technologies. Fearing this further expansion of U.S. culture, Europe and Canada joined the former Soviet Union and the Non-Aligned Movement countries in pushing for restrictions on global information flows. The real and imagined problems posed by manifest imbalances in the global exchange of information and entertainment remain unresolved. The matter is complicated, however, by emerging cultural theories that suggest alternative perspectives on cultural flow and emphasize the paradoxical fluidity and resilience of cultural identity, challenging the theoretical underpinnings of cultural imperialism in general and U.S. cultural hegemony in particular.

Material changes in global cultural trade since the 1970s likewise challenge the "one-way flow" thesis. The growth of alternative geolinguistic and culturally proximate markets alongside the U.S.-led English cultural-linguistic market demands a revision of the U.S.-centric worldview projected by the cultural imperialist idea. A more comprehensive concept, "globalization," emerged as a new social scientific theoretical paradigm in the early 1990s, substantially replacing the fatigued Cold War paradigm that had produced cultural imperialism. Globalization theories allow for the addition of multiple horizons to the U.S.-centric vista in order to account for the phenomena of changing flows of information and cultural goods on both global and local scales. Yet the classical concerns about hegemony and cultural imperialism have resurfaced within the globalization paradigm as particular sites of academic investigation. Revisionist political economists are concerned again about imbalances of power in and resulting from cultural exchange. Cultural theorists, on the other hand, propose an opposing, more celebratory view of global cultural exchange, holding that local cultures may prove resilient and that the balance of power always fluctuates. This optimism, however, is challenged by the economics of cultural production, the practical realities of ownership and profit that powerfully affect the strategic positions available within cultural production locally, regionally, and globally. Scholars who subscribe to the cultural industries approach consider dubious the assumption that the "internationalization of dominant imagery" has a homogenizing effect on subjectivities across cultures. Disenchanted with "grand narratives" such as cultural imperialism and postmodernism, the cultural industries approach has undertaken an empirical quest that has opened the way to considering cultural-linguistic markets as meaningful blocs in the complex context of a globalized cultural economy.

While recognizing the empirical strength of the cultural-linguistic markets construct, we must also recognize that it is a blunt instrument that begs the question of other audience formations within or alternative to the cultural-linguistic one. While it is evident that Chinese audiences gravitate toward cultural products in their native tongue, people in Hong Kong and Taiwan might feel more at home with U.S. popular culture than with propaganda-laced main-melody films and television programs from China.[12] What might be helpful in this instance and in other similar exceptions to the cultural-linguistic markets frame is cultural anthropologist Arjun Appadurai's "landscape" metaphor for identifying and describing complex, shifting cultural formations.[13] Appadurai (1996) asserts that the new global cultural economy has to be seen as a complex, overlapping, disjunctive order. In an effort to explore such disjunctures, Appadurai offers five "scapes": ethnoscapes, mediascapes, technoscapes, financescapes, and ideoscapes. The "-scape" suffix points to the fluid, irregular shapes of these figurative landscapes.

The relevance of Appadurai's metaphor here lies in its fluid grouping of media practices and markets. I propose that a practice and market can be formed simultaneously along lines of language, culture, politics, aesthetics, economics, and other factors. Individuals, groups, communities, nation-states, and regions carry multiple identities and constantly reposition themselves and therefore transgress various media practices and markets. As a Chinese-born but U.S.-trained academic with certain cultural predilections, I simultaneously consume Chinese-language media geolinguistically, the media of Masterpiece Theater and Bravo and art cinema alike geoaesthetically, the media of the left geopolitically, and the expensive world of ballet, opera, and concert music geoeconomically or geoculturally. I have little patience for martial arts drama, the cultural treasure of my birthplace.

This points to the difficulty, indeed the frustration, of sorting out global cultural affiliations. Appadurai's landscape analogy also recognizes that global cultural flows are inflected by the historical, linguistic, and political situatedness of different agents such as nation-states, multi-national corporations, diasporic communities, sub-national groupings and movements, and intimate face-to-face communities such as villages, neighborhoods, and extended families. This multiplicity of alliances and agencies points to a shortcoming of the cultural-linguistic markets model. The model thrives on the need of deterritorialized populations to maintain their bond to a homeland, imagined or real. Yet this "ethnoscape" is only one dimension of cultural alliances, albeit maybe the strongest. As I noted earlier, certain media practices in Hong Kong and Taiwan are more modern Western than distinctively Chinese if the measures are technology, economy, and ideology. Majorities in Hong Kong and Taiwan identify with the Western metanarrative of liberal democracy. An English-language program evincing liberal democratic values will be more accessible to them than the doctrinaire party line in some Chinese-language television dramas from China.

Likewise, self-proclaimed connoisseurs of any particular art (whether it is high or low, classical or pop, modern or postmodern) will generally identify with the cultural practices and products that fit their aesthetic sensibility, regardless of language barriers. The growing international art house film circuit attests to the viability of a global cultural market based on individuals' aesthetic propensities.

This is not to exaggerate the freedom with which individuals can flex their creative and consumer muscles. While Appadurai argues succinctly that these landscapes are navigated by agents who both experience and constitute larger formations in part according to their own sense of what these landscapes offer, one must also consider the historically contingent nature of linguistic, cultural, political, economic, and aesthetic affiliations. My reference to Appadurai's conceptualization of global cultural flows does not suggest that I share wholeheartedly his claim that the old center-periphery power dynamic is breaking down under the new dynamic of globalization. Far from endorsing his cheerful vision of autonomous "active" audiences in subversive pursuit of their pleasure, I recognize the very social construction of my linguistic, cultural, and political sensibilities, the larger forces that have shaped my consumption and transgression of certain media practices and products.

Understanding "grouping" beyond the center-periphery dynamic is imperative in our mapping of globalization as a process that defies the fatigued mode of analysis that always comes back to "national and transnational" or "local and global." The breakthrough of Appadurai's scheme lies precisely in his effort to map the process beyond the confines of nation-states as the most frequent site of investigation. Yet this is not to elide the fact that certain nation-states continue to wield dominating influence within associated cultural markets, leading us to the issue of hegemony.

The French effort to construct an alternative market based on shared Latin cultural and linguistic traits that would associate southern Europe with Latin America raised some concern that homogenization driven by U.S. popular culture might be overtaken by French cultural imperialism. This designed cultural-linguistic market never panned out, but cultural domination by Paris, as a production center, is a major concern among countries that share in the Francophone market that has emerged more or less organically. The Chinese cultural-linguistic market is likewise not the result of an elaborate effort by any of the three Chinese media production centers. Nevertheless, the mainland Chinese government has tried to shift some ideological freight onto its shoulders, and there has been some resistance in overseas Chinese communities to mainland-originated television channels perceived, rightly or wrongly, as ideological fronts. Moreover, linguistic tension between Mandarin and local dialects and the use of complex or simplified Chinese characters, as well as the overt ideological differences between Hong Kong, China, and Taiwan, all contribute to a dynamic of contested hegemony behind the scenes in Greater China.

There is also the issue of self-censorship. In the first half of 1994, Hong Kong's TVB decided not to broadcast two BBC documentaries deemed un-friendly to the mainland regime (To and Lau 1995). The Hong Kong film in-dustry has willingly undergone contortions to fit in with China. The 2003 Closer Economic Partnership Agreement (CEPA) between Hong Kong and the mainland, a package of regulatory changes that provided favorable conditions for Hong Kong industries to do business on the mainland, was the savior of the Hong Kong film industry. Yet CEPA also tends to erode the range of creativity and experimentation in Hong Kong productions, precisely by making the main-land market loom so prominently in creative decision making. For instance, crime must not pay in films screened on the mainland. 2003's *Infernal Affairs III*, a Hong Kong–China co-production, was strongly anti-crime, but for the 2002 *Infernal Affairs I* (not a co-production), the producers shot two endings. Hong Kong audiences were given no clear indication as to the fate of the crimi-nal (portrayed sympathetically by pop star Andy Lau), while mainland viewers saw justice done and the criminal taken away in handcuffs (Martinsen 2005).

On a different front, Chinese-language media and their products, even with this very large cultural-linguistic market supporting them, are not in a position to challenge the global dominance of English-language media and cultural products. Chinese-language channels are minuscule in the overseas media landscape. The English-language market, not just transnational but also trans-*linguistic*, has a longer history of pursuing audience maximization, more advanced production capacity, and better consolidated distribution channels. The English-language market is especially blessed by its wealthy native speak-ing base in the U.S., Australia, Canada, the UK, New Zealand, and other countries. The global market for English-language cultural products also ben-efits from the legacy of colonialism. A reputation for quality and reliability is one byproduct of this historical legacy, equating English with superiority and credibility. Advantages like these will be a long time in fading.

UNESCO's newly adopted Convention on the Protection and Promotion of Diversity of Cultural Expressions translates the long-standing concern of most of its member states about cultural hegemony into international law (Moore 2005).

In a vote cast as a battle of global conformity vs. cultural diversity, delegates turned aside strong U.S. objections in October 2005, overwhelmingly approving the first international treaty designed to legitimize the efforts of governments to protect movies, music, and other cultural works from foreign competition.[14] The measure passed at a time of growing fear that globalization was bringing a surge of commercial cultural products across borders that could wipe out local cultural heritage. The legally binding measure recognizes the right of countries to "maintain, adopt and implement policies and measures that they deem appropriate for the protection and promotion of the diversity of cultural expressions on their territory" (Moore 2005). Advocates say it could also help small nations promote and distribute their cultural products on the world market.[15]

Films and music are among the United States' largest exports—the foreign box-office take for American movies was $16 billion in 2004. Assuring access to overseas markets for these products has been a prime U.S. goal at the World Trade Organization. French sociologist Eric Fassin says, "In the battles over issues critical to shaping the globe in the 21st century, each side is defending its own best interests" (Moore 2005). The "interests" referred to by Fassin are both cultural and economic, increasingly acting in tandem, like two hands of a new global power dynamic. The smug mentality of the U.S. notwithstanding, a unified stance against the U.S. and in favor of cultural protection should not disguise the fact that commercial interests are as much a part of the struggle as is resistance to cultural domination, and the fight is often between the local capitalist and the transnational capitalist. In the case of transnational Chinese television, the interest of global capital in exploiting such a market by producing localized products will inevitably clash with the interests of the existing production centers.[16] In 2002, Warner Brothers signed a deal to co-produce ten made-for-TV movies set in the Qing dynasty. In early 2003 it announced plans to co-produce its first ever Chinese-language film (Dolven and Granitsas 2002).

As the international market has become crucial, Hollywood has begun to notice the waning appeal of American pop culture, particularly television dramas. The overseas flop of the popular U.S. show *Desperate Housewives* is a recent example (Zhou 2005). The transcontinental niches that the Spanish- and Portuguese- and Chinese-speaking television markets have carved out for themselves are forcing U.S. producers to develop programming for the Latino and Chinese markets in the U.S., with Latin America, Spain, and the pan-Chinese audience in East Asia as aftermarkets. MTV's Latin America division is illustrative. In addition, some U.S. investment groups have joined Latin America's Cisneros Group to create a "pan-Ibero-American media network" based in Miami. The comparative advantage that Latin American media companies derive from working in their native language is under threat. Sinclair (2004) reports a CBS executive's observation that Latin America is more attractive than Europe for global media firms interested in regional ventures because the whole region requires products in only two languages, as against the several languages needed for regional ventures in Europe.

Developing Chinese-language programming is even simpler, since it requires only one language. Recognizing the potential, U.S.-based companies have ventured into producing Chinese-language television programs not just in Hollywood, but in Chinese-speaking countries. Frank Rose (1999) finds News Corp. and Columbia Tri-Star trying out a new business model that replaces U.S. popular culture created for the English-language market and exported for whatever it can get in "secondary," non-English markets with popular culture created in the local tongue for local audiences who are treated as new primary markets. For instance, Columbia Tri-Star went to Beijing to produce *Chinese Restaurant* in 1999, a Mandarin-language television drama series about a young Chinese woman and the multi-cultural crowd at her struggling Beijing Garden Restaurant in (ironically) Los Angeles. As William Pfeiffer, the brain behind the show, puts it, "We take the best of their very rich culture and marry it with the professionalism and the polish of Hollywood" (Rose 1999).

News Corp. has also learned to localize. It bought into China in 1993 when it bought into STAR TV, but it has yet to turn a profit on the deal. High on its list of missteps was an early attempt to blanket Asia with English-language channels. STAR's real success comes from its Mandarin-language Phoenix Channel. A niche player with enviable demographics, Phoenix claims an audience of 170 million educated, upscale viewers, most of them in Beijing and the prosperous southern city of Guangzhou. Obviously, neither Sony nor News Corp. is on a mission to promote multi-culturalism. What is at stake is not what global media conglomerates can do for local culture, but what local culture can do for the bottom line.

Over the last two decades a number of media markets cut along cultural-linguistic lines have emerged and thrived alongside the global U.S. English market, notably multi-linguistic markets in Western Europe and East Asia, a dual-language Latin American market, a Francophone market, an Arabic market, a Chinese market, and a Hindi-language South Asian market. We are witnessing the emergence of a two-tiered global system. English is the language of the international blockbuster, but lower-budget pictures can be made in almost any language for the home market and the nearest cultural-linguistic market, with the occasional breakout global hit.[17] Hollywood attempts to call the shots in both tiers. Given the attempts of global media conglomerates based in the U.S. and elsewhere to position themselves in the technological vanguard in non-English cultural-linguistic markets and to face up to the content issue by producing programs in local languages, the current configuration of a global media scene sporting multiple established and emerging cultural-linguistic markets led by native non-English-language production centers might soon be undermined.

While the emergence and initial expansion of the Greater China media market was a natural outgrowth of globalizing communications technologies paired with demand from Chinese audiences all over the world, the active cultivation of a Chinese cultural-linguistic market and media practice is driven by the desire of both local and global media firms to cash in on the huge Chinese-language market.[18] The presence of global media firms in the Chinese cultural-linguistic market threatens the current dominance of local products. As more global firms begin to adapt to the local tastes, the Chinese cultural-linguistic market will no longer be the sole domain of producers in Hong Kong, China, and Taiwan. Meanwhile, local and regional firms in East Asia must constantly absorb global trends and produce media products up to par with the global fashion. Robertson's term (1995) "glocalization" captures the dynamic of mutual adaptation among global producers trying to localize their products and local producers trying to meet global standards. In the case of TV drama, as format and formula are standardized according to global norms, narrative content still tends to be locally grounded, using local actors, idioms, and scenery.

My elaboration of a Chinese cultural-linguistic market is a start on broadening what has so far been a somewhat Euro- and Latin-centric perspective on this developing area. Future research should take an empirical look at the production and consumption patterns of Chinese-language television programming locally, regionally, and globally to determine, for instance, the extent to which audiences in Hong Kong, Taiwan, China, and overseas really distinguish themselves in their choices of different television content, and the extent to which audience preferences in one or more of these distinct markets in turn affect production choices and the availability of different content. Or even whether the Greater Chinese audience is really divided along these lines at all. Maybe socio-economic differences or regional dialect differences will turn out to be more important than political borders.

Notes

1. "Cantonese Losing Its Voice" (Pierson 2006) aptly captures the shifting linguistic landscape in overseas Chinese communities.
2. "Globalization for Kids: Chinese Nannies Are the Latest New York Trend" (*Spiegel Online* 2006) is an amusing account of how the newly acquired elite status of Mandarin is making Chinese au pairs New York's latest fashion as Manhattan's rich and powerful want to prepare their progeny for the economic world of tomorrow. Another interesting article, "Chinese Language Study Catching On in U.S. Classrooms" (Silverman 2006) reports a U.S. government–backed effort to encourage more American students to learn Mandarin. The effort is seen as a nod to China's emergence as a global superpower.
3. At a 2005 entertainment award show in Shanghai, Chinese reporters drowned

out Hong Kong celebrities speaking in Cantonese with exasperated shouts of "speak Mandarin."

4. An online petition protested the UN's decision to abolish the use of traditional Chinese: http://www.gopetition.com/r890-egion/237/8314.html (accessed 28 February 2007).

5. During the Chinese Spring Festival of 1999, more than ten provisional satellite TV stations scheduled the Jin Yong adaptation *Tianlong babu* for their prime-time programs.

6. The growth of these travel narratives also coincided with TVB's development of satellite broadcasting, which helps these shows travel faster and wider. The obsession with time and space in these narratives is perhaps a timely response to advances in telecommunications and technology. For details see Lee, this volume.

7. The titles of these dramas are taken from a wide range of sources, including *Taiwan News* 2006, Her 2005, and Her 2006.

8. Programs were also frequently exchanged between Taiwan and Hong Kong before the TV market in the PRC opened up.

9. In January 2005 I surveyed six major websites that sell and rent Asian audiovisual products: YesAsia.com (http://us.yesasia.com/en/index.aspx), Chinesetapes (http://www.chinesetapes.com), ehit.com (http://www.ehit.com/newreleased?type=tv&cursor=16), RamenCity (http://www.ramencity.com/eshop/dvdindex.asp?search= chinese +dvd:series), HK Flix (http://www.hkflix.com), and Moviesville (http://stores.moviesville.com/).

10. For a more detailed history of Hong Kong's television industry, see Cheuk 1999.

11. A significant number of leading Chinese-language print media in the U.S. are owned by companies with ties to Xinhua News in China.

12. "Main-melody" films are government-sponsored melodramas that serve as tools for both propaganda and entertainment.

13. I should acknowledge that cultural-linguistic markets describe media-consumption groups (in effect, audiences), whereas Appadurai's scapes are part of a more encompassing effort to describe changing conditions of identification (how people find, create, and understand their identity) in a globalized climate. I recognize the difference but still find Appadurai's scapes useful for fine-tuning our understanding of cultural-linguistic markets.

14. In the vote, only Israel sided with the United States. Four countries abstained.

15. According to Molly Moore (2005), the showdown came two years after the United States rejoined UNESCO following a two-decade boycott that began over objections to the organization's media policy. "The vote came less than a month after delegates at a U.N.-organized summit in Geneva sided against the United States to try to remove technical control of the Internet from U.S. hands. Talks deadlocked after the European Union refused to support the United States."

16. Claydon Gescher Associates, a Beijing-based media consultancy, estimates that TV penetration in China is around 93 percent, or about 328 million households, which makes China the largest television market in the world (Lu 2002).

17. Roberto Benigni's Italian-language *La vita è bella* (*Life Is Beautiful*) went on to win multiple Academy Awards and become an international hit.

18. There are about 35 million overseas Chinese scattered among 150 countries.

References

Anagnost, Ann. 1997. *National Past-Times: Narrative, Representation, and Power in Modern China*. Durham, N.C.: Duke University Press.

Appadurai, Arjun. 1996. *Modernity at Large: Cultural Dimensions of Globalization*. Minneapolis: University of Minnesota Press.

Bodeen, Christopher. 2004. "Awash in Dialects, China Relies on Mandarin as Common Tongue—But How Common Is It?" *Associated Press*, 4 December. http://www.signonsandiego.com/news/world/20041204-0958-polyglotnation.html (accessed 31 January 2005).

Cai, Xiang. 1993. "1981–1992: Chinese Television Drama; Looking Back and into the Future." *Dianshi yanjiu* 4:2–7.

Cheuk, Pak-Tong. 1999. "The Beginning of the Hong Kong New Wave: The Interactive Relationship between Television and the Film Industry." *Post Script* 19, no. 1:10–27.

Chua Beng Huat. 2004. "Conceptualizing an East Asian Popular Culture." *Inter-Asia Cultural Studies* 5, no. 2:200–221.

Cody, Edward. 2005. "On Chinese Television, What's Cool Is No Longer Correct." *Washington Post*, 29 September.

Dolven, B., and A. Granitsas. 2002. "Please, Let Us Entertain You." *Far Eastern Economic Review*, 26 December 2002–2 January 2003, 88–94.

Donohue, Steve. 1999. "China's CCTV Seeking North American Partners." *Electronic Media* 18, no. 5:33–36.

Embassy of the People's Republic of China in the United States of America. 2007. "CASS Report: Number of Overseas Chinese up to 35 Mln." 13 February. http://www.china-embassy.org/eng/qwgz/t297510.htm (accessed 13 March 2007).

Fitzgerald, John. 1996. *Awakening China: Politics, Culture, and Class in the Nationalist Revolution*. Stanford, Calif.: Stanford University Press.

Goldkorn, Jeremy. 2005. "China Launches Pan-Asian Satellite TV." *Danwei: Chinese Media, Advertising, and Urban Life*. 2 February. http://www.danwei.org/archives/001287.html (accessed 2 February 2005).

Her, Kelly. 2005. "Celebrity, Superstition, and Drama." *Taiwan Review* 55, no. 10. http://taiwanreview.nat.gov.tw/site/Tr/ct.asp?xItem=1133&CtNode=128 (accessed 28 February 2007).

———. 2006. "Media—The Remix." *Taiwan Review* 56, no. 6. http://taiwanreview.nat.gov.tw/site/Tr/ct.asp?xItem=1219&CtNode=128 (accessed 28 February 2007).

Jin Baicheng. 2005. "Facts and Flaws Make Up Epic TV Tales." *China Daily*, 2 February. http://www.chinadaily.com.cn/english/doc/2005-02/02/content_414251.htm (accessed 2 February 2005).

Jin, Bo. 2005. "Director Finds Different Take on Musical." *China Daily*, 6 December, p. 14.

Korea Times. 2005. "China to Begin Broadcasting through Asia: 'Great Wall' Programs Will Air in English and Three Chinese Dialects in Parts of Southeast Asia." 2 February. http://www.asiamedia.ucla.edu/article.asp?parentid=20266 (accessed 28 February 2006).

Li, Xiaoping. 2002. "'Focus' (Jiaodian Fangtan) and the Changes in the Chinese Television Industry." *Journal of Contemporary China* 11, no. 30:17–34.

Lu, Xingzhi. 2002. "Creativity Is Needed for Entering Chinese Media Market." [In

Chinese.] DoNews.com, 26 December. http://home.donews.com/donews/article/3/38691.html (accessed 28 February 2003).

Martinsen, Joel. 2005. "One Country, Two Versions." *Danwei: Chinese Media, Advertising, and Urban Life.* 3 February. http://www.danwei.org/archives/001293.html (accessed 3 February 2005).

McAnany, Emile, and Kenton Wilkinson, eds. 1996. *Mass Media and Free Trade: NAFTA and the Cultural Industries.* Austin: University of Texas Press.

Moore, Molly. 2005. "U.N. Body Endorses Cultural Protection: U.S. Objections Are Turned Aside." *Washington Post Online,* 21 October. http://www.washingtonpost.com (accessed 20 October 2006).

Pierson, David. 2006. "Cantonese Losing Its Voice." *Los Angeles Times,* 3 January, p. A1.

Robertson, Roland. 1995. "Glocalization: Time-Space and Homogeneity-Heterogeneity." In *Global Modernities,* ed. Mike Featherstone, Scott Lash, and Roland Robertson, 25–44. Thousand Oaks, Calif.: Sage.

Rose, Frank. 1999. "Think Globally, Script Locally: American Pop Culture Was Going to Conquer the World, but Now Local Content Is Becoming King." *Fortune Magazine Online,* 8 November. http://money.cnn.com/magazines/fortune/fortune_archive/1999/11/08/268531/index.htm (accessed November 8, 1999).

Shu Daqing. 1999. "The Chinese Language Television in Los Angeles" [Weiguo luosanji de huayu dianshi]. *China Radio and TV Academic Journal* [Zhongguo guangbo dianshi xuekan] 12:38–40.

Silverman, Julia. 2006. "Chinese Language Study Catching On in U.S. Classrooms, Including One in Portland, Ore." *Seattle Times,* 1 January. http://seattletimes.nwsource.com/html/localnews/2002715474_weblanguage01.html (accessed 1 February 2006).

Sinclair, John. 2004. "Geolinguistic Region as Global Space: The Case of Latin America." In *The Television Studies Reader,* ed. Robert Allen and Annette Hill, 130–138. New York: Routledge.

Sinclair, John, and Mark Harrison. 2004. "Globalization, Nation, and Television in Asia: The Cases of India and China." *Television & New Media* 5, no. 1:41–54.

South China Morning Post. 2004. "Leaders Ponder a Return to Society's Roots to Stop the Rot." 12 June. http://www.chinastudygroup.org/index.php?action=news&type=printer&id=7908 (accessed 1 February 2005).

Spiegel Online. 2006. "Globalization for Kids: Chinese Nannies Are the Latest New York Trend." 3 January. http://www.spiegel.de/international/0,1518,392784,00.html (accessed 1 February 2007).

Taiwan News. 2006. "GIO Mulls Scheme to Ban Foreign Dramas in Primetime." 11 January. http://english.www.gov.tw/TaiwanHeadlines/index.jsp?categid=8&recordid=90418 (11 February 2007).

Thomas, Amos Owen. 2000. "Transborder Television for Greater China." In *Television in Contemporary Asia,* ed. David French and Michael Richards, 91–110. London: Sage.

To, Yiu-ming, and Tuen-yu Lau. 1995. "Global Export of Hong Kong Television: Television Broadcasts Limited." *Asian Journal of Communication* 5, no. 2:108–121.

Weber, Ian. 2002. "Reconfiguring Chinese Propaganda and Control Modalities: A Case Study of Shanghai's Television System." *Journal of Contemporary China* 11, no. 30:63–75.

Wong, Tony. 2007. "Controversial Chinese TV Okayed for Cable Broadcast: China Rejects Group's Claim That Shows 'Incite Hatred.'" *Toronto Star,* 3 January. http://www.thestar.com/article/167333 (accessed 8 April 2007).

Yan, Liqun. 2000. "China." In *Handbook of the Media in Asia*, ed. Shelton Gunaratne, 497–526. New Delhi: Sage.

Zhou, Min, and Guoxuan Cai. 2002. "Chinese Language Media in the United States: Immigration and Assimilation in American Life." *Qualitative Sociology* 25, no. 3:419–441.

Zhou, Raymond. 2005. "Why 'Desperate Housewives' Flopped in China." *China Daily Online*, 31 December. http://www.chinadaily.com.cn/english/doc/2005-12/31/content_508261.htm (accessed 31 December 2005).

Zhu, Ying. 2003. *Chinese Cinema during the Era of Reform: The Ingenuity of the System.* Westport, Conn.: Praeger.

Appendix: Relevant Milestone Events in the Development of Chinese Television

Milestones in the Development of Chinese Television

Year	People's Republic of China	Hong Kong	Taiwan	Elsewhere
1957		Rediffusion cable TV established		
1958	Beijing TV station established; locally produced documentary programs debut on 1 May.			
1962			Taiwan TV launches first free-to-air service.	
1963		Rediffusion establishes the first Chinese-language channel.		Singapore: English-language TV launched in April; a second channel, channel 8, begins broadcasting mostly in Chinese in November.
1965			Island-wide coverage established.	

Year	People's Republic of China	Hong Kong	Taiwan	Elsewhere
1967		TVB establishes first free-to-air service in Hong Kong.		
1969			Taiwan TV experiments with live broadcasting of a variety show.	Malaysia: TV2, the second government TV channel, is launched in Malaysia, and includes Chinese-language programming.
1971			First TV exports to Hong Kong, on 31 October.	
1972			Japanese TV imports banned after Japan establishes diplomatic relations with the People's Republic.	
1973		Rediffusion becomes free-to-air.		
1975		88% of households have TV sets.	73% of households have TV sets.	
1976		TVB International established to market programming overseas.		
1978	Less than 1 TV set per 100 people. Beijing Television is renamed China Central Television (CCTV).			
1979	First commercial appears on Shanghai TV on 28 January.			

Year	People's Republic of China	Hong Kong	Taiwan	Elsewhere
1980	The news magazine show *Observe and Think* (*Guancha yu sikao*), which later becomes *Focus*, debuts on CCTV in July.			
1982	Chinese Academy of Social Sciences conducts first TV audience research.			
1983	CCTV's annual *Spring Festival Gala* program launched; it remains the most popular program on Chinese TV. New policy allows national, provincial, county, and municipal governments to establish TV stations, leading to rapid increase.	Asia Television Ltd. is granted a permit to co-produce TV dramas.		
1984				Hong Kong–based TVB launches U.S.-based cable stations.
1986	CCTV launches second channel and establishes China's first ratings system in Beijing.			
1987	First nationwide audience research conducted by CCTV. 10.7 TV sets per 100 people.			
1988	Controversial documentary *River Elegy* airs.			

Year	People's Republic of China	Hong Kong	Taiwan	Elsewhere
1989	Western media, in Beijing to cover Gorbachev's visit to China, broadcast the Tiananmen Square massacre live.		Programs on three Taiwan stations begin to enter the Chinese market.	
1990	Hunan Cable Station, the first provincial cable station, founded on April 18.			
1991		STAR satellite TV launched.		
1992	19.5 TV sets per 100 people.			
1993	CCTV's *Oriental Horizon* pioneers investigative reporting, sets ratings records, and spurs advertising expenditure.	20% of Hong Kong households have satellite, and 15% subscribe to cable. Rupert Murdoch buys majority share in STAR TV.	Taiwan's cable TV opened to imports; ban on Japanese television dropped. Japanese dramas soon become popular. Hong Kong's TVB establishes Super Channel cable operation in Taiwan.	
1994	STAR TV drops the BBC and enters mainland China. CCTV auctions off prime-time advertising slots for the first time.			Hong Kong–based TVB launches its own satellite services in the U.S. Singapore Broadcasting Corporation is fully privatized; TV arm becomes Television Corporation of Singapore (TCS).

Year	People's Republic of China	Hong Kong	Taiwan	Elsewhere
1995				Singapore's SBC launches 24-hour transmission in Mandarin.
1996	25 TV sets per 100 people. CCTV launches talk show *Tell It Like It Is* and consumer trends show *Life*. Nielsen ratings company begins China operations.	Rupert Murdoch's News Corporation invests in Phoenix Chinese-language satellite TV.		
1997			Five cable channels specializing in Japanese programming are in operation.	
1998		TVB launches Galaxy global satellite platform.	Public Television Service established.	
2001	Chinese TV stations amalgamate into entertainment conglomerates in preparation for entry into the WTO.		*Meteor Garden* idol drama series debuts in Taiwan and becomes a regional hit.	Phoenix North American Chinese Channel launched.
2002	Phoenix TV is allowed across the whole of the People's Republic. Total TV audience is 1.15 billion—the largest in the world.			

Year	People's Republic of China	Hong Kong	Taiwan	Elsewhere
2003	Hong Kong's TVB and ATV both allowed access to Guangdong Province.			TVB becomes available through DirecTV in the U.S. EETV Eastern Television launches a Taiwan satellite package in the U.S.
2004	CCTV has 16 channels. Hunan Satellite TV electrifies China with the *Super Girl* talent contest series. Viewers use mobile phones to vote for their favorites.		Political parties required to divest themselves of TV station interests by 2006.	CCTV launches Great Wall satellite platform in the U.S.
2005	94.4% of the population has access to a TV.	Korean drama *Jewel in the Palace* is watched by half the population.		
2006	CCTV's *Spring Festival Gala* webcast and broadcast live globally			

Contributors

CHRIS BERRY is Professor of Film and Television Studies in the Department of Media and Communication at Goldsmiths, University of London. His books include *Postsocialist Cinema in Post-Mao China: The Cultural Revolution after the Cultural Revolution; Chinese Films in Focus: 25 New Takes;* and (with Mary Farquhar) *China on Screen: Cinema and Nation.*

JOSEPH M. CHAN is Professor in the School of Journalism and Communication at the Chinese University of Hong Kong and the Changjiang Chair Professor of the School of Journalism, Fudan University, PRC. The books he has co-authored include *Global Media Spectacle: News War over Hong Kong* and *Mass Media and Political Transition.* His publications appear in such venues as the *Journal of Communication; Communication Research; Media, Culture & Society;* and the *Journalism and Mass Communication Quarterly,* among others. He is the founding editor-in-chief of *Communication & Society,* a Chinese journal.

HSIU-CHUANG DEPPMAN is Assistant Professor of Chinese at Oberlin College and working on a book to be titled *The Cultural Politics of Adaptation: Modern Chinese Fiction and Film.*

JUNHAO HONG is Associate Professor of Communication at the State University of New York at Buffalo. His publications include authored and edited books, dozens of research articles in various refereed journals, and numerous book chapters.

AMY LEE is a Ph.D. candidate in the English Department at the University of California, Berkeley.

XINYU LU is Professor in the Broadcasting Department of the Journalism School at Fudan University, PRC. Her publications include *Documenting China: The New Documentary Movement in China*; *Mythology, Tragedy, Aristotle's Art of Poetry: New Concepts of the Ancient Greek Tradition of Poetics*; and *Writing and What It Obscures*.

YANMEI LÜ is a visiting scholar at the Annenberg School for Communication and the Center for East Asian Studies at the University of Pennsylvania.

KARIN GWINN WILKINS is Associate Professor in the Department of Radio-TV-Film at the University of Texas at Austin.

CINDY HING-YUK WONG is Chair and Associate Professor of Communications in the Department of Media Culture at the College of Staten Island, City University of New York. She is co-author of *Global Hong Kong* and co-editor of the *Encyclopedia of Contemporary American Culture*.

JANICE HUA XU is Assistant Professor in the Department of Communication, Cabrini College, Pennsylvania.

HAIQING YU teaches in the School of Asian Languages and Studies at the University of Tasmania, Australia. She is author of *Media and Cultural Transformation in China*.

TONGDAO ZHANG is Professor in the College of Arts and Media, Beijing Normal University. He is author of *Documentary Masters*; *Observations on Chinese Television*; *The Survey of Chinese TV Viewers*; and *Analysis of Chinese TV Programs*; and the director of several documentaries aired on China Central Television.

YING ZHU is Associate Professor of Cinema Studies in the Department of Media Culture at the College of Staten Island, City University of New York. Her books include *Television in Post-reform China: Serial Dramas, Confucian Leadership, and the Global Television Market*; and *Chinese Cinema during the Era of Reform: The Ingenuity of the System*.

WILLIAM ZOU is Professor of English and Director and Chief Interpreter of the Translation Office at Ocean University of China. He has published eighteen books, including a novel more than 300,000 Chinese characters long.

Index

Weather Forecast (CCTV), 45
Wen Jiabao, 137
Wharf Cable, 60, 62. *See also* Hong
    Kong Cable Television (HKCTV)
Who Wants to Be a Millionaire?, 27
Winter Sonata, 31
Women in Control, 205
Wong, Faye, 30
Workers' Daily, 174
World Trade Organization, 3, 235; Chi-
    na's accession to, 48, 76, 247
Wu Guoguang, 207

Xingkong Weishi, 64
Xinhua News Agency, 42

Yang Weiguang, 155
Yangtze River, The Grand Canal
    (CCTV), *The*, 41
Ying Qiming, 76, 77, 85
Yu Guoming, 178
Yu Yongjing, 82
Yuan Yemin, 81, 82

Zee TV, 21, 28
Zelizer, Barbie, 130–31
Zhao An, 120–21
Zhao Ziyang, 208, 218
Zhong Nanshan, 139
Zhou Zhu, 163
Zhu Rongji, 43